CLASSIC GAME DESIGN

CLASSIC GAME DESIGN

From Pong to Pac-Man with Unity

Franz Lanzinger

MERCURY LEARNING AND INFORMATION

Dulles, Virginia | *Boston, Massachusetts* | *New Delhi*

Publisher: David Pallai

MERCURY LEARNING AND INFORMATION
22841 Quicksilver Drive Dulles, VA 20166
info@merclearning.com
www.merclearning.com
1-800-758-3756

This book is printed on acid-free paper.

Franz Lanzinger. *Classic Game Design: From Pong to Pac-Man with Unity.*

ISBN: 978-1-937585-97-6

Library of Congress Control Number: 2013937526

131415 321

Printed in the United States of America

Our titles are available for adoption, license, or bulk purchase by institutions, corporations, etc. For additional information, please contact the Customer Service Dept. at 1-800-758-3756 (toll free).

The sole obligation of MERCURY LEARNING AND INFORMATION to the purchaser is to replace the disc, based on defective materials or faulty workmanship, but not based on the operation or functionality of the product.

TABLE OF CONTENTS

Acknowledgments

I'd like to thank just some of the many people who made this book possible.

Most significantly, Eric Ginner and Robert Jenks read and worked through large portions of the book in draft form and gave voluminous feedback and suggestions. This book would be less without your valuable contributions.

For reading and commenting on sections of the draft I'd also like to thank Mark Robichek and Karl Anderson.

Special thanks to Mark Alpiger, Sam Mehta, Brian McGhie, Desiree McCrorey, Joe Cain, Eugene Polonsky, Bob Jones, Aaron Hightower, Ed Logg, Dave O'Riva, and Steve and Susan Woita. You taught me how to play and develop games.

A word of thanks is due to my parents, Klaus and Aida Lanzinger, for their humanity and love.

And last, but not least, a big hug and thank you to my wife, Susan Lanzinger, for helping throughout the years. I couldn't have done this without you.

About the Author

Franz Lanzinger is president of Actual Entertainment, an independent game development studio in Sunnyvale, California. He started his career in game programming in 1982 at Atari Games Inc., where he designed and programmed the classic arcade game *Crystal Castles*. Some years later he joined Tengen, where he was a programmer and designer for *Ms. Pac-Man* and *Toobin'* on the NES. Mr. Lanzinger co-founded Bitmasters, where he designed and coded games including *Rampart* and *Championship Pool* for the NES and SNES, and *NCAA Final Four Basketball* for the SNES and Sega Genesis. In 1996, Mr. Lanzinger founded Actual Entertainment, publisher and developer of the *Gubble* series for PC and iOS. Mr. Lanzinger has a B.Sc. in mathematics from the University of Notre Dame and attended graduate school at the University of California at Berkeley. In 1980, he started playing arcade games, and at one time held the arcade world record scores on *Centipede* and *Burgertime*. Franz Lanzinger is a professional accompanist, piano teacher, and avid golfer. He continues to design and code games. The companion Web site for updates and additional information is located at *www.authorcloudware.com*.

CHAPTER
1 Introduction

This is a hands-on book about game design, and what better way to learn about game design than to study and emulate the classics. You're going to make some games, not just read about them. Assimilating the classics is a time-honored tradition. Pianists play Bach, writers read Shakespeare, and painters copy the Mona Lisa. It's not just about experiencing them; it's about creating something very similar and grasping the process of creation that brings the most benefit.

INTRODUCTION: WHO ARE YOU?

This book is for everyone who loves to play and make games, preferably in that order. You should be somewhat computer literate, but it's OK if you've never written a line of code, never taken an art-class, and are tone-deaf.

Maybe you're a student concentrating your studies on programming, art, or design. This book can teach you about the basics of classic game design and introduce you to the major classic games and design techniques that every game developer should know. It's these classics that led the way and showed future generations of designers how to make games.

Maybe you're just a fan of the old games, the ones that started it all. It's just plain fun and relatively easy to recreate the old games using modern tools. Maybe you own a few classic arcade games and you like to change the option switches to see what happens. This book will allow you to do a lot more than that. Not only are the sample games fun by themselves, you'll learn how to make changes to them without being a professional programmer. With a little bit of effort, you'll learn the basics of how to add new features, change the way the scoring works, and replace the graphics and sounds with something entirely different.

Possibly you're just interested in learning Unity, Blender, GIMP, or Audacity. These development tools are the basis of this hands-on approach and enable you to get started making your own games right away. All of these tools are free to use, no strings attached. In the case of Unity, there is a professional version available that costs some serious money, but the free version is very good and perfectly fine for this book. All of these tools are extremely powerful. By using Unity, Blender, GIMP, and Audacity to make some games you'll gain a good introductory understanding of the entire process. You'll then be able to more easily tackle a myriad of advanced topics in game design and development. Detailed installation instructions are available later in this chapter.

Just as composers need to listen to music, artists should look at art, and writers had better read, so game designers ought to play games, especially their own games. There's a word for it, "dogfooding," which literally means that if you're making dog food, you need to eat it too. In the classic era of the '70s and '80s, it was possible to keep up with the industry and play all the top games. Nowadays you have to pick and choose, but that's no excuse for not playing at all. Whether you're a newbie designer or a thirty-year veteran with dozens of credited titles, you need to also be a player.

WHAT ARE CLASSIC ARCADE VIDEO GAMES?

Let's take a look at each of those words. What exactly is a game? Here's how we define a "game":

A *game* is an activity involving players and a referee. At the end of the game, the referee must assign a score to each player according to the rules.

It's just that simple. There are many other definitions out there, but this one really captures the essence of games.

Let's examine this definition in more detail. *Players* can be people, computers, or groups of these. For example, soccer is a game with two players; each player is a team of eleven people. Games can have as few as one player or huge numbers of players.

Scores can be numbers or sequences of letters. In classic video games, scores are always integers, but there are games out there where the score is simply a *win*, *lose*, or *disqualified*, for example.

Referees can be people, computer programs, or teams of these, just like the players. The strangest thing about this book's definition of game is the referee. Referees are often hidden, but they're required for every game. Sometimes people can do double duty, and be both referees and players at the same time. For example, when two people play a casual game of tennis, the referee is the group consisting of the two players. The players, as a group, decide what the score is going to be by following the rules of tennis to the best of their ability. They might not agree or fight about it, but because it's a casual game it's not that much of a problem.

As you can see, the rules of the game are interpreted and enforced by the referee. Sometimes the referee has trouble following the rules because the rules are poorly formulated. Sometimes the rules are incomplete, vague, or contradictory. This is why there has to be a referee. All decisions by the referee are final. Once the referee assigns the scores you are done. If you, the players, or the spectators don't like what the referee did, too bad. You can try to change the rules for next time or get a different referee.

Look at the next word: "video." *Video games* display a *game world* to the players using a *video display*. The players interact with the world using *game controllers*. You might ask, wait a minute, how do all these things fit into our broad definition of game? The word "game" describes all kinds of events, including ones that don't have a game world. In video games, we have a game world residing inside computer memory, and the video display shows the world to the players. The referee is usually embedded in the same computer program that displays the world.

Next, look at arcade video games. These are coin-operated machines, where players pay money in the form of coins or tokens to play a game. They are sometimes called *coin-op games* for short. The early arcade games were built and designed to be played in arcades and street locations such as restaurants, movie theaters, or airports. Arcade video games work as a business because they provide a game experience that's hard to duplicate at home. Ever since home console and PC video games became hugely popular in the late '80s arcade video games have been relegated to the few remaining arcades and street locations.

From a game design perspective, arcade video games are no different from the console games of today, for the most part. Some coin-specific features such as "add-a-coin" or dealing with a ticket dispenser only apply to arcade games, but the basics of controlling a character on a rectangular screen haven't really changed since 1972 and apply to arcade games, computer games, console games, and even mobile games.

The heyday of these types of games started in 1972 and ended in about 1984 when the arcade game industry collapsed in the United States. New arcade games are still manufactured today, but in much lower numbers than in the '80s.

Finally, to complete the definition, this is what is meant by a *classic*. A classic should be of high quality, timeless, and influential. These are somewhat subjective criteria, but they'll have to do. Amazingly, a very large proportion of the top selling arcade video games from the heyday of arcade video games fit this description. This almost seemed inevitable. There weren't that many arcade games made when compared to the huge number of new games released in the following decades. In the '80s, this art form was so new and resulted in such huge growth that most any reasonable idea would get reused countless times in the coming years. It was much easier to create an influential game back then compared to the present day. The high quality and timeless aspects were more difficult to achieve, especially because the technology was new and often cumbersome. Still, the '70s and early '80s were nothing less than the golden age of video game design.

From this book, you will take a detailed look at five featured classic arcade video games from this time period: *Pong, Breakout, Space Invaders®, Scramble™,* and *Pac-Man™.* In the interest of learning the basics well rather than doing a comprehensive survey, the scope of this book is limited to those five featured games. There are probably several dozen other classic arcade video games from this period that are similarly influential and important, games such as *Asteroids, Missile Command, Galaxian, Defender, Joust, Frogger®,* and *Pole Position,* just to name a few. It is left up to you to look at, play, and learn from the many other classic arcade video games out there.

Each of the featured games is responsible for countless imitators. They pioneered some of the most important game categories. The games you will be creating come from six categories: a paddle game, a brick game, a vertical shooter, a scrolling shooter, and a maze game. Furthermore, you'll be looking at some of the methods and design decisions that go into making these types of games.

This is a book about design, so it won't dwell too much on the now outdated technologies used to make the original featured games. Rather, it'll try to answer some very basic design questions that every game designer needs to tackle: What do the players do? What's their motivation? What are the strategies and tactics? What are the basic design elements?

The influence of classic arcade video games on modern games is undeniable. When you see a player getting points for running into something, or dying when colliding with something, it's because some arcade video game in the '70s or '80s pioneered it. Much of the history of these early days is lost, so it's difficult to give proper credit to the people and companies who are responsible.

The real fun comes when you try to reconstruct some of the game elements from the classics. The paddles in *Pong,* the bombs in *Scramble,* the shots in *Space Invaders*: these are basic game elements that every video game designer needs to understand. There's no better way to gain this understanding than by building some simple games that use these elements.

In the next section, you'll be taking a closer look at the tools you'll be using to make your own classic games.

UNITY, BLENDER, GIMP, AND AUDACITY!

Yes, you'll dive right in and use professional tools to make some games. Here are free to use, modern professional game development tools: Blender for 3D graphics, GIMP for 2D graphics, Audacity for sound effects, and Unity for creating the logic for the games and putting it all together. These are some of the same tools that a large number of professional game developers use when making commercial games. Just a few years ago it would have cost many thousands of dollars to get access to game development tools of this caliber. Via the generous efforts of these open source projects and the free version of Unity even the smallest of budgets is sufficient to make a good looking, good sounding, and high quality video game.

Please download and install the following software packages on your Mac or Windows PC:

Unity 4.0 or later, free version at www.unity3d.com

Blender 2.65a or later at www.blender.org

GIMP 2.8.2 or later at www.gimp.org

Audacity 2.0.2 or later at audacity.sourceforge.net/download/

These four applications are extremely powerful. It will take you some time to do the installations. Please be aware that if you have older versions installed on your system this would be an excellent time to upgrade. If you install even newer versions, for example version 2.66 of Blender instead of 2.65a, then there's a good chance that you'll be OK, but be aware that the screenshots might not match exactly due to future changes in the graphic look of the user interfaces. If you're reading this book many years after it was first published then you should probably not install the latest versions but rather the exact versions recommended in the NOTE.

Next, look at how you're going to make your graphics. You will go the 3D route. Figure 1.1 shows the art pipeline.

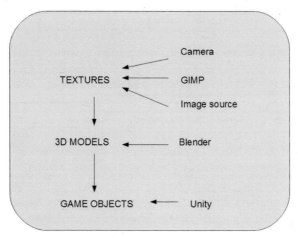

You will start with making some 2D images, use them to make textured 3D models, and then import them into the game engine, Unity.

GIMP is the open source graphics editor that you'll be using. It allows you to quickly sketch some 2D art that you can use as textures.

Alternatively, you can use a camera or scanner to make graphics files. Do you want to put a picture of yourself or your pet into the game? No problem. Just take a digital photo and put it into our Images directory. You'll also have the option of using GIMP to add effects to your images.

Blender is an open source tool that allows you to create 3D models and export them into your game engine. You'll use the textures from your Images directory to make the 3D models look better. Strictly speaking, you don't really have to have textures, especially for really simple games. But to make your games look more realistic you'll want to use textures.

Each graphic model gets imported into Unity. Whether it's a spaceship, an alien, or an elaborate scene, it all goes through the art pipeline in order to be usable by Unity. Unity will be described in much more detail in the next chapter.

But hold on, don't forget about sound! You'll be adding some simple sound effects to your classic games. You'll be using the open source tool Audacity to help make the sound effects. It would be easy to just use a bunch of sound effects from an effects library. However, in the spirit of classic gaming, you'll be creating all sound effects from scratch.

HOW TO USE THIS BOOK

This book is written to be read cover to cover all the while carefully following with the hands-on step-by-step instructions. This will give you a good foundation in the basics of classic game design and development. Along the way you'll learn some of the history and gain an appreciation of the pioneering arcade games that launched the video game industry.

If you're an experienced programmer and game developer, you can dive right into any or all of the projects and follow along as we build some fun games. You could also just load the projects as starting points for your own experiments.

The projects are all available on the companion DVD for this book.

If you're just interested in the programming aspects of these projects, you can just use the art and sound assets and follow along with the programming steps. Similarly, if you want to learn how we made the graphics, you can skip our programming and sound discussions.

You can just read the chapters about the featured classic games and learn about design without worrying about the technical implementations. However, it's strongly recommended that you work through at least one or two of the classic game projects. The best way to learn anything is "learning by doing." This is especially true for the daunting task of learning how to be a game designer.

In the next chapter, you'll get started by taking the software out for a quick spin.

2 Tools of the Trade

IN THIS CHAPTER

In this chapter, you'll be introduced to the tools that you're going to use to make your games. They are all professional level tools, and yet they are free. In the classic era only a select few developers could afford the software and hardware necessary to make even the simplest games. Now there's nothing standing in your way to making a professional quality game. All you need is an inexpensive PC and an Internet connection, and you're on your way. The goal for this chapter is to use all of these development tools to create a very small demo application with 3D graphics and sound.

INSTALLING UNITY

If you haven't done so already, your next step is to get Unity installed and working on your computer. None of the software tools in this book require a high-end system, but it's a good idea to use your fastest system with the best monitor setup for this kind of work.

In order to run the tools in this book, you need access to a PC or Mac made sometime after 2007. If your computer is older, it might still work depending on the particular capabilities of the system. Go to unity3d.com/unity/system-requirements and check the "System Requirements for Unity Authoring." Once you've determined that your system meets or exceeds the requirements, the next step is to install the latest free version of Unity and try it out.

This book fully supports both PC and Macs. The projects in this book were originally developed on a PC, and then tested on a Mac. The step-by-step instructions are designed to work on both PCs and Macs. The screen shots used to generate the illustrations in this book were captured from a PC, so if you're using a Mac you might notice some minor differences between your screen and the PC screen shots in the book.

It is recommended, but not strictly necessary, to use an HD monitor, preferably with a resolution of 1920x1080 or better. A dual monitor setup with two HD monitors is definitely a plus and well worth it, considering the low cost of HD monitors.

It is also highly recommended that you connect a real three button mouse with a scroll wheel and, especially when you're doing 3D modeling with Blender, a full keyboard with a numeric keypad. If you're missing a numeric keypad there's alternatives that aren't too bad, but all other things being equal it's slightly easier and faster to use a physical numeric keypad.

Once you've selected your computer it's time to get started with Unity. Go to www.unity3d.com and, if you haven't done so already, install the free version of Unity 4. This book uses Unity 4, Version 4.0.0f7. If you install a subsequent version, you should be able to still follow along with this book using that newer version, but it's not guaranteed. This install file is somewhat large, so be prepared for the process to take some time depending on the speed of your Internet connection.

To see the current version number of Unity, find the "About Unity" dialog under Help for the PC or under Unity on the Mac.

HELLO WORLD

The phrase "Hello World" has taken on a special meaning for programmers. It has become a tradition to make a "Hello World" application when first encountering a new programming language or development environment. A "Hello World" application simply displays the words "Hello" and "World". This is about as simple as it gets. It's not intended to be a true test of the power of Unity, but rather it's a simple exercise to make sure you can do something very basic.

This is the first step-by-step process. This book has a bunch of them, so get ready to follow along on your own computer. It's easy to get lost, skip a step, or to not quite follow the instructions exactly as written, so read each step very carefully before trying the step on your own.

After the initial description of a step, there often follows a more detailed explanation, for example in Steps 1 through 4 below.

Step 1: Start Unity.

Make sure you've successfully installed Unity 4 on either your PC or your Mac as described in the previous section. It doesn't matter if you have the free or the professional or a trial version installed. The free version is what is used in this book.

At this point, you'll either get the main Unity workspace or the Project wizard. If you have the Unity workspace with a menu, do the following step, otherwise skip to Step 3.

Step 2: Click on **File – New Project…**.

In this book, drop-down menu items are indicated using the dash character "–". In this step, you should click on "File" and then on "New Project…" in the resulting drop-down menu.You will see a new window pop up with the title Unity - Project Wizard, or just "Project Wizard" on the Mac.

Step 3: Click on the **Create New Project** tab.

This may not really be necessary, but it's easier to just click on it to make sure it's selected.

Step 4: In the Project Location (Project Directory on a Mac), replace "New Unity Project xxx" with "HelloWorld".

The xxx is a placeholder for a number or a blank. Notice that there's no space between Hello and World.

Step 5: Click on the **Create** box (or **Create Project** on a Mac).

Your screen should look similar to Figure 2.1.

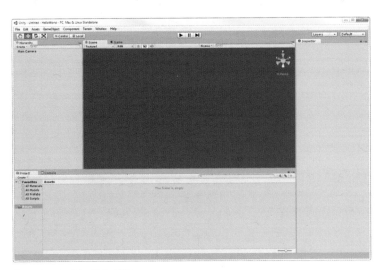

▲ **FIGURE 2.1** The Unity Editor.

If, due to prior usage of your installation of Unity, your screen looks substantially different, it's probably because you have a different layout selected. In that case, look for the Layout drop-down menu at the top right of the Unity window. It's the one immediately to the right of the "Layers" dropdown.

Step 6: Click on the Layout drop-down menu and select the **Default** layout.

If you wish, go ahead and try out the other layouts, but switch back to the Default layout before continuing on. Notice the text on the top middle or top left of the window. It should say:

```
Unity - Untitled - HelloWorld - PC, Mac & Linux Standalone
```

The first word of the title, "Unity" is missing in the Mac version. The "Untitled" refers to the scene which you haven't named yet. You will do that next.

Step 7: Click on **File – Save Scene** and name the scene **HelloWorldScene**.

The window title now includes HelloWorldScene, the new name of your scene. The scene is stored in a file with that name. It's important to know that in Unity there are both *scenes* and *projects*. Every project is typically a game and includes one or more scenes.

You're now ready to create your "Hello World" object.

Step 8: Click on **GameObject – Create Other – GUI Text**.

Your screen now looks like Figure 2.2.

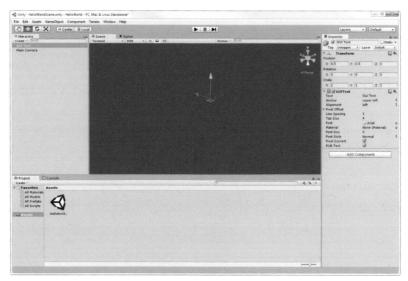

▲ **FIGURE 2.2** Creating a GUI Text Object.

Before you move on and create the Hello World text, take a closer look at the Unity window. This causes a great many changes to the screen. Let's go through all the panels and try to understand what just happened.

First, the window title now has a star at the end of it (PC version only). This is an indication that something has changed since you last did a save. Earlier in Step 6, we selected the Default layout. If for some reason you have a different layout selected, please change it back to "Default" so your screen more closely matches the screen shots in the book.

There are four visible panels: Hierarchy, Scene, Inspector, and Project. There are also two hidden panels, the Game and the Console. The hidden panels are displayed if the user clicks on their corresponding tab. Let's look at each of the panels in more detail.

Figure 2.3 illustrates the Hierarchy panel.

The Hierarchy panel shows the two game objects in the current scene. Their names are "GUI Text" and "Main Camera." The "GUI Text" object is highlighted because it's the one currently selected.

▲ **FIGURE 2.3** The Hierarchy panel.

The Scene panel is shown in Figure 2.4. It contains a graphical view of the game from the developer's perspective. As you can see, there are three bizarre looking arrows in the middle of the panel.

They indicate that there's a game object there and the arrows show the orientation of the object. The object is very simple. It's a string of text with the current value of "Gui Text."

▲ **FIGURE 2.4** The Scene panel.

You will shortly change the text to say "Hello World." The text itself can be seen in the Game panel as shown in Figure 2.5. Clicking on the "Game" tab makes the Game panel visible. You can then see the text superimposed on a blue background.

The Game panel is at the same location as the Scene panel depending on the tab selection. It shows the game as it appears to the players. The players don't need to see the arrows. They just see the text in the middle of the screen.

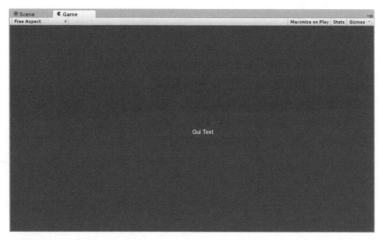

▲ FIGURE 2.5 The Game panel.

Next, on the right side of the window you have the Inspector panel as illustrated in Figure 2.6. It shows the properties of the currently selected game object. Here is where you change the properties of your game objects by pointing and clicking. You'll be doing that shortly.

Figure 2.7 shows the Project panel, which also includes the Assets subpanel.

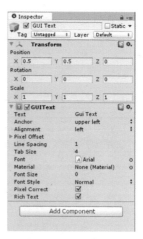

▲ FIGURE 2.6 The Inspector panel.

The Project panel shows items that make up the project. Currently, there's just one item in the project, the "Hello-WorldScene." Notice that there's a slider at the bottom right of the Project panel. Sliding this makes the asset names appear larger or smaller.

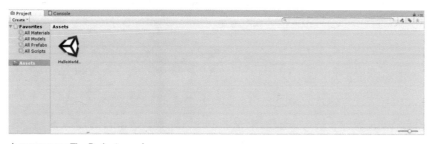

▲ FIGURE 2.7 The Project panel.

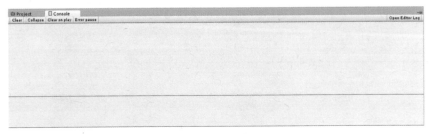

▲ **FIGURE 2.8** The Console panel.

Figure 2.8 shows the Console panel. It is usually hidden behind the Project panel. To view the Console panel, click on the Console tab to select it. This is a panel used to display system messages. If you have an error of some kind this is where the messages are listed for future reference. Click on the Project tab again to go back to displaying the Project panel.

You're now ready to change the text in the GUI Text object. In the Inspector panel near the middle of the panel, you'll see the property named "Text" with the value "Gui Text" on the right of it. Be careful not to confuse this with the "GUI Text" edit box at the top just below the title of the panel.

Step 9: Select the Game panel if necessary, then, in the Inspector panel, click on "Gui Text" to the right of **Text** and change it to **Hello World!**.

Notice that when you're making edits there, the display of the "GUI Text" object changes in real-time in the Game panel and that the line that you're editing gets highlighted in blue.

You could stop right now, but it's just too tempting to experiment with some other properties in the Inspector panel.

Step 10: Change the **X** Position to **0.1** and **Y** Position to **0.9**.

These data entry boxes are located in the Transform section. These changes move the text to the upper-left section of the Game and Scene panels. The Rotation and Scale properties aren't used when displaying GUI Text. Any changes you make in the inspector take effect immediately. It's not necessary to hit Enter on the keyboard.

If you want to make the text larger, you'll have to change the font size.

Step 11: In the **GUIText** section look for **Font Size** and change it from 0 to **48**. This has the effect of making the text larger and more readable. Your screen should now look like Figure 2.9.

▲ **FIGURE 2.9** Hello World.

Now, "run" the application. This application doesn't do much, but that's OK. This is simply a test to see if you know how to run applications in Unity.

Step 12: Click on the **Scene** tab to display the Scene panel.

This will better show what happens when you run an application.

Step 13: To run the application, click on the arrow button on the top middle of the window.

When necessary, the Game panel gets automatically shown in response to your click on the arrow. The game itself doesn't do anything yet other than display your Hello World text.

Step 14: In the Inspector panel, Change the **X** position to **0.5**.

You can change the properties of objects while the game is running. This is one of the things that make Unity extremely powerful. But watch out, these changes are only temporary.

Step 15: To stop running the application, click on the arrow button again.

The Scene panel just came back, but notice that the X position is back at 0.1, just like you never changed it to 0.5.

Step 16: Run the application again by clicking on the arrow button.

You can see that the text has moved back to the upper-left hand corner of the Game panel.

Step 17: Click the arrow button yet again to stop the application. Save your work.

Step 18: Click on **File – Save Scene** and then **File – Save Project**.

Step 19: Exit Unity. There are multiple ways of exiting Unity. Do you know them all? You can close the window, use a dropdown menu, or possibly a keyboard shortcut. The details of this differ for Macs and PCs.

It's a good idea to save your scenes and your project frequently. The most recent scene that you worked on will be automatically loaded next time you start up Unity with the same project. If you load an older project, you'll probably need to explicitly load one of the scenes in that project before continuing to work on that project.

This HelloWorld project was simply a test to see if you can do the very basics of Unity. Of course, Unity can do a whole lot more than displaying text, but you took your first steps. This philosophy of trying out the simple features first before moving on to more complex and difficult ones fits in with a recurring theme in software development: test everything early and often.

Finally, it's time to do some programming.

C# OR JAVASCRIPT?

Before you proceed with programming with Unity, you need to choose your programming language. Unity supports three languages: C# (pronounced C sharp), JavaScript, and Boo. All three languages are interpreted and relatively easy to use. In general, professional developers have a slight preference for C#, mainly because that language is similar to C++, whereas beginners like JavaScript. Currently, Boo is only used by a small percentage of Unity developers.

This book uses JavaScript, mainly because it's a better fit for beginners. There are some technical advantages to C#, but they are outweighed by the steeper learning curve. There's an obsolete misconception that JavaScript is slower than C#. While it is true that some JavaScript code can be very slow, the main culprit of the slowness, dynamic typing, can be easily avoided by including the "#pragma strict" directive in all of your script files.

PROGRAMMING WITH JAVASCRIPT

You're going to get started with programming by diving right in and writing a few very small programs. Your first goal is to add 2 and 2 and to display the result on the Hello World game panel.

Step 1: Look at Appendix I, Programming for Beginners, at the back of this book.

If you're very new to programming, it would be good to carefully read that appendix before continuing. If you're a professional programmer, you can safely skim through that appendix and move on to the next step.

Step 2: Open Unity and, if necessary, load the **HelloWorld** project.

Step 3: Double-click on **HelloWorldScene** in the Assets section of the Hierarchy panel.

Step 4: Click on **GUI Text** in the Hierarchy panel.

The Inspector will now show the properties of the Gui Text object. At the bottom of the Inspector panel, there's an "Add Component" box. You'll be using that box to add a small JavaScript program to this object.

Step 5: Click on the **Add Component** box.

Step 6: Click on **New Script** at the bottom, and then change the name of the script to **Testing123**.

Step 7: Make sure that the language is set to **JavaScript** and then click on **Create and Add**.

Step 8: Click on **Testing123** in the Assets panel.

Depending on your window resolution, you might notice that the script name is truncated to something like "Testing1...". The ellipsis (the three dots) appears if the asset name is too long to fit underneath the asset icon. To see the full asset name, slide the icon slider at the bottom right of the Assets panel all the way to the left, or all the way to the right.

There is now a default script in the Inspector right below the label "Imported Object," consisting of the following:

```
#pragma strict


function Start () {
}


function Update () {
}
```

This is the code you're going to change so that you can compute 2+2. You'll be editing this script in the following steps.

Step 9: Double click on **Testing123** in the Assets panel.

After a delay of several seconds, the MonoDevelop window will appear. It contains the same code you saw earlier, but now it's editable and color coded. The pragma statement is orange and the function keywords have turned blue. This is to help you read the code more easily and to give you immediate feedback when typing in code.

Step 10: Edit the script so it looks like the following:

```
#pragma strict


function OnGUI()
{
    var Result: int = 2 + 2;
    GUI.Box(Rect(10,10,240,40),"Result is " + Result);
}
```

This is the first time you're editing text into Unity, so it's time to do some experimentation. In the following steps, you'll test the code to see if it's working.

Step 11: Save the code! Use **File – Save** or the keyboard shortcut Ctrl-S on the PC, Command-S on the Mac. This is a truly important step and you can easily get bitten if you forget to do this. This is a good keyboard shortcut to learn because you'll need to save frequently.

Step 12: Run the game by clicking on the run arrow. If you're somewhat lucky, you'll see the message telling you that "Result is 4." If you're not so lucky, you'll get some kind of error message. Carefully check all of your code and make sure that it exactly matches the text in the book. If nothing is happening at all, check the function name "OnGUI" for typos. If, for example, you typed "OnGui" instead, you'll get no error messages and no output from the function.

Now we'll carefully go through the six lines of code and fully understand them. The pragma line is customary at the top of all of the script files. It ensures that your code uses strict typing rather than dynamic typing. You'll be using strict typing throughout the book for the sake of efficiency of your code. For now, all you need to know is that this is a good line and you want it right at the top.

The "OnGUI" function is a built-in feature of Unity and gets executed periodically to display user interface items. As stated above, if you have a typo in that name you won't get an error message but the function then just sits there and doesn't get executed. Try temporarily changing the name to OnGui for instance and watch how suddenly the message is no longer there.

The variable name "Result" is one that's made up. It could have easily been something else, such as "WeirdValue." The only thing that matters is that the two occurrences of the name in your code match each other exactly.

The GUI.Box line creates the output that you see in your window. The numbers 10, 10, 240, 40 are coordinates of the rectangle that contains your output. The "Result is" string gets displayed together with the value of the Result variable. The plus sign before Result is not addition but string concatenation, an operation that takes two strings and merges them together. Notice the space at the end of the "Result is " string. That's there to keep the 4 from running together with the word "is." The Result variable contains an integer but automatically gets converted to a string when concatenated with another string.

The last line contains a single curly bracket. It closes an earlier open curly bracket. The two brackets contain the code for the OnGUI function.

Step 12B: Experiment with the code by changing some things and seeing what happens. This is a somewhat free-form step. Keep your changes small and make sure to undo them when you're done. Some possible examples of what to try is to try multiplication with the star character, such as 12*12, or the change the string from "Result is" to "I can put any old string in here."

If you've been lucky enough to avoid compiler error messages, this would be a good time to try out what happens when you do something wrong, such as forgetting a semicolon or a bracket.

It's time to move on and create some graphics.

USING GIMP TO MAKE AN IMAGE

GIMP is a great free program for creating graphic images for use in your game projects. If you haven't done so already, go to *www.gimp.org* and install GIMP on your system. If you have GIMP installed already, please verify that you have version 2.8.2 or later. If you have a later version, or even a slightly older version, everything in this book should still work, but that can't be guaranteed. In the following steps, you'll take GIMP for a quick spin and make an image.

Step 1: Start up GIMP.

Take a look at the main window. The title of the window is GNU Image Manipulation Program. GIMP is an abbreviation of that. It looks like Figure 2.10.

Depending on your previous usage of GIMP you may see additional windows. These additional windows are called "Dockable Dialogs." In this book, Single-Window

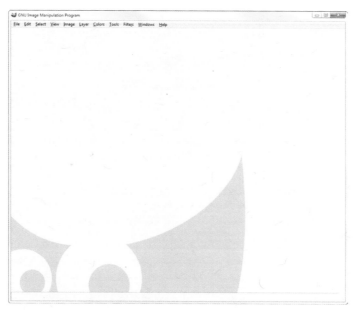

▲ **FIGURE 2.10** GIMP main window.

mode will be used, a mode where these dialogs become panels on the right and left side of the main window.

Step 2: Select **Windows – Single-Window Mode** from the main window.

The main window should look like Figure 2.11.

The group of icons on the left is called the Toolbox, and below it is the Tool Options dialog. If you are using a small monitor, or if your GIMP installation isn't brand new, then your screen may look quite a bit different. This doesn't really matter as long as you can see the tool box icons and the Tool Options.

If you wish, you can use the following procedure to match our screenshot more closely: Disable **Single-Window mode**, and click on **Windows – New Toolbox**. Click on **Windows – Dockable Dialogs – Tool Options**. Then move the Toolbox – Tool Options window to the left of the main window, and then enable Single-Window mode again. Resize the window and adjust the panel layout by dragging the borders left-right, if necessary. Your screen should now match Figure 2.11 more closely.

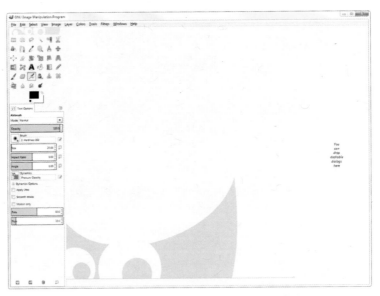

▲ **FIGURE 2.11** GIMP Single-Window mode with Toolbox and Tool Options.

You're now ready to start using GIMP.

Step 3: Select the **File** menu and select **New…**.

Step 4: Activate the **Template** drop-down menu by clicking on the drop-down arrow on the right.

Step 5: Select **1024x768** and click **OK**.

Next, you'll need the Tool Options dialog. The next step is only necessary if you don't have that dialog visible.

Step 6: Select **Windows – Dockable Dialogs – Tool Options**.

Now comes the fun part. You're going to fill your image with dried mud.

Step 7: Select the **Bucket Fill Tool** icon in the Tool box.

It's the icon that looks like a paint bucket. Once you have it selected, the Tool Options area will change to show the options for the Bucket Fill tool.

Step 8: Select a **Fill Type** of **Pattern Fill**.

Step 9: Select the **Dried Mud** built-in pattern.

To select the pattern, first clear the text entry box. Then start typing the name of the pattern and hit return once the autocomplete shows the words "Dried mud." Move the mouse into the image area and notice that the mouse now has a paint bucket icon to let you know that you're about to do a bucket fill.

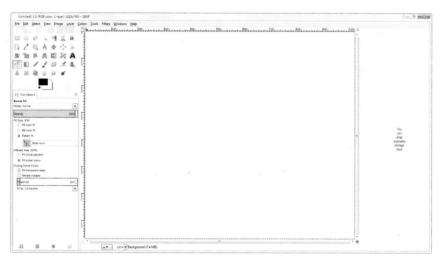

▲ **FIGURE 2.12** Getting ready to fill the image with dried mud.

Step 10: Click anywhere inside of the image.

Your image fills with dried mud and should look like Figure 2.13.

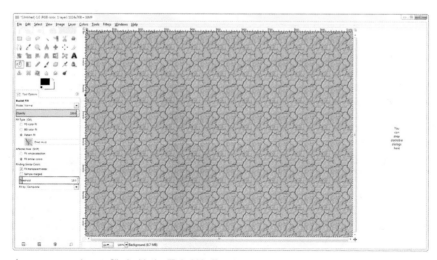

▲ **FIGURE 2.13** Image filled with the "Dried Mud" pattern.

This is going to be your texture image for your demo application. In this book, images are saved in *png* format.

Step 11: Do **File – Export...** with name **MudBackground.png**.

Use the default export settings and use any folder that you can easily find later, such as your Documents folder. You just created a new image containing a repeating dried mud texture. Later on, you'll use GIMP to do some basic drawing with brushes and to manipulate existing images.

Step 12: Do **File – Quit** to exit GIMP and **Discard Changes**.

You did an export, so there's no need to do the save as well.

In the next section, you'll get introduced to yet another tool, Blender, and use it to make a 3D object for your application.

USING BLENDER TO MAKE A 3D OBJECT

Blender is an incredibly powerful, useful, and free program that allows you to make 3D objects for your games. If you haven't done so yet, install the latest version of Blender. It can be downloaded at *www.blender.org*. If you already have Blender installed, make sure that you have version 2.65a or later.

Step 1: Run Blender and left-click the mouse to dismiss the splash screen.

If you're an advanced Blender user, you may skip the following step.

Step 2: Click on **File – Load Factory Settings**.

Your screen should look similar to Figure 2.14.

The loading of the factory settings isn't really necessary if you just installed Blender, but if you've used this particular installation of Blender before it's a good idea to go back to the factory settings so your settings match the ones used by the book.

Before you start to use Blender, the instructions in this book assume that you have a three-button mouse with a scroll wheel and a keyboard with a numeric keypad. If you're using a laptop without a mouse, for example, you can still follow along by learning how to emulate a numeric keypad and scroll wheel on your laptop. This

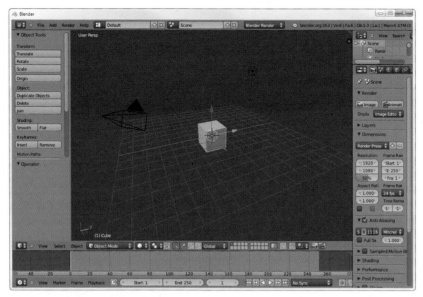

▲ **FIGURE 2.14** Blender initial screen.

works, but it can be cumbersome at times. The Blender interface was designed to be used with a "real" mouse and a full-size keyboard.

Step 3: Delete the cube by moving the mouse to the center of the window, press the **x** key and hit the **Enter** key.

Blender has this default cube set up every time you start the program. You don't need the cube this time, so you can start by deleting it from your 3D world.

Step 4: Click on **Add – Mesh – Monkey**.

Yes, Blender has a monkey object built in. Her name is Suzanne. You'll put this monkey into your application.

Step 5: Hit the **1** key on your numeric keypad.

Step 6: Use the mouse scroll wheel to enlarge the view of the monkey head.

Your screen should now display Suzanne, as shown in Figure 2.15.

Blender is an enormous program. This book only scratches the surface. You can try out one of the more popular and powerful features of Blender by doing the following step.

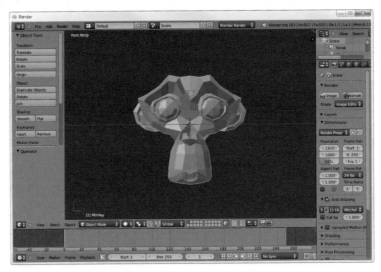

▲ **FIGURE 2.15** Blender monkey Suzanne.

Step 7, PC only: Hit **Control-2** to add a Subdivision Surface Modifier. Another way to get the same effect is this:

Step 7: Click on the **wrench icon** (Object Modifiers), click on **Add Modifier – Subdivision Surface**.

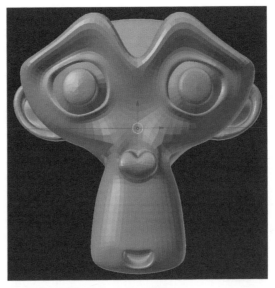

▲ **FIGURE 2.16** Smooth monkey head.

The monkey head magically looks much smoother. It's not really magic, but just a mathematical algorithm that inserts more faces for a smoother appearance. The smooth monkey head is shown in Figure 2.16.

Step 8: Save the file and name it **monkey.blend**. Make a note of where the file is on your system. You'll be using the monkey.blend file later in this chapter when you bring it into Unity.

Now take a look at Audacity, the free audio editor and use it to make a cool sound effect.

USING AUDACITY TO MAKE A SOUND EFFECT

Audacity can be downloaded at *http://audacity.sourceforge.net/*. If you have Audacity installed on your system already, please verify that you have version 2.0.2 or later.

It's surprisingly easy to make sound effects with Audacity.

Step 1: Start Audacity.

Step 2: Click on **Generate – Pluck….**

You will be using one of the built-in sound effects, a synthetic plucking sound.

Step 3: Set the **Pluck MIDI pitch** to **32**.

Step 4: Set the **Fade-out type** to **gradual**.

Step 5: Set the **Duration** to **4.0 seconds** and click **OK**.

You just made a very cool looking audio waveform. Make sure that you have speakers or headphones attached to your computer and that the volume is set to a medium level.

Step 6: Press the **green arrow**.

You should hear four seconds of a distorted sound effect, just what you want. If you don't hear anything, test out your computer with some other sound source, such as an online video.

This sound is a good start, but it's too long.

Step 7: Select the **right two seconds** of the waveform with the mouse.

You select portions of the waveform by clicking and holding the left mouse button, then dragging the mouse, then letting go of the left mouse button. The selected portion of the waveform is now highlighted in a darker shade of grey.

Step 8: Press the **delete** key.

Step 9: Test your change by clicking on the **Skip to start** icon (a double left arrow), followed by the **Play** arrow.

Make the sound more interesting.

Step 10: Click on **Effect – Wahwah...** and **OK**, then click on the **Play** arrow to listen to it.

Your window now shows the new waveform as illustrated by Figure 2.17.

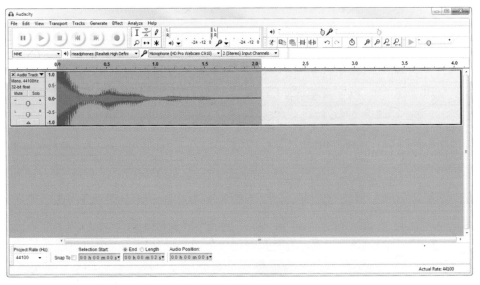

▲ **FIGURE 2.17** Audacity window showing Sound Effect Waveform.

Step 11: Click on **File – Export...**, use the filename **monkeysound.wav**, and use the WAV filetype. Be sure to remember or take a note of the directory where you're saving this file, because you'll be using it shortly in your demo project.

Step 12: Exit Audacity.

The program will ask you if you want to save your work. That may seem strange because you just exported the sound effect. You may save now if you wish, but strictly speaking it's not necessary because the exported .wav file is all you need.

As you saw when you selected the Effect menu, Audacity has a large number of effects. Don't be afraid to try a few of them to see what they do. You're always just a few clicks away from creating something weird and brand new. It's also fun to record sound effects with a microphone and to then unleash some effects on the recordings. More details on how to use Audacity for making realistic and strange sound effects will be discussed later on in this book.

Next, you're going to put the texture image, 3D object, and sound effect together in a demo Unity project.

PUTTING IT TOGETHER: MY FIRST DEMO

In this section, you'll be making a demo application. The plan is to have the monkey head from Blender bouncing up and down on a textured playfield. You'll insert the sound effect and have it looping just because it's very easy to do that. This isn't a game yet, but simply a demo of how the development tools interact with each other.

Step 1: Start up Unity 4.

Unity loads the most recent project that you worked on.

Step 2: Click on **File – New Project…**.

Step 3: Change the name of the project to **ClassicProjectDemo**.

Step 4: Click on the **Create** button.

Step 5: Select **File – Save Scene** and use the name **DemoScene**. Your screen should now look like Figure 2.18.

If your screen looks very different from this, it might be because you have a different layout selected. Make sure that you are using the "Default" layout. If the top right

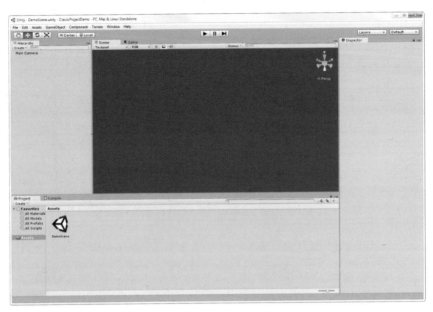

▲ **FIGURE 2.18** Getting started with Unity demo project.

box in your Unity window doesn't say Default, click there and select Default from the drop-down menu.

First, you'll create your playfield. It starts out as a cube and then you'll stretch it.

Step 6: Click on **GameObject – Create Other – Cube**.

Step 7: In the Inspector panel, change the **Position X** value to **0**, **Y** value to **0**, and **Z** value also to **0**, if necessary. Those positions are probably at 0 already, but if they're not, change them to 0.

Step 8: Change the **X Scale** to **10**, leave the **Y Scale** at **1**, and change the **Z Scale** to **10**.

To illuminate your scene, add a light.

Step 9: In the Hierarchy panel, click on **Create – Directional Light**.

Your Unity window should look similar to Figure 2.19.

You're now ready to start importing *assets*. The word "asset" refers to pieces of graphics, code, or sound that might be used in your scenes. The assets are all listed in

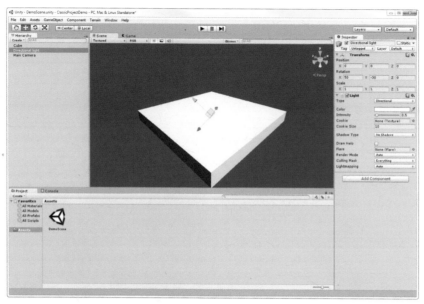

▲ **FIGURE 2.19** A stretched cube acting as the Playfield.

the Project panel in the Assets subpanel. It's easy to add assets to a project. Just drag them into the Project panel using the mouse.

Step 10: Find the file **MudBackground.png** and drag it into the Assets panel. This is the texture file that you created using GIMP a couple of sections ago. The Assets panel should now list three items: DemoScene, MudBackground, and the Standard Assets folder.

Step 11: Drag the **MudBackground** asset on top of the **Cube** object in the Hierarchy.

Now the cube is textured with dried mud! Notice that you now have a Materials folder in the Assets panel. This folder was created automatically when the mudbackground texture was assigned to the Cube.

The texture is hard to see, so you can fix that.

Step 12: Select the **Cube** and change the **tiling** to **0.2** for both **x** and **y** in the Inspector panel.

Step 13: Select the **Cube** again, move the mouse into the Scene panel and scroll the mouse wheel to adjust the zoom level on the playfield so that you see all of the playfield.

After all that, your screen should look similar to Figure 2.20.

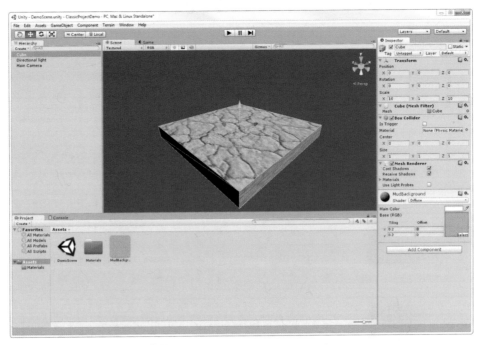

▲ **FIGURE 2.20** Texturing the Playfield.

Your next asset is the monkey. Even though this is a very different file from the mud texture file the importing of this asset works the same way.

Step 14: Drag the file **monkey.blend** into the Assets panel.

Step 15: Drag the **monkey** asset from the project panel to the Scene and drop it near the center of the playfield.

Step 16: With the **monkey** still highlighted, change the **X Position** to **0**, **Y Position** to **4**, and the **Z Position** to **0**. Also, change the **Y Rotation** to **180**. Then click on the cube to get a better view of the monkey.

It's easy to change the color of the monkey as follows:

Step 17: Click on the **monkey**, then click on the white rectangle next to **Main Color** at the bottom of the Inspector panel. This brings up a color dialog. Feel free to experiment with the sliders in this dialog to get familiar with it.

Step 18: Pick a **green color** and exit the color dialog.

Step 19: Click on the layout drop-down menu in the upper-right corner of the window, currently at **Default**, and select **2 by 3**. You should now see a green monkey head in the Game panel as shown in Figure 2.21.

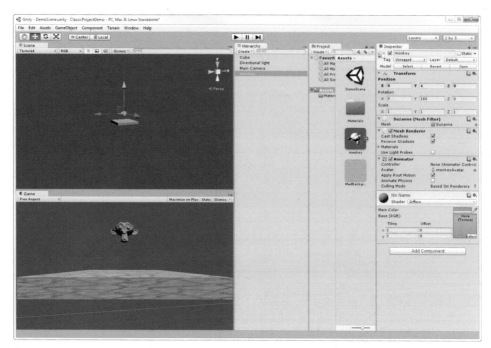

▲ **FIGURE 2.21** Green monkey demo.

Step 20: In the Game panel, select Maximize on Play.

Step 21: Click on the Play arrow at the top of the window.

Running the demo right now causes the Game panel to cover the entire screen. The monkey sits there and doesn't do anything. How can this be fixed? First, notice the Animator section in the Inspector panel. You want to remove this because you don't wish to use the imported Blender animation for the monkey.

Step 22: Stop running the game by clicking on the Play arrow again.

Step 23: Click on the small star on the right side of the Animator component and select **Remove Component**.

Then add a Rigidbody component to the monkey to give it gravity and have Unity's built-in physics engine move the monkey for you.

Step 24: Highlight the monkey in the Hierarchy panel and select **Component – Physics – Rigidbody**.

Now when you run the demo, the monkey falls right through your playfield into a bottomless pit. That's better, but the monkey should collide with the playfield.

Step 25: Click on **Component – Physics – Sphere Collider**.

Now the monkey falls to the playfield and gets stuck there. Try to make it bounce.

First, you need to create a *Physic material*. This unusual terminology refers to a set of physical properties.

Step 26: Click on **Create** in the Project panel and select **Physic Material**.

Step 27: Rename the new Physic material to **Bounce**.

Step 28: Notice the **Bounciness** property in the Inspector and change it to **1**.

You might as well remove the friction as well, so do this:

Step 29: Change the **Dynamic Friction** and **Static Friction** from 0.4 to **0**.

Step 30: Drag the **Bounce** material from the Project panel on top of the monkey in the Hierarchy panel.

Now the monkey bounces but the bouncing is very damped and the bouncing stops very quickly. Why is this? You haven't set the physic material of the playfield yet.

Step 31: Drag the **Bounce** material onto the **Cube** in the Hierarchy panel.

Now when you run the demo the monkey bounces and keeps on bouncing.

Finally, add some sound. Again, you're going to simply drag your sound asset, monkeysound.wav, into the Project panel.

Step 32: Find the file **monkeysound.wav** and drag it into the Assets panel.

Having an asset in your project doesn't actually do anything. To activate it do the following:

Step 33: Select the **Cube** object and click on **Component – Audio – Audio Source**.

Step 34: Drag the **monkeysound** asset on top of the **Cube** in the hierarchy panel.

Step 35: Click on the **Check** for the **Loop** property in the Inspector.

The loop property makes your sound repeat over and over. Notice that the "Play on Awake" property is already checked. That means that the sound will start looping as soon as you start the program running.

Step 36: Run the program and admire your handiwork.

Step 37: Save your scene and project, then **exit** Unity.

Now you know the very basics of running the tools and creating some assets with them. In the next chapter, you'll take a quick look at the early history of video games and a closer look at the arcade video game that started it all, *Pong*.

Pong is generally considered to be the first successful commercial video game. Released in 1972 by a then unknown company, Atari, it had a great name and was an instant hit. *Pong* is truly the game that launched the commercial video game industry. In this chapter, you'll look at the history and design of *Pong* from various perspectives. You'll also get introduced to our first two classic game design rules.

BEFORE *PONG*

Before *Pong* there were tennis and table tennis (also known as Ping Pong). Both are Olympic sports with hundreds of years of history. More important, in the '70s both tennis and table tennis enjoyed great popularity around the world. Back then a majority of the U.S. population knew the basic rules and had at least some experience with trying to play these games.

Pong wasn't the first video game. There's some debate on which one was in fact first, but the first commercial *arcade* video game was *Computer Space*, shown in Figure 3.1.

Amazingly, eight years before *Asteroids*, this game had Asteroids controls! You're flying a space ship with a thrust and two rotation buttons and you shoot at flying saucers.

▼ FIGURE 3.1 Computer Space screenshot.

Computer Space was created in 1971 by Nolan Bushnell and Ted Dabney who would soon after found Atari. Computer Space was not a big commercial success, probably because it was too difficult to learn. The screen also looks a bit busy, in great contrast to its much simpler and better looking successors.

Going farther back in time, *Spacewar!* (see Figure 3.2) is very similar to Computer Space. It was developed on a PDP-1 mainframe computer at MIT in 1962 by Steve Russell and others. DEC distributed this game with all PDP-1's and consequently it ended up at a large number of universities. Even more amazing, this game also had Asteroids controls.

▼ **FIGURE 3.2** *Spacewar!* PDP-1 (1962).

"Easy to learn and hard to master" has become a mantra for many game designers, especially arcade game designers in the '70s and '80s. Arcade games times average three minutes, so there just isn't much time for potential players to learn the games. Ideally the players would watch someone else play the game for a minute or two and would immediately feel that they too could do that.

All this led up to *Pong*. If *Pong* isn't easy to learn, nothing is.

PONG, ATARI (1972)

The gameplay for *Pong* is incredibly simple, even for 1972. Two players each control a paddle with a knob and try to keep the bouncing ball in play. The only differences between *Pong* and Ping Pong are that it takes place on a TV screen, the physics are simplified, and the players control their paddles with knobs instead of holding a physical paddle. When you first encounter the screen, it looks like Figure 3.3.

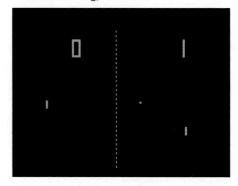

▼ **FIGURE 3.3** *Pong*, Atari 1972.

The design elements consist of just six items: two scores for the players, two paddles, a ball, and a net. Figure 3.4 illustrates the design elements.

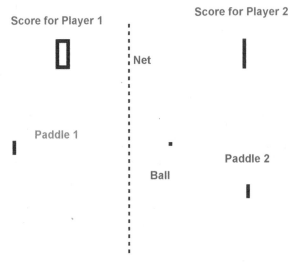

▲ **FIGURE 3.4** *Pong* design elements.

The players control the paddles and they have nothing else to do but to move the paddles up and down and try to make contact with the ball. The scoring is very familiar and self-explanatory.

The physics are simple and a bit unrealistic. There is no gravity, no friction, and no spin effect. Basically it's like Ping Pong in space. None of that matters though. In fact, it's partly because of the clean look and feel that the game was so successful.

This book introduces eight classic game design rules. Here is the first one:

Classic Game Design Rule 1: The Simple Rule: Keep it simple.

Simplicity is the hallmark of great design, and not just in games. The iPhone, *Pong*, the four note theme for Beethoven's fifth symphony, Ernie Els's golf swing, and the pyramids of Egypt: all have a startlingly similar elegance. Designers often arrive at this simplicity via an arduous and complex path. Only rarely does the final design appear fully formed. Rather, years of development are needed to get there.

The enemy of Rule 1 is "featuritis," a disease that can afflict even the best designers. Looking at the sequels of hit games, it's often apparent that the addition of features merely dilutes and spoils the original game. There are exceptions, of course, but great care must be taken when trying to improve upon a successful product.

Examples of Rule 1 are everywhere. Consider Apple's iPod, iPhone, and iPad. Their phenomenal success is often attributed to their optimally simple user interface.

Here's the second rule:

Classic Game Design Rule 2: Immediate Gameplay Rule: Start gameplay immediately.

All too many modern games break this rule. People are impatient. They don't want to wait around, or read a bunch of rules. They want to start playing the game right away. It takes some judgment to deal with this rule. A good way to look at it is this: Estimate the duration of the playing session, and allow for about 5% of that time for instructions, cut-scenes, or the traversing of menus before starting with the actual gameplay. In the coin-op days of the '80s, 3 minute game times were the norm, which is 180 seconds; thus the games wouldn't go over 9 seconds of introduction or instruction before allowing people to play. Ideally, like in *Pong* for instance, the players would insert a coin and start playing just a few seconds afterwards.

It's tempting to write more rules now, but that would be a violation of Rule 1!

COIN-OP, THE REAL ATARI

Pong was the first product made by Atari. The people who made the games were hardware engineers. There were no programmers because the game was made entirely in hardware. It would take several more years until commercial games were programmed by game programmers rather than designed by hardware engineers. In the mid-seventies, Atari split into two groups: coin-op and consumer. The coin-op group always considered itself the "Real Atari" because most of the big hits originated as coin-op games. The consumer group, however, would soon be responsible for the vast majority of revenues.

PONG SEQUELS AND CLONES

Predictably, *Pong* led to a whole slew of arcade sequels and clones including *Pong Doubles* (1973), *Super Pong* (1974), and *Quadrapong* (1974), all by Atari. *Pong Doubles* added two more paddles so that four players could play. Atari also got into the home video game business with the *Home Pong* console. If you haven't done so already, this would be a good time for you surf the Web and look at some images and videos of *Pong* and its sequels.

BITMASTERS, DAY ONE

Over 20 years later, in 1994, Bitmasters got a development contract to do a basketball game for Mindscape on the Genesis and SNES home video game systems. Bitmasters was a small game development company located in Sunnyvale, California, just a few miles from the old Atari buildings. This was no coincidence because several of the people at Bitmasters were ex-Atari employees. Day one of the basketball project was also day one for several new programmers. None of them had ever seen a SNES system, much less programmed for it. So what would be the best way to teach them the basics? They all spent the day programming *Pong* using 65816 assembly language and proprietary Bitmasters software tools developed for previous SNES games. Amazingly, it took just one day for the new programmers to get a very good version of *Pong* up and running on their development systems.

PONG AT FORTY

Is *Pong* still a viable game forty years later? Yes! In 2012, Atari held a high publicity contest called the Pong Indie Developer Challenge. The winning entry was *Pong World*, published in November of 2012, four decades after the first *Pong* hit the arcades. This modern sequel is a much more complex game than the original, but the basic ideas behind *Pong* are still there.

What can you learn from this? Just as good literature, music, and art continue to thrive tens or even hundreds of years after their creation, so do the great classic video games. All game developers should keep this in mind when negotiating contracts with publishers. It's also good to consider the far future when designing games. Can you imagine what a game console will look like in fifty years? Chances are the resolution will be higher, the processors faster, the storage larger. The controls will be different, maybe even unrecognizable. The constants are the rules, the product trademarks, the characters, the stories, and to some extent the basic game mechanics. A reasonable attempt to future-proof your game would include the following: stay away from fad controls, avoid cultural references to current events, and develop your art assets in a resolution independent way.

In the next chapter, you'll start by developing your very own paddle game inspired by *Pong*.

CHAPTER 4 — Classic Paddle Game

In this chapter, you're going to build your first game, a two-player paddle game similar to Pong. It's an exercise in building a prototype from scratch using Unity.

GETTING READY

As you can see, the title is Classic Paddle Game. This is a working title, intended to be replaced by the real title as some point. It is up to you to create a better title. Working titles are often chosen to be intentionally unusable for a commercial product, and this one's no different. You're going to do a game that's a very abstract version of ping pong. There are two players, and all they do is control their respective paddles to hit a ball back and forth across the screen. If a player misses hitting the ball, the other player gets a point. The first player to get to eleven points wins. That's the game in a nutshell, and this description is a rough guideline. You're perfectly free to change some things along the way. This game, unlike *Pong*, will use a physics engine and, just for fun, it'll be in color with 3D lighting effects.

VERSION 0.01: THE PLAYFIELD

Your first goal is to display the playfield. This is a very common first step in making games. Whether it's a detailed world in *Skyrim™* or a blank canvas in *Pong*, you always need some kind of background. Your background in this game is going to be a rectangular shape with borders on the top and the bottom. That's about as simple as it gets, but like in all software development, this first step can be the most difficult.

This would be a good time for you to create a directory where you'll be storing all of your Unity projects, if you haven't done so already. Then proceed with Step 1:

Step 1: Create a new Unity project with the name "ClassicPaddleGame" in your Unity projects directory. Import the "Physic Materials.unityPackage".

We're loading the Physic Materials package when creating the project, but if you forget to do this you can load this package later on. Your screen should look similar to Figure 4.1.

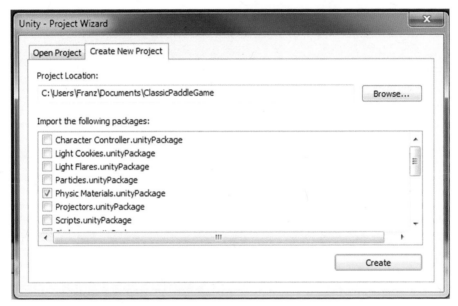

▲ **FIGURE 4.1** Using the Physic Materials package.

Step 2: Use the **2 by 3** layout.

Upon startup, there is a blank workspace as shown in Figure 4.2. You should see the text "2 by 3" in the upper-right hand corner of the window. If you don't, activate the layout drop-down menu and select "2 by 3". You're now ready to create your game.

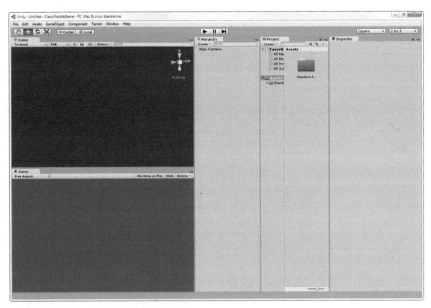

▲ **FIGURE 4.2** Starting workspace in Unity.

Step 3: Click on **GameObject – Create Other – Cube** from the main menu and rename the Cube to **Playfield**. Renaming can be done either in the Hierarchy or in the Inspector.

Step 4: Use the **Top Isometric** view. To do this, manipulate the Scene Gizmo in the upper right corner of the Scene panel. Your goal is to see the text "Top" and three parallel lines next to it. You can click on the four arms of the gizmo to change views, and you can click on the text to change from perspective to isometric view.

Step 4A: Select the **Playfield** object, hover the mouse over the Scene panel, and then press the **f** key.

You should now see a cube in the upper left window as shown in Figure 4.3. The "f" key focuses on the currently selected object. It's very useful for finding your current game object when it's gotten lost off-screen someplace, or if the zoom level is much too large or too small.

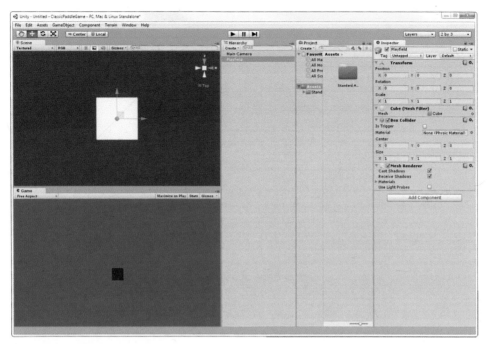

▲ **FIGURE 4.3** Creating a cube in Unity.

This is your starting point for the playfield. Make the Playfield larger by changing the scale.

Step 5: Set the **Scale** of the **Playfield** to (**30, 30, 1**). This is done by clicking on X, Y, and Z in the Scale section of the Inspector window and entering the new values for X and Y. The Z Scale is already set to 1.

Step 6: Use the **Front** view and **focus** on the **Playfield**.

Select the "Front" view by clicking on the triangle below the "z" in the Scene Gizmo. Then focus on the Playfield like this: select it, hover the mouse in the Scene panel, and press the "f" key. Your screen should now look like Figure 4.4.

Next, you'll change the color of the playfield object. You'll do this by creating a material, assigning it to the object, and adjusting the color of the material.

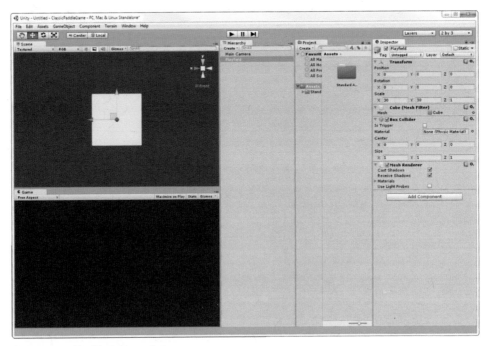

▲ **FIGURE 4.4** The Playfield rescaled.

Step 7: Click on **Create** in the Project panel and select **Material** and give it the name **Mat Playfield**. Rather than renaming the material later, it's possible to immediately type the new name after clicking on "Material."

Step 8: Change the **Main Color** of **Mat Playfield** to a dark shade of green. As you might recall from Chapter 2, to change color, click on the rectangle to the right of "Main Color" in the Inspector. Then use the pop-up Color Dialog to select a dark green color.

To get a dark green color, first select green in the rainbow strip, and then select a dark green from the main square.

Step 9: Assign the **Mat Playfield** material to the **Playfield**. This is done by dragging the material with your mouse from the Assets panel to the Playfield in the Hierarchy panel or alternately in the Scene panel. Your screen should now look like Figure 4.5.

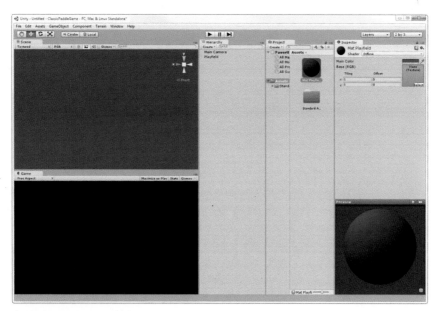

▲ **FIGURE 4.5** A green playfield.

You might have noticed that the Playfield appears much darker in the Game panel than in the Scene panel. That's because the camera is right next to the playfield and because the lighting isn't set up yet. Move the Main Camera farther back to see the playfield properly.

Step 10: Click on **Main Camera** and move it to **(0, 0, -30)**.

As usual, you do this by entering the new position in the Transform section. The playfield still looks dark in the Game panel, so go ahead and add a light.

Step 11: Click on **Create** in the Hierarchy panel and select **Point Light**.

Step 12: Move the Point light to **(0, 0,-10)** and change its **Range** to **100** in the Inspector panel.

Step 13: Select the **Top** view in the Scene panel by clicking on the triangle below "y".

Step 14: Select the **Main Camera** object by clicking on it.

You should now get a good view of what's happening as shown in Figure 4.6.

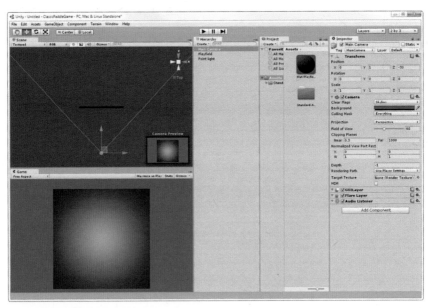

▲ **FIGURE 4.6** Camera moved back to reveal the entire playfield.

Step 15: Experiment with the Field of View. Be sure that the "Main Camera" is still selected. The top view shows that the camera is in front of the playfield and the view lines emerging from the camera encompass the entire playfield. You can move the "Field of View" slider with your mouse to see the effect of changing the field of view. When you're done playing with the slider, put it back at 60 degrees.

You've done quite a bit of work and all you have is a green square! Still, this is a good point to test the game, just to see if you can see the green square when you hit the play button.

Step 16: Turn on **Maximize on Play** in the Game panel, if it's not already on.

Step 17: Hit the **play** arrow. You should see Figure 4.7.

It's now time to save your work. First, stop playing the game by clicking on the Play triangle again.

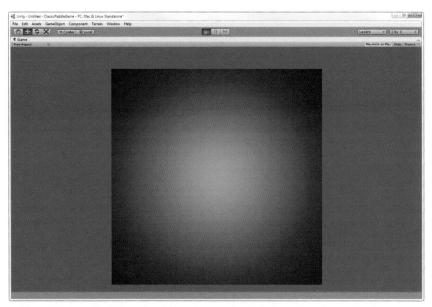

▲ **FIGURE 4.7** Looking at the maximized playfield in Play mode.

Step 18: Stop playing. **Save** the Scene as **PaddleScene**. **Save** the Project. **Exit** Unity.

Your next goal is to create boundaries at the top and bottom of the playfield. Also, please note, that from here on the instructions are slightly less detailed, now that you're getting more familiar with the Unity interface.

Step 19: Launch Unity. You should see the scene just as you left it when you saved it.

The scene got reloaded, not because you saved it, but because it was the most recent scene. If you worked on other Unity projects in the interim, you'd have to now explicitly load "PaddleScene" by double clicking on it in the Assets panel. You can try this out by loading one of the old projects from Chapter 2, then loading this project.

Step 20: Create a cube, **Scale (30, 1, 1)**, **Position (0, 15, 0)** and rename to **BoundaryUpper**.

Step 21: Select the **Back** view in the Scene panel. To get to the Back view, click on one of the horizontal triangles until the Back view appears. The horizontal triangles cycle through the sequence left, front, right, back.

Step 22: Select **Playfield** and give it a new **Z Position** of **1.1** instead of 0.

The playfield just got a cool 3D quality to it. Your screen should look like Figure 4.8.

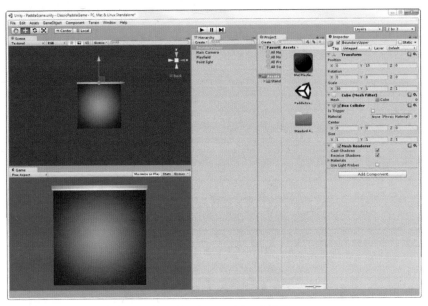

▲ **FIGURE 4.8** Upper boundary positioned at the top of the playfield.

Why did the instructions direct you to move the playfield back? The ball is going to have a z-coordinate of 0, so you want the playfield behind it rather than at the same position. Notice the subtle 3D effect of the boundary because it is no longer overlapping with the playfield.

Step 23: Select **BoundaryUpper**, then right-click and select **Duplicate**.

Step 24: Rename one of the duplicates to **BoundaryLower**.

Step 25: Select **BoundaryLower** and change the **Y Position** to **-15**.

Your screen should look like Figure 4.9.

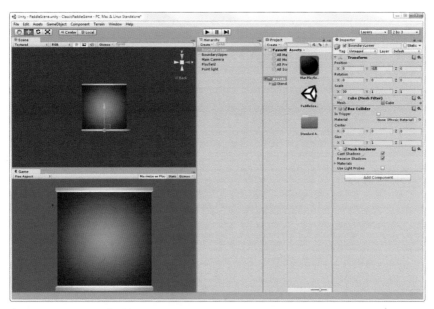

▲ FIGURE 4.9 The playfield for your game.

Step 26: **Save** your work by saving the scene and the project, then **exit** Unity.

This is about as simple a playfield as you can have in a game. Commercial game projects spend millions of dollars developing just the playfields for their large worlds, but essentially they are all just the stage and background for the true stars of the games, the animated characters. While it's certainly possible to skip making the playfield entirely, it's usually a good idea to have a simple playfield in place before doing anything else.

For the next version, you'll add the paddles for your paddle game and control them with your computer keyboard.

VERSION 0.02: THE PADDLES

The paddles are the player characters in this two-player game. They will be created by starting with cubes and scaling them.

Step 1: Launch Unity and load the project.

Your screen should look like you left it in Figure 4.9. As usual, it may be necessary to explicitly load PaddleScene.

Step 2: Create a **Cube** and name it **PaddleLeft**.

Step 3: Change the **Position** of **PaddleLeft** to (-14, 0, 0) and the **Scale** to (1, 4, 1).

In case you're wondering, the 14 was determined by trial and error. The playfield is 30 units wide, so you'd think that -15 would be the correct x position, but you want the paddle to be offset a little bit away from the edge, so -14 seems about right.

Next, let's make the paddle red.

Step 4: Create a **Material** in the Project panel, name it **Mat Paddle**.

Step 5: Change the **Main Color** of **Mat Paddle** to **red**.

Step 6: Drag **Mat Paddle** onto **PaddleLeft**.

The paddle should now be red instead of grey. Next, you need to make the other paddle.

Step 7: Duplicate PaddleLeft.

This is done by selecting it, right clicking, and selecting "Duplicate" from the menu.

Step 8: Rename one of the duplicates to **PaddleRight**.

Step 9: Move **PaddleRight** to (14, 0, 0) by deleting the minus sign for the X position.

The screen should now show the two new paddles, ready for action, as shown in Figure 4.10.

What just happened? Well, you made two red paddles out of cubes and placed them on the playfield. You're now ready to make the paddles move in response to player inputs.

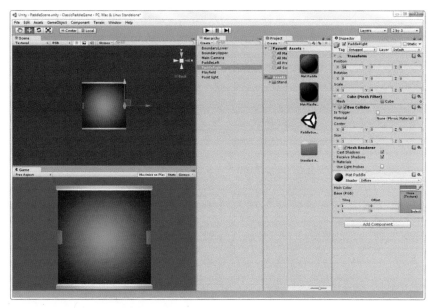

▲ **FIGURE 4.10** Two new paddles, ready for action.

Step 10: Save your scene and project.

Step 11: In the Project Panel, click on **Create – JavaScript** and rename it **P1** instead of NewBehaviour.

This is where you start putting in some code to make the left paddle move up and down.

Step 12: Select **P1** and click on **Open...** in the Inspector as shown in Figure 4.11.

▲ **FIGURE 4.11** Getting ready to edit the P1 script.

A new window opens up. This is MonoDevelop, the code editor for Unity. You'll be editing your code in this window as shown in Figure 4.12.

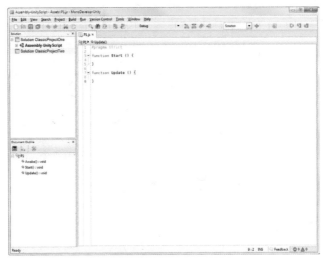

▲ FIGURE 4.12 MonoDevelop window.

You should see nine lines of code. There are two functions, `Start` and `Update`, and they are empty. These are placeholder functions to help you get started.

Step 13: Replace the placeholder code in P1.js by deleting it and typing in the following code:

```
#pragma strict

function Update ()
{
    if (Input.GetKey ("w"))
    {
        transform.Translate (0, 20 * Time.deltaTime,0);
    }
    if (Input.GetKey ("s"))
    {
        transform.Translate (0, -20 * Time.deltaTime,0);
    }
}
```

Step 14: Save your editing work in MonoDevelop by clicking on **File – Save** in the MonoDevelop Window.

Always save your code right away. Notice that the filename P1.js has a star next to it whenever there are unsaved changes present.

This `Update` function periodically checks the keyboard. When the "w" key is pressed down, it moves the current object by a few units of distance. In this case, the "w" key makes the object move up. The "s" key makes it go down.

Step 15: Drag the **P1** script onto **PaddleLeft**.

You'll need to click on the Unity window to make it the active window before doing this.

Step 16: Run the game and press the **w** and **s** keys. They should move the left paddle up and down.

There's a chance that you made a typo when you typed in that code. If so, you'll probably get a compiler error. To fix the error go back to MonoDevelop, fix the problem, using the error message as a guide, save your changes, and try again. You may need to do this several times. This is normal, even for experienced programmers, so don't give up if it doesn't work for you right away.

Step 17: Exit Play mode.

It's *very important* that you leave play mode by deselecting the play arrow whenever you make changes that you wish to be permanent. If you forget to do this, everything you do during play mode will be lost when you finally remember to stop game-play mode! This is a nasty surprise waiting to happen. As long as you have "Maximize on Play" selected it's much less of a problem, so be sure to continue to use Maximize on Play when possible.

Now do this all again for the other paddle in the following steps.

Step 18: Create another JavaScript, call it **P2**, and open it.

You'll be back in MonoDevelop and see two tabs for the two script files, P1.js and P2.js.

Step 19: Select the P1.js tab, do **Edit – Select All**, the copy it using **Edit – Copy**.

Step 20: Select the P2.js tab, again select all the code, then do **Edit – Paste**.

Both P1.js and P2.js should now contain the same code.

Step 21: Change "w" to "up" and "s" to "down" in P2.js.

The "up" and "down" refer to the up arrow and down arrow keys on your keyboard.

Step 22: Save the file in MonoDevelop.

Step 23: In Unity, drag **P2** from the Project window on top of **PaddleRight**.

Step 24: Run the game and try out the new controls. We can now control both paddles.

Step 25: Save the scene and project, and **exit** Unity.

VERSION 0.03: THE BALL

It's time to create a ball to knock around with your paddles. Fortunately, this is really easy to do in Unity.

Step 1: Start up Unity.

If you need to, load the project and scene that you saved at the end of the last section.

Step 2: Create a **Sphere** in the Hierarchy panel and rename to **Ball**.

Step 3: Select **Ball** and change the **Position** to (**0, 0, 0**), if necessary.

Step 4: Make it yellow by creating the material **Mat Ball**, making it **yellow**, and dragging it onto the **Ball** game object.

The code for the ball is a little tricky. You'll launch the ball from the middle of the playfield in a somewhat random direction.

Step 5: Create a new JavaScript, call it BallScript, and assign it to the Ball object. Then type in the following code:

```
#pragma strict

function Start ()
{
   rigidbody.freezeRotation = true;
   yield WaitForSeconds (3);
   rigidbody.AddForce (Random.Range(6,8) , Random.Range(-4, -3) ,0);
}


function Update ()
{
   transform.position.z = 0;
}
```

If you were to try and run the code right now, you'd get an error message because the ball doesn't have a Rigidbody component yet. Here's how to fix that:

Step 6: Select **Ball** in the Hierarchy. Click on **Component – Physics – Rigidbody**.

Step 7: In the Inspector **uncheck Use Gravity** and set the **Mass** to **0.01**.

It's critical that you enter the mass correctly, or the ball will behave strangely. For example, with a mass of 0.1, the ball would move much too slowly.

Step 8: In the **Sphere Collider**, click on the small circle next to the Material box. A new window will pop up. Assign the **Bouncy** material to the Sphere Collider. This makes the ball bouncy. If you don't see bouncy as one of the choices, you forgot to import the Physic Materials package when you created the project. In that case, you can import that package now by clicking on **Assets – Import Package – Physic Materials**.

Step 9: Click on **Bouncy** in the **Sphere Collider** of the **Ball**.

This makes the "Bouncy" material appear in the Assets panel.

Step 10: Drag the **Bouncy** material onto **both paddles** and **both boundaries**.

Finally, remove all friction from the bouncy material.

Step 11: Click on **Bouncy** and, then, in the Inspector panel, change the Dynamic Friction and the Static Friction from 0.3 to **0**.

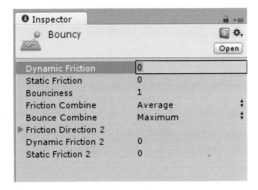

▲ **FIGURE 4.13** Removing friction from the Bouncy Physic Material.

Look at Figure 4.13 for a view of the Inspector panel.

Step 12: Save your work and test it.

You have reached a major milestone. The game is now playable. There's still quite a bit of work left to do, but you've made a good start. The ball is bouncing off the walls and the paddles as long as you keep the ball in play. You do have a problem in that if the ball gets by one of the players, you have to restart the game if you want to play again. You'll fix this in the next section.

VERSION 0.04: A BETTER PLAYFIELD

You've reached your first major milestone, but there are still some major missing elements. You also have some problems with the game. There are two separate philosophies on how to proceed in such a situation. Do you fix what you have, or do you add more features and fix the problems later?

In general, it's a better approach to fix your problems early. This has many advantages, the main one being that it's easier to fix problems while your project is still small. It's just a better feeling to have a working game rather than a broken game. This also allows you to do more early testing. A broken game is difficult or maybe even impossible to test.

So rather than adding scoring or audio, you're going to first fix this problem of the ball flying off into space when a player misses it.

Step 1: Start up Unity and load your project. Make sure you're still using the 2 by 3 layout.

You're now going to create an empty object and manually add a box collider to it.

Step 2: GameObject – Create Empty.

Step 3: Rename to **BoundaryLeft**.

Step 4: Move **BoundaryLeft** to position (**-15**, **0**, **0**).

Step 5: Component – Physics – Box Collider.

Step 6: Change the **Size** of the **Box Collider** to (**1**, **30**, **1**).

You should now see a green outline of a skinny vertical box in the Scene panel. Notice that you didn't change the Y Scale in the Transform section, although that would have had the same effect.

Step 7: Check the **Is Trigger** box in the Inspector.

You'll see the effect of the trigger checkbox later, when you code your collision script.

You now have a box much like the upper and lower boundaries on the left side of the playfield, except that it's invisible! You'll be using this invisible box as a way to detect when the ball is out of bounds.

Step 8: Create a JavaScript, call it **BallRelaunch**. Then enter the following code:

```
#pragma strict

function OnTriggerEnter (other : Collider)
{
    other.transform.position = Vector3(0, 0, 0);
}
```

Step 9: Save the code and drag the **BallRelaunch** script to the **BoundaryLeft** Object.

Step 10: Duplicate BoundaryLeft, rename it **BoundaryRight**, and move it to (15, 0, 0).

Now, if you test the game (and you should), then you'll see that the ball gets magically transported to the middle of the screen whenever it gets by one of the players.

Step 11: Save your Scene and Project and **exit** Unity.

Feel free to keep the MonoDevelop application running or not, but make sure that you don't have any unsaved editing left in MonoDevelop.

You've just made the game quite a bit better but you're still missing a couple of major features: audio and scoring.

VERSION 0.05: AUDIO

In this section, you'll add a simple sound effect to your game. You'll be using Audacity.

Step 1: Open Audacity.

Step 2: Select **Generate – Pluck** from the drop-down menu.

Step 3: Change the **Pluck MIDI pitch** to **80** and click on **OK**.

Your Audacity window should look like the window in Figure 4.14.

▲ **FIGURE 4.14** Audacity used to create a simple sound effect.

If you play this sound, you'll hear that it can work as a collision sound in your game, which is what you want.

Step 4: Select **File – Export**, give the file the name **pluck.wav**, and save it to the Assets folder of the ClassicPaddleGame Unity project.

One of the convenient features of Unity is that by saving your externally generated files into the assets folder, they automatically get imported into Unity. Try out this feature right now.

Step 5: Exit Audacity and don't bother saving because you just exported the sound.

Step 6: Open Unity and look for Pluck.wav in the Assets panel.

Because presumably ClassicPaddleGame was the most recent project, you won't need to load it. And, if everything went according to plan, the pluck audio file should be in the Assets panel, ready for inspection. You may need to scroll down in the Assets panel to see the pluck.wav file.

Step 7: Select the **pluck** sound and **play** the sound in the preview section of the Inspector panel.

Your Unity screen should look like Figure 4.15.

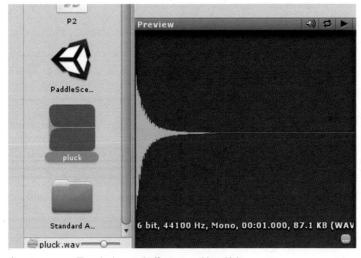

▲ **FIGURE 4.15** The pluck sound effect moved into Unity.

That was pretty easy so far. Of course, you could have used any other short .wav file instead of pluck.wav.

Your next goal is to have your sound effect play when the ball collides with something. This takes quite a few steps:

Step 8: Select **Ball** in the Hierarchy. Then do **Component – Audio – Audio Source**.

This makes the ball a source of audio by adding an Audio Source component to it.

Step 9: Drag the **pluck** sound from the Assets Panel on top of the **Ball** object.

The pluck sound should appear as the Audio Clip in the Inspector panel as shown in Figure 4.16.

▲ **FIGURE 4.16** The pluck sound appears as the Audio Clip.

Next, you need to change the code for the BallScript.

Step 10: Add the following variable declaration at the beginning of **BallScript**. Insert between the pragma and the Start function as follows:

```
#pragma strict

var BeepSound: AudioClip;

function Start () {
    ...
```

This is where the script stores a reference to the sound.

Step 10B: Add the following function at the end of **BallScript**:

```
function OnCollisionEnter (other : Collision)
{
    audio.PlayOneShot(BeepSound);
}
```

Step 11: Save the BallScript.js file in MonoDevelop.

Step 12: Select the **Ball** in the Hierarchy. In the **Ball Script** section of the Inspector, click on the small circle to the right of **Beep Sound**. A window will pop up. Select the **pluck** sound.

Step 13: Save your work, then **test**.

During testing, you discover that the sound plays for no apparent reason on startup. To fix this unwanted behavior, do the following:

Step 14: Select the **Ball** object in the Hierarchy panel and **uncheck Play On Awake** in the Inspector.

Step 15: Save your work, then test, again.

Step 16: Exit Unity.

The audio for the classic arcade games is famous for being extremely primitive. The basic formula for sound design was to have a few simple sound effects when something collided with something else. Recorded music and speech didn't become common until later. In this book, you'll stick with very simple sound effects in keeping with the spirit of early classic gaming.

In the next section, you'll finally add scoring to your game.

VERSION 0.06: SCORING

Your paddle game isn't really a game unless you add scoring. In the classic era, all games had numbers as scores. As games migrated to home systems numerical scoring became less important, so it was either made irrelevant or dropped altogether, like in many of today's first person shooters.

Step 1: Start Unity and load ClassicPaddleGame if necessary.

Step 2: GameObject – Create Empty, name it **Score**.

Step 3: Add a new script component to Score with the name **Scoring** and enter the following code for it:

```
#pragma strict

static var scorep1: int;
static var scorep2: int;

function Start ()
{
    scorep1 = 0;
    scorep2 = 0;
}

function OnGUI()
{
    GUI.Box (Rect (10,10,90,30), "Player 1:    "+scorep1);
    GUI.Box (Rect (Screen.width - 100,10,90,30),
            "Player 2:    "+scorep2);
}
```

A few words of explanation are in order. "scorep1" and "scorep2" are integer variables that store the score for the two players. Our "Start" function automatically gets called at the beginning of the game, so that's a good place to initialize the scores to zero.

The OnGUI function is similar to the code you used for the HelloWorld project. This is where you display the two scores plus labels.

If you now run the game, you'll see the score display as shown in Figure 4.17, but the scores aren't changing!

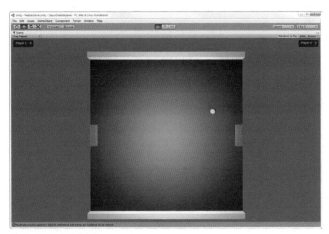

▲ **FIGURE 4.17** Adding scoring to your game.

To make the scores update according to the gameplay, you also need to change the "BallRelaunch" script as follows:

Step 4: Edit BallRelaunch to look like this:

```
#pragma strict

function OnTriggerEnter (other : Collider)
{
    if (other.transform.position.x > 0)
        Scoring.scorep1++;
    else
        Scoring.scorep2++;

    other.transform.position = Vector3(0, 0, 0);
}
```

The "++" command in JavaScript increments the variable by 1. Test the x coordinate of the ball and if it's greater than 0, it's on the right side of the screen, which means that the ball was missed by player 2. With this somewhat convoluted logic we conclude that in this case Player 1 gets a point, otherwise Player 2 gets the point.

Step 5: Run the game to test it out. Stop running it, and save the scene and project, then exit Unity.

VERSION 1.0: FIRST RELEASE!

Is this game ready for release? Probably not, but you're going to release it anyway! It's an old joke among developers to say "ship it" right after fixing a bug or adding a feature. For you, in this book, *release* means something a little different. It merely means that you're done with the main development of the game and ready to move on to other things. Of course if your game is fun and people like it, then the release is just the beginning of development.

The classic arcade video games that you're studying in this book were developed in an environment where games were tested extensively before release. This testing would happen in focus groups and field tests. For this first game in your book you're going to be lazy with the testing because this game wasn't really intended to be a real product. It's basically a prototype and an exercise to get you started. Your testing will merely consists of making sure the game runs when you build it. In your subsequent games, you'll be tougher on yourself during testing.

So how do you release this game? This is really easy in Unity. You simply select **File – Build Settings...** and you will see a new Window as shown in Figure 4.18.

▲ **FIGURE 4.18** Building the game.

Select PC and Mac Stand-alone, click on Add Current, to add the current scene, select your target platform (windows or Mac), click on Build and Run, and give it a name. You will then have to wait a while for the game to build, though this should take less than a minute depending on the speed of your computer. You'll then be able to try out the game in various environments, different graphics settings, and different window sizes. It might also be interesting to take the resulting game and move it to a different computer to see if or how it runs. For example, Figure 4.19 shows how the game looks in a 640x480 window under the "fastest" setting.

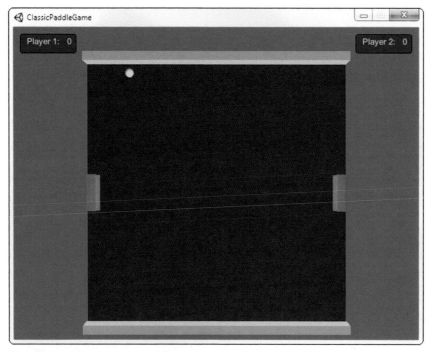

▲ **FIGURE 4.19** Running the game in fastest setting.

Notice that the lighting effect of your Point light isn't working any more. This is all part of testing the release. You need to test what the game looks like and plays like in different environments. So far you can conclude that your game is still playable even in the lowest quality setting.

It's a good idea to test your game on several different computers before releasing it to a large audience. You'd be amazed how frequently additional problems surface

during this process. This is also a good time to show the game to some fresh players and to get their feedback.

POSTMORTEM

A *postmortem* is a medical term having to do with studying a medical case after the patient has died. Literally, it is Latin for "after death." This word is also used in the game development community to take a look back at a project after it's been released and to try to learn what went wrong and what went right. You're now going to do that for your first classic game project.

Here's what went right. We designed, built, and tested a prototype for a very simple paddle game. It works. It compiles and doesn't crash. It looks way better than the original paddle games from the seventies, but that's not really saying much. All you had to do is add color and use a 3D engine. The game feels pretty good and it took very little code.

What went wrong? Well the obvious problem is that you're not really done yet. There's no game over, no title screen, and there's no "Player x wins" message. This is somewhat deliberate. After all, this is just a prototype. You do have a worse problem though: the physics aren't quite right. When the ball hits the paddle the player doesn't really feel like he can control where he wants the ball to go. In real table tennis you can control how fast and where the ball goes. We'd kind of like to have that in this game. Oh well, that's what sequels are for.

EXERCISES

There's always more that can be done to a game. Here are a few suggestions for readers who would like to reinforce what they just learned in this chapter.

1. Adjust the speed of the ball to make it faster, thus making the game more difficult.
2. Adjust the speed of the paddles to make them slower. Experiment with slower and faster speeds. What is the effect of a very fast paddle speed? A very slow speed?

3. Add two more paddles to make it a four player game.

4. Create a new and different sound effect using Audacity and use it in the game.

5. Add a circular obstacle in the middle of the playfield. Try adding several obstacles. Is the game better or worse when you do that? Explain.

6. Implement two ball speeds. Have the speed depend on a button press by one of the players.

   Which player should control the ball speed? Why?

Advanced exercises for experienced Unity users:

7. Make it a one-player game by adding AI to player 2.

8. After completing the previous exercise, add a menu to select one-player or two-player.

9. Add graphics for the net in the middle by adding a texture to the Playfield object. Create the texture using GIMP.

CHAPTER 5 — *Breakout*

Breakout is the first successful single-player arcade video game. It's a good example of a simple game with the kind of addictive quality that foreshadowed the golden age of arcade gaming in the early eighties. With *Breakout*, it's just you against the machine, an experience similar to golf or bowling, where you try to outdo your own past efforts.

WOZ

Steve Wozniak, aka Woz, so the story goes, built a working prototype of this game in four days, together with Steve Jobs. Jobs was a brand new technician at Atari and had been assigned the task of making this game. He immediately enlisted his friend and hardware guru, Woz. Getting little sleep the duo worked nonstop to pull off this stunning feat. Nowadays, games such as *Breakout* can be implemented in software in just a few hours, but this was 1976. In order to keep costs reasonable, the game needed to be built using custom hardware. This is one of the earliest anecdotes of people working crazy overtime hours to make a video game. Things haven't changed, and it's still very common for game developers to work late into the night. On the other hand, there are plenty of successful and even famous designers who work normal hours and have a life.

BREAKOUT, ATARI (1976)

Just like Pong, *Breakout* is a ball and paddle game, but with the goal of breaking the bricks in a wall. Every time the ball hit a brick it would magically disappear and you would score points. You would start with three balls and you'd lose a ball every time you'd miss hitting it with the paddle. *Breakout* gets more difficult as the game progresses by speeding up the ball and making the paddle smaller. You can see a game design diagram of the original coin-op *Breakout* in Figure 5.1.

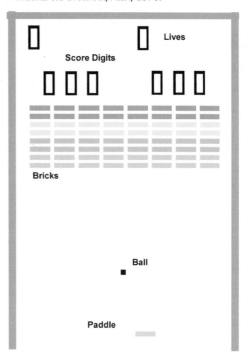

▼ **FIGURE 5.1** *Breakout*, Atari, 1976.

The text in the diagram isn't in the original. The colors were changed to make the diagram easier to see in print. The original background color is black and the digits were white. The number of bricks in the original *Breakout* coin-op version was fourteen columns across and eight rows high.

The details of the difficulty progression are interesting. The paddle gets smaller when the ball hits the top boundary for the first time. The ball speeds up after it hits the paddle four times and again after it hits the paddle sixteen times. Also, the angle of the ball path changes after it hits the paddle four, eight, twelve, and sixteen times.

The reason those numbers are powers of two, or related to powers of two (i.e., $12 = 8 + 4$) has to do with the efficiency and cost of the hardware, not just because the game designers liked powers of two.

The scoring is fairly simple, rewarding the player with 1, 3, or 5 points depending on the color of the brick. In the original arcade game, the color was faked by putting a colored overlay on top of the black and white monitor.

The difficulty resets every time the player loses a ball, giving a moment of relief to the player. On the other hand, there's a slow difficulty progression happening in the background because every time a brick gets destroyed, the difficulty increases slightly. When there are less bricks out there, it's more likely that the ball will hit the back border, which dramatically increases the difficulty due to the much smaller paddle.

Difficulty ramping is a central concept of classic game design and deserves its own design rule:

Classic Game Design Rule 3: Difficulty Ramping Rule: Ramp difficulty from easy to hard.

Almost all games need to deal with the issue of how fast to ramp difficulty, if at all. *Pong* had no ramping, at least not explicitly. In multiplayer games, the ramping usually happens by having your opponents getting better with practice. Successful single-player games almost always ramp difficulty at a steady pace, with periods of relief thrown in to reward the players. Look at Figure 5.2 for a way to visualize this.

▼ **FIGURE 5.2** Typical Difficulty Ramping in Single-Player Games.

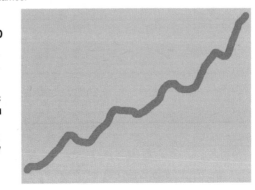

Game Time

How are you to know if a game is difficult or easy? Game developers tend to have tunnel vision when it comes to their own games. They may think it's easy when it's actually hard, especially for novices. The next rule:

Classic Game Rule 4: Test Rule: Test the game to make sure it's fun.

It's just that easy. You need to test the game. In the days of custom hardware, testing was an expensive proposition. Now that video games are developed using incredibly powerful software tools, it's much easier and cheaper to test. You need to test early and often. People have careers consisting of testing video games. Mostly, the career video game testers look for bugs and try to figure out how to duplicate them. But even more important than bug testing is testing for fun and suitability. Is the game too easy or too hard? Or even both? These questions can only be answered by extensive testing, preferably by representatives of the target customers.

It's critically important to test new video games first on yourself, but then with children, expert players, casual players, players of all sizes, ages, and abilities. In the old days of arcade game development, this was a common practice. Arcade game companies put prototype games into arcades and street locations. They carefully measured how many quarters each game earned when compared to the other popular arcade games. If a game didn't have top earnings, the project would be cancelled.

In these days of Internet distribution, testing is very easy, but it still takes some effort. Just release the game as a beta, or in a limited geographic region, and gather statistics on how long people play the games, where they have trouble, and how far they get into the game. It's also a good idea to talk to the players.

BREAKOUT SEQUELS

It's no surprise that *Breakout* inspired sequels, including *Super Breakout*™ Atari (1978) and *Arkanoid*™, Taito (1986). In the sequels, the basic control stays the same. You still try to break the bricks, and if you break all of them, you move on to the next screen. In *Super Breakout*, you have multiple balls and a progressive mode where the bricks shift down the screen at you.

In *Arkanoid*, various powerups are introduced which make the game much more interesting. For example, you get a capture powerup which, when enabled, lets you catch the ball and have it stick to the paddle. When you're ready, you can then release the ball with the launch button.

WHERE ARE THEY NOW?

Right after their *Breakout* adventure, Steve Jobs and Steve Wozniak founded Apple Computer, Inc. Steve Jobs was largely responsible for growing Apple Computer into the most valuable company on the planet. Apple Computer dropped the "Computer" in its name and is called just Apple, Inc. as of 2007. Woz continues to be an iconic presence in Silicon Valley. *Breakout* sequels are still showing up, most recently *Breakout Boost*™ by Atari in 2011.

CHAPTER 6 — Classic Brick Game

PADDLE GAME FOR ONE

This is going to be your first one-player game, building upon what you learned in the classic paddle game project. You will be starting "from scratch," even though it's tempting to reuse the framework from your first project. The two projects are different enough that it's better to just start over. This is a good lesson, by the way. When in doubt, just make a fresh start. Often the baggage from an old project is more of a hindrance than a help.

This game is basically a mash-up of Pong and pinball. There will be a paddle at the bottom of the screen and a wall of bricks. There's the familiar bouncing ball, and the goal is to keep the ball bouncing, much like in a pinball game. You start with three balls, and if you lose all of them, it's game over. In a way, this is a very simple pinball game without the gravity.

This project has another big difference with the paddle project. You'll be using "fake" physics rather than the physics engine built into Unity. It's good to remember that all the classic games of the seventies and eighties didn't use physics engines, but instead used custom code to move and animate game objects. This was due to the very limited compute resources available at the time. It wasn't until the '90s that floating point computations were commonly used in games, and even then, there was a large cost associated with them. Today, floating point computations are actually faster than integer, so the world has really changed in this regard. In the classic era, integers were king, and the whole idea of using a floating point physics engine was a distant dream.

In your project, you will use the classic technique of updating your object positions using explicit code, and you'll do collision reaction explicitly as well. The object positions will be represented using floating point numbers, just because it's easier to do it that way in Unity.

VERSION 0.01: THE PLAYFIELD

Once again, your first goal is to display the playfield. This is an easy step for you now because you just built a very similar playfield in the previous project.

Step 1: Run Unity and create a **new project** with the name **ClassicBrickGame**.

There is no need to load the Physic Materials package for this project. Note the project folder location for your reference so you can find the project outside of Unity.

Step 2: Use the **2 by 3** layout.

You're now ready to create your game.

Step 2B: GameObject – Create Other – Cube, rename it **Playfield**.

Step 3: Focus on the **Playfield** by hitting the **f** key.

You should now see a cube in the upper-left window. This is your starting point for the playfield. Make the playfield larger:

Step 4: Change the **Scale** of **Playfield** to **(30, 30, 1)**.

Step 5: Use the Scene Gizmo to select the **Front iso** view and refocus with the **f** key.

Click on the Scene Gizmo text to select the iso mode, if necessary. Iso mode is indicated by three horizontal lines. Your screen should now look like Figure 6.1.

Next, you'll change the color of the playfield. Just as in ClassicPaddleGame, you'll do this by creating a material, assigning it to the object, and adjusting the color of the material.

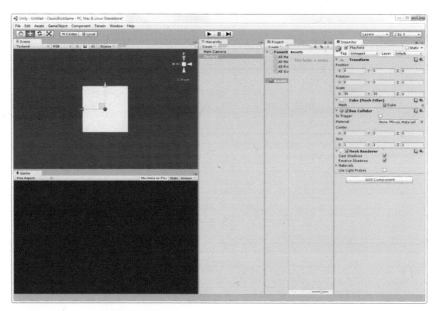

▲ **FIGURE 6.1** The Playfield rescaled.

Step 6: Click on **Create** in the Project panel, click on **Material** and immediately type the new name for it: **Mat Playfield**.

The text entry is highlighted in blue to tell you that you can type a new material name, if you wish.

Step 7: Make the material color **dark green** by clicking in the white rectangle to the right of **Main Color** in the Inspector. Then use the pop-up Color Dialog to select a dark green color.

Step 8: Drag the **Mat Playfield** material onto the **Playfield** game object.

The Playfield game object now appears to be dark green in the Scene panel. The Game panel is temporarily very dark green.

Step 9: Move **Main Camera** to **(0, 0, -30)**.

The Game panel now shows the entire playfield.

Step 10: Create a **Point Light** at **(0, 0, -10)** and change its **Range** to **100** in the Inspector panel.

Step 11: Select the **Top iso** view in the Scene panel by clicking on the top triangle of the Scene Gizmo.

Step 12: Select **Point Light** and use the **f** key to focus on it in the Scene panel.

Step 13: Click on the **Top label** in the Scene Gizmo repeatedly a few times.

This shows you how the point light is sitting in relation to the playfield. The perspective view is shown in Figure 6.2.

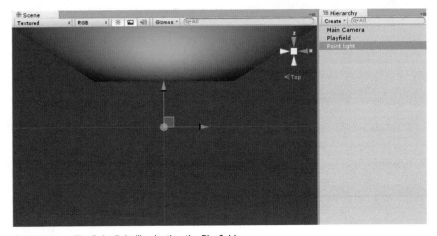

▲ **FIGURE 6.2** The Point light illuminating the Playfield.

Step 14: Click on the **Top label** one more time, if necessary, to go back to the isometric view.

Just as in the paddle game, this is a good time to do your first test.

Step 15: Select "Maximize on Play" in the Game panel. Then hit the Play arrow.

Just as in the Paddle game there's no animation yet, just a still view of the Playfield. You might have noticed that these initial steps are almost exactly the same as in the Paddle game. This concludes your review and you're now ready to do some new things.

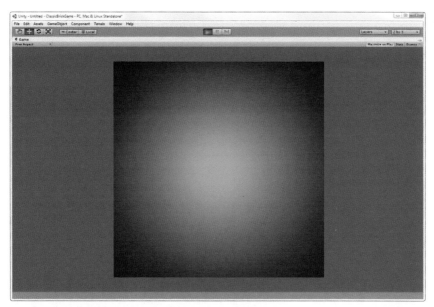

▲ **FIGURE 6.3** Looking at the maximized playfield in Play mode.

Step 16: Stop play mode by clicking on the Play arrow again.

The five panels appear again.

Step 17: File – Save Scene with the name **BrickScene**.

Step 18: Save the project.

Saving here isn't truly necessary, but it's a good habit to save your work at a good stopping point.

Your next goal is to create the boundaries of the playfield. For this game, the boundaries are at the top, left, and right, with an open area at the bottom.

Step 19: Create a **Cube** with **Position (0, 15, 0)** and **Scale (30, 1, 1)**.

Step 20: Rename it **BoundaryUpper**.

The Scene panel is still using the Top view, which isn't what you want any more.

Step 21: Select the **Back** view in the Scene panel using the Scene Gizmo. You can right-click on the Gizmo to quickly select the back view.

Step 22: Select **Playfield**, hover the mouse in the Scene panel, and press **f**. Then **zoom in** on the playfield with your **scroll wheel**. It's a little strange that you're looking at the Playfield from the back, but that's what you need to do because there are negative Z coordinates for the Point light and the Main Camera.

Step 23: Enter a new **Z Position** of **1.1** instead of 0. Note that the position is 1.1 instead of 1 just as you did in the previous project. Your Scene panel should look like Figure 6.4.

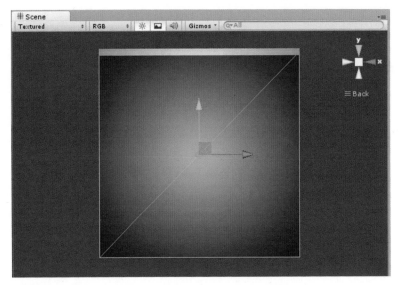

▲ **FIGURE 6.4** Upper boundary positioned at the top of the playfield.

Step 24: Right-click on **BoundaryUpper**, click on **Duplicate**, and rename the duplicate to **BoundaryLeft**.

Step 25: Set **BoundaryLeft Position** to (-15.5, -0.5, 0) and **Scale** to (1, 32, 1).

Step 26: Duplicate **BoundaryLeft**, rename the duplicate to **BoundaryRight** and change the **X Position** to **15.5**. Your screen should look like Figure 6.5.

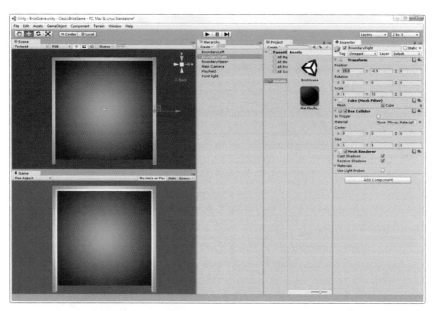

▲ **FIGURE 6.5** The playfield for the Brick game.

Step 27: Save your work by saving the scene and the project. In the next section, you'll add the player character, which for this game is a paddle at the bottom of the playfield.

VERSION 0.02: THE PLAYER

Just as in the ClassicPaddleGame project, the player character is a paddle, but this time it moves left to right, and there's only one of them.

Step 1: Start up Unity and load the project and scene, if necessary. Your screen should look like Figure 6.5.

Step 2: Create a **Cube** and name it **Paddle** at **Position (0, -15, 0), Scale (4, 1, 1).**

Notice that the origin of your coordinate system is in the center of the playfield, so to move the paddle to the bottom requires a negative Y Position.

Step 3: Create a **Material** in the Project Window, rename it **Mat Paddle**, make it **red**.

Step 4: Drag **Mat Paddle** on top of **Paddle**.

The paddle should now be red instead of grey.

You're now ready to create a script for the Paddle so it's controlled by the player.

Step 5: Select **Paddle** and create a JavaScript for it using **Add Component** with name **PlayerScript**. Then enter the following code:

```
#pragma strict

function Update ()
{
    if (Input.GetKey ("left"))
    {
        transform.Translate (-20 * Time.deltaTime,0,0);
    }
    if (Input.GetKey ("right"))
    {
        transform.Translate (20 * Time.deltaTime,0,0);
    }
}
```

This `Update` function is pretty much the same as in ClassicPaddleGame except it moves the paddle from left to right instead of up and down. It does this by changing the x coordinate in the `Translate` calls instead of the y coordinate.

Step 6: Save the file in MonoDevelop and then run the game. Test the left and right arrow keys. When you're done testing, click on the play arrow again to stop play mode. The arrow keys should move the paddle left and right and your screen should look similar to Figure 6.6.

Controlling the paddle using arrow keys is not nearly as much fun as using the mouse, so you'll add that feature. The arrow controls can stay, just because they don't do any harm.

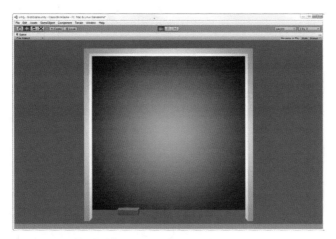

▲ **FIGURE 6.6** The Paddle controlled by arrow keys.

Step 7: Modify PlayerScript as follows:

```
#pragma strict

function Start ()
{
    Screen.lockCursor = true;
}

function Update ()
{
    if (Input.GetKey ("left"))
    {
        transform.Translate (-20 * Time.deltaTime,0,0);
    }
    if (Input.GetKey ("right"))
    {
        transform.Translate (20 * Time.deltaTime,0,0);
    }

    var h = 30.0 * Time.deltaTime * Input.GetAxis ("Mouse X");
    transform.Translate (h, 0, 0);
}
```

You added a "Start" function which turns off the mouse cursor display when playing the game. To turn the mouse cursor back on, the player has to use the "Esc" key. This is necessary when the player wants to exit the game. You also need this when testing the game so you can get back to Unity when you're done testing.

Step 8: Try it out by saving your editing session in Monodevelop and then running the game and moving the mouse left and right. Try doing both the mouse control and the arrow control at the same time. It's a bit strange to allow both arrow and mouse controls at the same time, but it really doesn't matter.

Step 9: Save and **exit**.

VERSION 0.03: BASIC BALL MOVEMENT

It's time to add the ball. It's not exactly a powerful sword, but it'll have to do.

Step 1: Start up Unity.

Step 2: Create a **Sphere** in the Hierarchy window, rename to **Ball** at (**0, -7, 0**).

This is the initial ball position. It's a little lower on the screen to make room for the bricks later.

Step 3: Make the Ball **yellow** using a new material called **Mat Ball**.

As you should know by now, you do this by creating the material "Mat Ball", making the material yellow, and dragging it on top of the Ball.

Step 4: Select **Ball**, do **Add Component** with name **BallScript** and enter the following code:

```
#pragma strict

var BeepSound : AudioClip;

static var launchtimer: float;
static var xspeed: float;
static var yspeed: float;
static var collflag: boolean;
```

```
function Start ()
{
    launchtimer = 2.0;
    xspeed = 8.0;
    yspeed = 8.0;
    collflag = true;
}


function Update ()
{
    transform.position.z = 0;
    launchtimer -= Time.deltaTime;
    if (launchtimer <= 0.0)
    {
        transform.Translate(Vector3(xspeed,yspeed,0) * Time.deltaTime);
        launchtimer = 0.0;
    }
}


function OnTriggerEnter (other: Collider) {
    audio.PlayOneShot(BeepSound);
}
```

Your screen should look something like Figure 6.7.

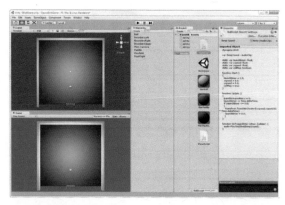

▲ FIGURE 6.7 Unity workspace showing the Paddle, Ball, and BallScript.

The `Time.deltaTime` variable is a built-in Unity variable that returns the amount of time, in seconds, since the last time the Update function was called. For more information on this and many other Unity features, do Help – Scripting Reference and do a search.

Step 5: Save your work and start testing.

The ball should be stationary for a while and then move to the upper right and off the screen without bouncing. The audio isn't working yet.

This is a great example of incremental development. You eventually want the ball to bounce off the boundaries, but first you just want it to sit there for two seconds, and then move along the specified velocity vector with the components xspeed and yspeed.

This was about as much code as you should ever write all at once without testing. There are software developers out there who spend days, weeks, or even months writing thousands of lines of code without testing any of them. Then they start testing, and they have hundreds of bugs. Needless to say, that is a horrible situation. How can you find, fix, or even test such a mess of buggy code? It's much better to write a little, test a lot, fix and repeat.

While you were at it, you added the audio code and a declaration for an as yet unused variable. This is also an example of what not to do, but people often do this anyway. It would have been cleaner and better to keep it simple and to not yet add the dead code (code that's not used right now).

Even though you added some code for audio, the audio isn't working yet, which is what you would expect because you don't even have your audio asset yet, nor is it connected to the Ball object. Next, you'll get the audio working by reusing the pluck.wav file from the Assets folder of the previous project.

Step 6: Open a window that shows the pluck.wav file used in ClassicPaddleGame. Drag pluck.wav into the Assets panel, or copy it into the Assets folder. Test the asset by previewing it.

Step 7: Select **Ball** and then click on **Component – Audio – Audio Source**.

Step 8: Assign the **pluck** sound to the **Ball** object.

Step 9: Click on the small circle next to **Beep Sound** in the Inspector and select the **pluck** sound for it.

Step 10: Test the game.

You should hear the pluck sound at the beginning, but then never again.

Step 11: Uncheck Play on Awake.

Step 12: Save your work and **exit** Unity.

Because you unchecked Play on Awake, there's no audio at all in the game now. That's because the Beep Sound isn't getting triggered yet. That will happen as soon as you add collisions. You need to remember to test the audio at that time. You might have been better off adding the audio code after implementing collisions.

VERSION 0.04: COLLISIONS

To do collision with the playfield, you'll start by writing a short script for the right and left boundaries.

Step 1: Start Unity and load the project and BrickScene, if necessary.

Step 2: Create a **JavaScript** and call it **WallScript** with the following code:

```
#pragma strict

function OnTriggerEnter (other: Collider) {
    BallScript.xspeed = -BallScript.xspeed;
    BallScript.collflag = true;
}
```

Step 3: Drag it on top of **BoundaryLeft** and **BoundaryRight**.

This isn't quite it yet. It's easy to forget to set the triggers and rigidbody setting.

Step 4: Select the **Ball**, and select **Component – Physics – Rigidbody**.

Step 5: Uncheck Use Gravity.

The physics engine supports gravity by default, but in this game there's no gravity.

Step 6: Select **BoundaryRight** and **Is Trigger** box in the Box Collider in the Inspector panel. Do the same for **BoundaryLeft**. Now you should be able to run the game and have the ball bounce off the right wall. Of course, because you haven't put in the collision code for the upper boundary yet the ball will behave strangely when hitting it. The next steps add proper collision for the upper boundary.

Step 7: Create a **JavaScript** and name it **WallTopScript**. Open it and copy the code from WallScript into it.

One fast way to do this is to open WallScript.js in another tab, Edit – Select All, Edit – Copy, select the WallTopScript tab, and Edit – Paste. It's even faster if you use the keyboard shortcuts.

Step 8: Replace both instances of xspeed with yspeed on line 4. Your code should look like this:

```
#pragma strict


function OnTriggerEnter (other: Collider) {
    BallScript.yspeed = -BallScript.yspeed;
    BallScript.collflag = true;
}
```

Step 9: Save WallTopScript in MonoDevelop and assign the script to **Boundary-Upper**.

Step 10: Select **BoundaryUpper** and **check Is Trigger** in the Box Collider component.

When the game is played now, the ball should bounce off the right, top, and left boundary, and then fall through the bottom. Also, it acts weirdly when it hits the paddle. So, you've got two more collision cases to deal with, ball vs. lower boundary and ball vs. paddle.

First, you'll create the lower boundary as an invisible barrier.

Step 10B: Select **GameObject – Create Empty**, rename it **BoundaryLower**. Move it to **Position (0, -17, 0)** and **Scale (35, 1, 1)**.

Step 11: Select **Component – Physics – Box Collider** and **check** the **Is Trigger** box in the Inspector. This invisible box is a way to detect when the ball has escaped from the playfield at the bottom. The screen should now look like Figure 6.8.

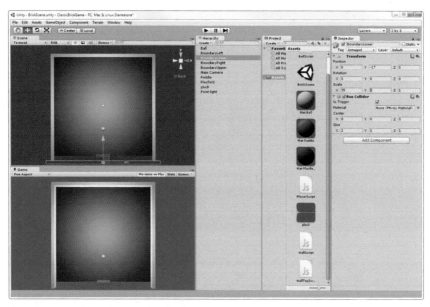

▲ **FIGURE 6.8** Unity workspace showing BoundaryLower.

Notice that BoundaryLower is visible in the Scene panel but not in the Game panel, which is exactly how you want it. Next, you need to write a script that handles what to do when the ball hits that lower boundary.

Step 12: Create a **JavaScript**, rename it to **BallRelaunch**. Then open the script and enter the following code:

```
#pragma strict

function OnTriggerEnter (other: Collider) {
    other.transform.position = Vector3(0,-7,0);
    BallScript.xspeed = 8.0;
    BallScript.yspeed = -8.0;
    BallScript.launchtimer = 1.0;
}
```

Step 13: Assign **BallRelaunch** to **BoundaryLower**.

This script deserves some explanation. The variable `other` is the object that collides with our lower boundary. This code magically repositions that object, presumably the ball, to its starting position and resets the speed. It also resets the `BallScript.launchtimer` variable to one second so that the player has a little bit of time to get ready for more action.

To add collision with the paddle, first make the Paddle object a trigger:

Step 14: Select **Paddle** and **check** the **Is Trigger** checkbox in the Inspector.

Step 15: Enter the following function at the bottom of **PlayerScript**:

```
function OnTriggerEnter (other: Collider) {
    BallScript.yspeed = -BallScript.yspeed;
    BallScript.collflag = true;
}
```

Go ahead and try it. You now have a bare bones brick game without the bricks. The ball bounces the way it's supposed to, and the player character works. You even have rudimentary sound.

There's one serious flaw in your current code, and it won't really become apparent until later. You don't have any way of controlling what the ball does when it hits the paddle. In real table tennis, you would have smashes, strange spin shots, and of course, you'd have some way of aiming where the ball goes. There are countless ways to implement ball control, but the simple way in the original arcade *Breakout* is a good starting point: if the ball hits the left side of the paddle, it bounces to the left, and if it hits the right side, it bounces to the right. The following modified trigger code does that.

Step 16: In **PlayerScript** modify the **OnTriggerEnter** function as follows:

```
function OnTriggerEnter (other: Collider) {
    BallScript.yspeed = -BallScript.yspeed;

    if (other.collider.gameObject.transform.position.x >
    gameObject.transform.position.x)
```

```
    {
        BallScript.xspeed = Mathf.Abs(BallScript.xspeed);
    } else {
        BallScript.xspeed = - Mathf.Abs(BallScript.xspeed);
    }
    BallScript.collflag = true;
}
```

The `Mathf.Abs` function is the absolute value function that returns the positive value of a number. The code checks to see if the ball is on the right side of the paddle. If it's on the right, then the x component of the ball velocity is set to be positive, otherwise it's set to be negative. In any case, the y component of the ball velocity is reversed.

The variable `other.collider.gameObject.transform.position.x` looks complicated. You read it from back to front like this: the x-coordinate of the position of the transform of the gameObject of the collider of the other object. That's a long way of saying the x coordinate of the colliding object, which happens to be the ball.

This is a great example of the kind of "fake" physics that is prevalent in classic games. Real physics requires compute power that wasn't yet feasible at the time. Much of the development time and effort was spent on technical issues such as this.

Step 17: Test it, **save** it, **exit** Unity.

It's time to add some bricks. After all, this is a brick game.

VERSION 0.05: BRICKS

You're ready for another new programming technique. How can you add an array of bricks to your playfield? It's tempting to create them the same way as you've been creating all of your objects, but this would be very time consuming. Instead, you'll be creating a "BrickMaker" object and create your bricks using a double loop in the associated script.

First, you'll just make the display of the bricks. Then, you'll add collision handling so that the bricks actually disappear when they get hit by the ball.

Step 1: Start up Unity and load the project and scene, if necessary.

Step 2: Click on **GameObject – Create Empty** with name **BrickMaker**.

Step 3: Create **MakeBricksScript**, assign it to **BrickMaker** and enter:

```
#pragma strict

function Start () {
    for (var y = 0; y < 8; y++) {
        for (var x = 0; x < 15; x++)
        {
            var cube = GameObject.CreatePrimitive(PrimitiveType.Cube);
            cube.transform.position = Vector3 (x*2 - 14, y - 1, 0);
            cube.transform.localScale = Vector3 (1.9,0.9,1);
//          cube.AddComponent("BrickScript");
            cube.collider.isTrigger = true;
            cube.renderer.material.color = Color(0.2 + y*0.08,0.3,1.0);
        }
    }
}
```

That's quite a bit of new code all at once! First take a look at what it does, and then carefully go through it. The screen should look like Figure 6.9.

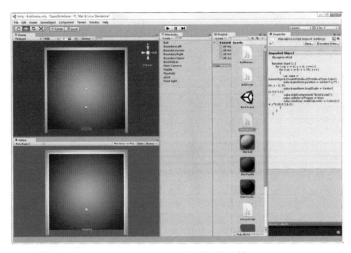

▲ **FIGURE 6.9** Unity workspace showing BrickMaker object.

Notice that the bricks aren't showing up yet. That's because they get created by the BrickMaker object when the game is running. The script is displayed on the right side of the Unity window, but the formatting is ugly. This is OK, because you don't do your editing there, but rather inside of MonoDevelop.

Step 4: Run the game.

So go ahead and run the game. The screen now looks like Figure 6.10.

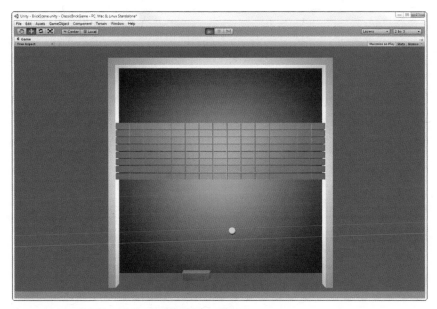

▲ **FIGURE 6.10** Bricks made by the BrickMaker object.

Pretty amazing! Just a few lines of code and you generated 120 bricks. They don't do anything yet, but you can see them, and that's a good start.

Let's go through the code together and try to understand what it does.

The two `for` statements set up the 2-dimensional array of bricks. The y variable traditionally keeps track of vertical position. Here you have eight rows of bricks and the y variable ranges from row 0 to row 7 (which adds up to 8 rows). Programmers like to count starting at zero because that usually makes the geometrical formulas simpler and thus, more efficient. The x variable keeps track of the fifteen horizontal brick locations, ranging column 0 to column 14.

Inside of your double loop you create a brick using the `CreatePrimitive` statement. Then you compute the position and scale of each brick. The position depends on the x and y variables. The scale is set to make your bricks a width of slightly less than 2 and height slightly less than 1. The depth is 1 as always for all of your objects. The two slashes on the next line indicate a comment. This means that the line doesn't get used, but is just there for future reference. You'll be "uncommenting" this line later on by simply deleting the slashes. The next lines turn on the "Is Trigger" property for the bricks and then finally set the color of the bricks. The color effect is a little strange right now because you're using a point-light. Change the point-light to a directional light.

Step 5: Select the **Point light** object, rename it to **Light**, and in the inspector change the Type to **Directional** and the **Intensity** to **0.63**. If you run the game again, your screen will look like Figure 6.11.

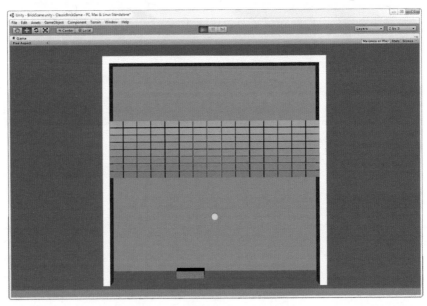

▲ **FIGURE 6.11** Effect of having a directional light.

Note the rather dramatic effect lighting can have on your scene. You now have a much more cartoon-like look.

You can have a more dramatic color change from row to row.

Step 6: Replace the color statement with the following code:

```
if (y<2)
cube.renderer.material.color = Color.yellow;
else if (y<4)
cube.renderer.material.color = Color.cyan;
else if (y<6)
cube.renderer.material.color = Color.blue;
else
cube.renderer.material.color = Color.red;
```

When you run the game now, you'll see something like Figure 6.12.

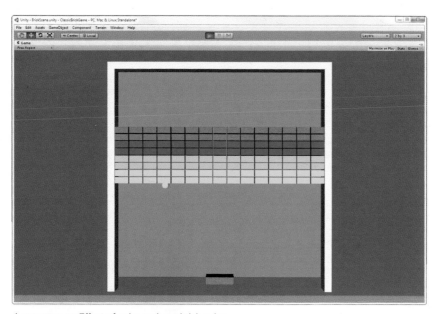

▲ **FIGURE 6.12** Effect of color code on brick color.

You used some of the built-in colors of Unity. You could also explicitly set the RGB values of each color using the Color function.

Step 7: Save your work, **exit** Unity.

In this section, you saw the amazing power of programming. Rather than creating all those bricks manually, you wrote just a few lines of code that do the same thing. In the next section, you'll put in some code to make the game playable.

VERSION 0.06: FIRST PLAYABLE

Now it's time to make those bricks disappear when the ball hits them.

Step 1: Start up Unity and load the project and scene, if necessary.

In the MakeBrickScript, there's a green line. It's commented out because it would cause an error otherwise. Each of those bricks will have a script, so first, let's write it.

Step 2: Create a **JavaScript** and call it **BrickScript**. Enter the following code:

```
#pragma strict

function OnTriggerEnter (other: Collider)
{
    if (BallScript.collflag == true)
    {
        BallScript.yspeed = -BallScript.yspeed;
        BallScript.collflag = false;
        Destroy(gameObject);
    }
}
```

Step 3: Delete the **slashes** at the beginning of the commented line in **MakeBricksScript**.

Step 4: Save the changes for both files in MonoDevelop and try running the game.

Magically, the game is now playable. Figure 6.13 shows it in action.

The BallScript.collflag variable is a boolean variable which is true when you want collisions to be active and false when you don't. The idea behind this variable is that after the ball hits the first brick you don't want the ball colliding with other bricks but to instead have it immediately bounce back to the player or a wall. This is a somewhat weird piece of logic, but it works and it's simple. The

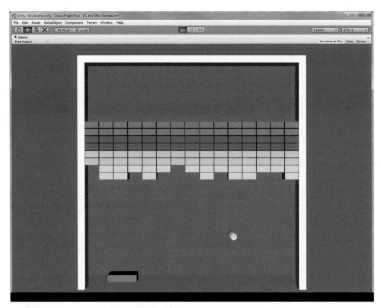

▲ FIGURE 6.13 Screen shot of first playable version.

original *Breakout* used similar logic, but the sequels went for something more realistic.

Once the script has determined that the collision should be done, it flips the y component of the ball velocity, turns off the collision flag, and finally destroys the brick that called it.

You can now better understand the reason behind the collflag statements in WallScript and WallTopScript. Those statements turn collisions on again when a ball hits a wall, thus allowing the ball to bounce back and forth between walls and bricks.

Step 5: Save and **quit.**

You now have a playable prototype. You even have some sound, just because it was easy to put in. If you're not hearing any sound, turn on your computer speakers, turn up the volume, and verify that you're getting the pluck sound every time there's a collision between the ball and something else. In the next section, you'll add scoring to your game because a game without scoring isn't much of a game.

VERSION 0.07: SCORING

In this section, you'll create the score display, design the scoring rules, and finally implement them in your code. In general, it's good practice to make your games playable first. Only then does it make sense to add the scoring code.

Step 1: Start up Unity and load the Project and Scene, if necessary.

Step 2: Create a Score object by selecting **GameObject – Create Empty**, name it **Score**.

Step 3: Create a new **JavaScript**, call it **Scoring**, and enter the following code for it:

```
#pragma strict

static var score: int;
static var lives: int;

function Start () {
   score = 0;
   lives = 3;
}

function OnGUI () {
   GUI.Box (Rect (10,10,90,30), "Score:    "+score);
   GUI.Box (Rect (Screen.width - 100,10,90,30),"Lives:    "+lives);
}
```

Step 4: Assign the **Scoring** script to the **Score** object as usual by dragging.

To make the scores update, you now need to find a place in your code where the bricks get destroyed. You just wrote that code in the previous section.

Step 5: Edit **BrickScript** by inserting a single new line of code as follows:

```
#pragma strict

function OnTriggerEnter (other: Collider)
```

```
    {
        if (BallScript.collflag == true)
        {

            BallScript.yspeed = -BallScript.yspeed;
            BallScript.collflag = false;
            Destroy(gameObject);
            Scoring.score += 10;

        }

    }
```

The "+=" command in JavaScript adds the following number to the preceding variable. In this instance, 10 gets added to the score. Not every new feature can be implemented in just one line. You just added simple scoring but now it's time to update the lives counter. This is also very easy.

Step 6: Insert the following line of code at the beginning of the OnTriggerEnter function in the **BallRelaunch** script:

```
Scoring.lives--;
```

The two minus signs are the decrement operator in JavaScript. This has the effect of decreasing the number of lives by 1.

Step 7: Save your work, **test** it, and **exit** Unity.

You should see the lives display in the upper-right corner of the game count down when you lose a ball off the bottom of the screen. That's a good start, but there's a problem. You don't have a game over screen! Instead the lives counter goes negative. Not good. In the next section, the concept of multiple Scenes in Unity is introduced.

VERSION 0.08: TITLE SCREEN

In this section, you'll build a very simple title screen. It'll be a single image with the instruction to press a key to start the game. Pressing any key will go to the game. When the game is over, this title screen will appear again. That's about as simple as it gets, but because you're building everything from the ground up, it still takes some careful work to have this happen.

Step 1: Run GIMP and create a new image with dimensions 256 x 240 pixels.

Any dimension will do, but these dimensions were selected as a reminder of this common and very low resolution that was used by raster arcade games of the early eighties.

Step 2: Add the text "Brick Game, press any key" using the Text tool in GIMP.

It doesn't really matter how you do this as long as the text is legible.

Step 3: Export the image into the Assets folder of your Unity game project. The image should be in .png format and have the name **BrickTitleImage**.

Step 4: Exit GIMP.

You may save to the GIMP native file format too, if you wish, but it's not necessary.

Step 5: Open Unity and load the **ClassicBrickGame** project and **BrickScene**, if necessary.

Notice that BrickTitleImage automatically shows up in the Assets panel.

Step 6: Do **File – New Scene**, then **File – Save Scene** and call it **BrickTitleScene**.

Step 7: Create a new **Java Script** with name **MainTitle**. Enter the code:

```
#pragma strict

var backgroundTexture: Texture;

function OnGUI() {
    GUI.DrawTexture(
        Rect(0, 0, Screen.width, Screen.height),
        backgroundTexture);
    if (Input.anyKeyDown)
    {
        Debug.Log("A key or mouse click has been detected");
        Application.LoadLevel("BrickScene");
    }
}
```

Step 8: Assign the **MainTitle** script to the **Main Camera** game object.

Step 9: Select **Main Camera** and drag **BrickTitleImage** to the slot next to **Background Texture** in the inspector.

Running the game now will display the image, but when you press a key you will get an error because you haven't yet included both scenes in the build settings for the project.

Step 10: File – Save Scene.

Step 11: Select **File – Build Settings...** and add the current scene to the build settings by clicking on the **Add Current** button. **Exit** the build settings window.

Step 12: Load **BrickScene** by double-clicking on it in the Assets panel, select **File – Build Settings...** again, and click on **Add Current** just like in the previous step.

You'll now have two scenes in the current build settings for this project.

Step 13: Click on **BrickTitleScene** in the Assets panel to select it. **Run** the game and press some key after the title screen appears.

You're now ready to go back to solving the problem that started all this. What should happen when the player runs out of lives? You just go back to the title screen. To do that, add this new code to the BallRelaunch script:

```
if (Scoring.lives == 0)
{
    Application.LoadLevel("BrickTitleScene");
}
```

Step 14: Insert the code fragment from above after the line that says "Scoring.lives–" in the **BallRelaunch** script.

Notice the two equal signs next to one another. That's not a typo. You need both of those equal signs. Unlike in mathematics, in JavaScript and most other modern programming languages, one equal sign is used for assignment, but two are needed when testing for equality.

Step 15: Test it by **losing on purpose** and then **playing** a **second game**.

Well, guess what, there's a bug! By the way, the automatic answer when someone says this is "Just one?" The nature of programming, and especially game programming, is that there're going to be bugs. A lot of bugs. The best defense against having buggy code is to test frequently and to fix all known bugs as soon as possible.

The bug is that when you start a game, the ball gets launched up instead of down and bounces off of a brick. This isn't really a big deal. It could even be called a feature, but you should fix it, because it's easy to do.

Step 15B: Make sure you've exited play mode.

Step 16: In the `Start` function of BallScript, change the initialization for yspeed to -8.0.

Step 17: Test, **save**, and **exit**.

This game is in pretty good shape now, so now you can release it.

VERSION 1.0: FIRST RELEASE AND POSTMORTEM

There's a relatively new adage in the game business: release early and release often. So you're releasing this game even though it's still very basic. The procedure for releasing this game in Unity is pretty much the same as for Project One, so the instructions won't be repeated here.

It's time for a quick postmortem of the Brick game. Here's what went right. You made a simple brick game and it works. It sure looks a lot like the many similar brick games from the '70s and '80s, though the graphics are much better with the nice 3D effect of the bricks. The best part is that you learned quite a bit about how to make this kind of game in Unity.

What went wrong? Well, the game isn't very fun yet. There's no difficulty ramping and the game is just too simple, even by the standards of 1976. Nevertheless, the following exercises will help with this.

EXERCISES

1. Adjust the speed of the ball to make it faster, thus making the game more difficult. Put in a counter that increases the speed of the ball after the ball has had eight collisions.

2. Adjust the numbers in the mouse control code and see what happens. What happens to playability if the mouse control is too sensitive or not sensitive enough?

3. Add a second paddle just above the first paddle and have the mouse control it simultaneously with the first. Try using different mouse sensitivities with the two paddles.

4. Create several different sound effects in Audacity and have different sounds for different types of collisions. If you did Exercise 1, increase the pitch of the collisions when the ball speed increases.

5. The title screen text is fuzzy. Experiment with the texture import settings in Unity to improve this. Hint: try the different filter settings.

Advanced Exercises for experienced Unity users:

6. Make it a two-player game by adding a second paddle of a different color and have the second paddle be controlled by a different set of keys.

7. Create a texture in GIMP and use it in the playfield.

CHAPTER 7 Space Invaders

Space Invaders is the first mega-successful video game, surpassing everything before it exponentially. The success is a result of great design that made the game much deeper than anything before. It was the first arcade video game that celebrated the skill of the players, a game where millions of players would play every day to get better and better, get higher scores in the process, and feel a sense of accomplishment much like in golf, bowling, or pinball.

HUGE MONEY, HUGE

In terms of money, *Space Invaders* broke new ground. By some estimates, *Space Invaders* grossed a coin drop of two billion dollars by 1982, making it the highest grossing entertainment product of all time. It is also the top selling arcade game of all time, having sold 300,000 units in Japan alone and responsible for a shortage of 100-yen coins. It's easy to forget the huge impact of this game. It showed that the public was willing to spend serious cash on video games.

THE DESIGN OF *SPACE INVADERS*, TAITO (1978)

Space Invaders is the first vertical shooter. You control a laser gun with a two-directional joystick and you shoot at a horde of alien attackers by pressing the fire button. To give the player a better chance to survive early on, there are four destructible barriers near the bottom of the screen as depicted in Figure 7.1.

This game is still fun to play over forty years later. It introduced the basic gameplay formula of having three lives and getting an extra life after reaching a point goal. Countless games after it imitated the style of having a character move side to side and shoot up at an onslaught of enemies. Even today's FPS extravaganzas can be viewed as fancy sequels to *Space Invaders*.

This game was also the first major video game to get people to REALLY care about their score.

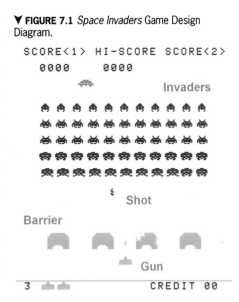

▼ **FIGURE 7.1** *Space Invaders* Game Design Diagram.

SCORE EQUALS SKILL

Classic Game Design Rule 5: Score Rule: Score equals skill.

In *Space Invaders*, having a score higher than your friends was meaningful, just like in pinball. It also introduced the High Score display at the top of the screen. Furthermore, *Space Invaders* didn't forget about the expert players and made the score mean something even for the elite players. *Breakout* has no meaningful world record because, well, if you're an advanced player then it's no problem for you to get the maximum possible score of 896. On the other hand, *Space Invaders* requires expert skill to get a world class score.

There are at least three major ways that Rule 5 is violated by designers: capping the score, allowing marathoning, and allowing score milking. Here's a look at all of these in turn.

Capping the score means there is an easily achievable and known maximum score for the game, for example, the maximum score of 896 in single-player *Breakout*.

Claiming to have the world record on this game is somewhat misleading because thousands of players have achieved it.

Marathoning is the practice of playing arcade games up to the limits of human endurance. Achieving a large score is more an indication of the ability to keep playing rather than a measure of skill. This happened with major games such as *Asteroids* and *Missile Command* and countless others.

Score milking occurs when players easily build up their score indefinitely without actually playing the game as intended. This was uncommon in arcade games, but this is frequently possible in home games, for example, *Super Mario Brothers*.

 One of the great achievements of *Space Invaders* is that the scoring is truly meaningful.

Now remember Rule 4? How are you going to test your scoring system? Well, for starters, it's important to get yourself an advanced player playing the game for a few weeks to see if he's still breaking his own scores and still has the desire to improve. If you don't have access to a top player or two, make sure that you're ready to respond when your game gets into their hands after you've released your game!

In *Space Invaders*, the waves of enemies would start a little bit lower on the screen when compared to the previous wave. This simple device is a great way to ramp up difficulty, and is a verification of the Difficulty Ramping Rule. The majority of classic arcade games, starting with *Space Invaders*, would use this device. Compare this to *Breakout* where, if you finished the first wave of bricks, you were handed another wave without any ramping.

GOING STRONG 34 YEARS LATER

Even though the arcade business faded away in the '80s and '90s, *Space Invaders* sequels continue to be sold. The latest version is *Space Invaders Infinity Gene*™

released for IOS in 2009, Xbox Live Arcade and Playstation Network in 2010, and Android in 2011.

The *Space invaders* characters are really the first video game characters to achieve iconic stature in popular culture. The aliens have been featured in street art, t-shirts, and even furniture.

Space Invaders changed the video games from casual to hardcore, from diversion to hobby. We owe a debt of gratitude to game designer Tomohiro Nishikado and Taito. It's hard to imagine how video games would have evolved without the seminal influence of *Space Invaders*.

CHAPTER 8 — Classic Vertical Shooter

DESIGNING A SHOOTER

The third classic project is going to be quite a bit more ambitious if the size of this chapter is any indication. Your goal is to build a simple vertical shooter, similar to the great many arcade vertical shooters from the '70s and '80s. You're going to start by sketching the basic layout of the game.

The setting is an outer space battle where you control a spaceship near the bottom of the screen and shoot at alien spaceships and creatures that are attacking you. You are seeing the beginnings of some story elements here, but don't be too concerned about telling the story. Classic games are all about the gameplay.

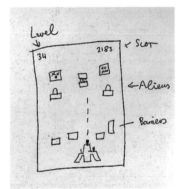

▼ FIGURE 8.1 Game sketch of vertical shooter.

Take a look at Figure 8.1. It's a very rough sketch of the layout. You'll want to display the score and the level, the enemies and the playfield, and, of course, the player character.

In the next section, you'll start by building the playfield.

VERSION 0.01: THE PLAYFIELD

Because you're in outer space, you'll choose to display the playfield as black with a background of scrolling stars. There are two approaches to displaying a star field, both valid: each star can be its own object or you can simply display an image of the star field created in a paint program or captured with a camera.

▼ **FIGURE 8.2** Star field for the classic vertical shooter.

Step 1: Run Unity and do **File – New Project...** for a new project with the name **ClassicVerti-calShooter**.

To keep things simple, draw a star field image in GIMP using the mouse. If you wish, you can create your own star field, or use the one provided on the DVD. Figure 8.2 shows what the star field looks like.

Step 2: Create a Star Field using GIMP. Make it 1024 x 1024 pixels and export it to **starfield.png** in the Assets folder of our Unity project.

It's OK to leave Unity open while you do this. It's up to you how you want to draw the starfield. It should be mostly black or some very dark color with some outer space objects on it like stars of varying colors and sizes. The starfield on the DVD was created using a large brush of size 20 and a smaller brush of size 5. The colors are white, light yellow, light red, and light blue.

The size of 1024 by 1024 is no accident. Today's 3D hardware has an easier time displaying textures with dimensions that are powers of two. It probably doesn't matter much in this case, but it's a good habit to use powers of two for image sizes in games and 3D applications. The reason for this has to do with "mipmapping," a technique used by 3D display hardware to efficiently display textured objects that are far away from the camera.

In this game, the playfield will be scrolling, but first you'll just display it. In this project, you'll be using a 2D approach. It's a bit strange to do 2D graphics in Unity. Unity is designed to do 3D graphics, so you still have to deal with some 3D concepts.

Step 3: GameObject – Create Other – Plane, name it **starfield**.

Step 4: For **starfield**, set **Position (0, 0, 3)**, **Rotation (270, 180, 0)**, **Scale (1, 1, 1)**.

Step 5: Assign the **starfield** asset in the **Assets** panel to the **starfield** object in the **Hierarchy** panel. This step automatically created a Materials folder and a starfield material in that folder.

Step 6: Place **Main Camera** at **Position (0, 0, 10)** and **Rotation (0, 180, 0)**. Set the **Projection** to **Orthographic**. Change the **Size** to **3.5**.

The rotation coordinates are in degrees, and were found via experimentation. The starfield texture is one-sided, so if it's facing away from the camera it becomes invisible. The Size controls the zoom factor of the orthographic camera.

Step 7: Create a **Directional Light** with Rotation (0, 180, 0).

Step 8: Select the **Front iso** View in the Scene panel, use **2 by 3** layout, then **select** and **focus** on the **starfield** using the **f** key.

Step 9: Save your **scene** with the name **mainscene**.

That's quite a few steps. Make sure that your screen matches Figure 8.3.

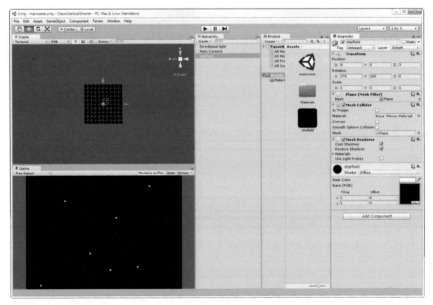

▲ **FIGURE 8.3** Starfield displayed in Unity.

The starfield game object is only visible from one side. You can verify this by looking at the back view in the Scene panel. Make sure that you go back the Front view when you're done.

You're now going to do some housekeeping to prepare yourself for this somewhat larger project.

Step 10: In the Project panel, **create** a new **Folder** called **Textures** and drag the **starfield** texture into it.

CAREFUL! You have three objects, all with the name "starfield." There's the game object, the texture, and the material which was automatically created back in Step 5. The game object is in the Hierarchy panel, the material is in the Materials folder of the Project panel, and the starfield texture is in the top level of the Project panel. You're moving only the texture into the newly created Textures folder.

Next you're going to create a Scripts folder where you'll be keeping all of your scripts.

Step 11: Create a **Scripts** folder at the top level of the Assets panel. **Double-click** on the Scripts folder to select it and **create** a new **JavaScript** called **scrollme**. Then open the script and enter the following code:

```
#pragma strict

var scrollSpeed: float;

function Start () {
}

function Update () {
    renderer.material.SetTextureOffset(
        "_MainTex",
        Vector2(0,scrollSpeed * Time.time)
        );
}
```

Step 12: Save the script, and **assign** it to the **starfield** object.

Step 13: Select **starfield** and set **Scroll Speed** to -0.2 in the Inspector section for scrollme.

If you don't see Scroll Speed in the Inspector, it might be because you had an error in your script. Check for any red error messages at the bottom of your Unity window.

Step 14: Make sure you have the **2 by 3** layout with **Maximize on Play** enabled and then hit the **Play** arrow.

The starfield should be continually scrolling down at a moderate speed.

Step 15: Save and **exit** Unity.

What did you just do here? You created a plane and assigned a texture to it. Then you created a script that changes the y texture offset depending on the time. This has the effect of scrolling the starfield down in a vertical direction. To scroll horizontally, you would animate the x coordinate instead.

VERSION 0.02: THE SPACESHIP

Now that you have a playfield, it's time to make your main player character, the spaceship. This is one of those situations where it takes a lot of work to do something very simple. Fortunately, you'll be able to reuse much of this work later on, so it's well worth it. Here's the plan for this section. You're going to draw a spaceship in GIMP and then display it in Unity. The spaceship is going to be a nonanimated 2D sprite with alpha. Let's first explain what that is:

- Nonanimated is simple enough. You just have a single image for your spaceship. There's really no need to animate the spaceship because it's a solid object without moving parts.
- The word *sprite* just means that the image can be moved on the screen. In the early days of video game development the hardware commonly supported both sprites and stamps. Stamps, as opposed to sprites, were rectangular chunks of graphics that couldn't be moved relative to each other, though it was typically possible to move all the stamps as a unit.

- *Alpha* is a term used to describe transparency. The spaceship will fit into a 32 x 32 grid. Some of the pixels in the grid will be used to display the spaceship, whereas other pixels will be transparent. The transparent pixels will have an alpha value of 0, the solid pixels 1. It's possible to have an alpha value in between. For example, an alpha of 0.5 would mean that the pixel appears to be transparent when displayed on top of background graphics.

You're ready to begin.

Step 1: Run GIMP.

Step 2: Select **Windows – Dockable Dialogs – Channels**. Then drag the Channels dialog to the right side of the window using the Channels label as a handle.

Step 3: Do **File – New** and choose an image size of **32 x 32** pixels.

Your screen should look something like Figure 8.4.

Notice that you have three channels: Red, Green, and Blue. Soon you'll have an Alpha channel as well. The image looks tiny, so zoom in on it so you can better see what's happening.

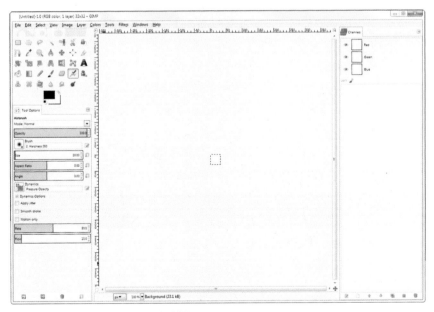

▲ **FIGURE 8.4** The Channels dialog in GIMP.

Step 4: Select **View – Zoom – 8:1**.

Step 5: Select the **Pencil** tool (the tool that looks like a diagonal pencil).

Step 6: In the Tool Options dialog, make the **Size** 1 pixel.

Step 7: Choose a **foreground** color of **dark green**.

This is done on the color selection area at the bottom of the toolbox. The foreground box is the upper-left rectangle. Click on it to get the color selection dialog.

Step 8: Use the mouse and the left mouse button to **draw** a shape like the one shown in Figure 8.5. This is the right half of your spaceship.

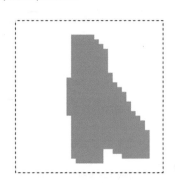

▼ **FIGURE 8.5** Starting to draw the spaceship in GIMP.

It's not important that your drawing matches the book's version pixel for pixel. Feel free to draw something else that looks similar to a top view of a spaceship. This is just a starting point. The first thing you're going to improve is the symmetry. Your goal is to take the right half, flip it, and copy it on top of the left half of the image.

Here's one way to do this.

Step 9: Use the **Rectangle Select Tool**, the upper-left tool in the tool box, and select the right half of the image. The size of the selection should be **16 x 32**. You can watch the bottom of the window to see the size change as you drag the mouse. This looks like Figure 8.6.

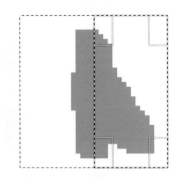

▼ **FIGURE 8.6** Selecting the right half of the spaceship.

Step 10: Edit – Copy and **Edit – Paste As – New Layer**. Make sure you're still using the Rectangle Select tool and **select** the left half of the image as shown in Figure 8.7.

You're now ready to flip the left half of the image.

Step 11: Select the **Flip tool** as shown in Figure 8.8.

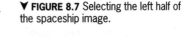

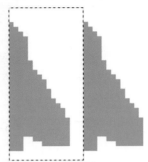

▲ **FIGURE 8.8** Using the Flip tool.

Step 12: Click on the **left half** of the image.

This is quite an improvement! Symmetry is the secret to making great looking pixel art. It often doesn't matter how well you can draw as long as you incorporate symmetry.

You're not done yet. The left half of the image is still sitting in a separate layer. You need to merge the layers.

Step 13: Select the **Rectangle tool**, click on the **right half** of the image, and do **Layer – Merge Down**. Your image should now look like Figure 8.9.

▼ **FIGURE 8.9** Basic spaceship.

Next, you'll use the "Cartoon" filter to add a nice black edge to your spaceship.

Step 14: Select **Filters – Artistic – Cartoon…** and use a **Mask radius** of **1.3** and **Percent black** of **0.5**. Feel free to experiment with these values or even to try some of the other filters. Your result should look something like Figure 8.10.

You're now ready to add alpha to your 2D image. You might have noticed that the Channels dialog now displays an Alpha channel, but it doesn't have any content yet. Adding alpha to this particular image is really easy because you didn't use white when drawing your spaceship.

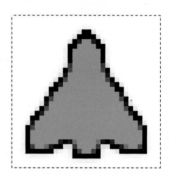

▼ **FIGURE 8.10** Final 2D spaceship, no alpha.

Step 15: Do **Colors – Color to Alpha** and make sure that the **From** color is **white**, which is the default. You now have an outline of the spaceship in the Alpha channel in the Channels dialog as shown in Figure 8.11.

The spaceship itself now has a checkerboard background to indicate transparency. It should look like Figure 8.12.

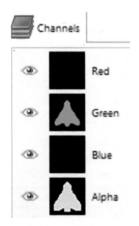

▲ **FIGURE 8.11** Alpha channel for the spaceship.

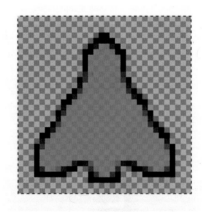

▲ **FIGURE 8.12** Final 2D spaceship with alpha.

Next you'll save your work. There are two files that you want to save, .xcf and .png.

Step 16: Click on **File – Save As** and use the name **ship.xcf** in the directory "ClassicVerticalShooter/Assets/Textures".

Step 17: Do **File – Export** to save **ship.png** in the same directory. IMPORTANT: Use **compression level 0**. This is a very small file so there's no need to compress it and, if you use compression with alpha sprites, you can easily get artifacts when displaying them in Unity.

Step 18: Exit GIMP.

You're done with GIMP for now and it's time to open Blender.

Why do you need Blender? Blender is a 3D program and you're doing a simple 2D image. The reason is that you need a quadrilateral made up of two triangles. Unfortunately, Unity doesn't have this object as a built-in mesh, so you need to create it in Blender instead.

Step 19: Run Blender and **delete** the default **cube**. To remove the default cube, right click on it to select it, then press x and enter.

One of the potentially confusing things to deal with when switching between Blender and other applications is that in Blender, you use the right mouse button to select objects, whereas in other applications you usually use the left mouse button to select things. If you accidentally left click in Blender, it moves the Blender cursor, which doesn't do anything to the scene, but does affect the location of where new objects get placed in the scene.

In the next steps (20 – 23) you'll test this out.

Step 20: Left click on the scene **somewhere**. This moves the Blender cursor to a new location.

Step 21: Create a cube with **Add – Mesh – Cube**. Notice that the cube is now created at the new location for the cursor.

Step 22: Undo with Ctrl-Z (Command-z on the Mac).

Step 23: Object – Snap – Cursor to Center. The Object drop-down menu is along the long, horizontal window at the bottom of the Blender window. The

Cursor to Center command moves the cursor to the center of the scene, right where you want to have it.

Step 24: Add – Mesh – Plane. It should look like Figure 8.13 in the center of the world.

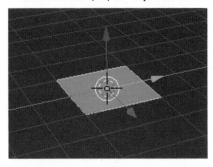

This object is made up of a single face, which in turn consists of two triangles. The next steps in Blender are necessary to paint your spaceship texture onto this object.

Step 25: In the Properties panel, click on the **Material icon**. This icon looks like a sphere and it's the eighth icon in a horizontal series of icons. The Properties panel should now look like Figure 8.14.

▼ **FIGURE 8.14** Activating the Material dialog in Blender.

Step 26: Click on **New** and a bunch of new dialogs appear. Fortunately, you can leave those alone and move on.

Step 27: Click on the **Texture icon**, which is immediately to the right of the Material icon and looks like a checkerboard. You may need to widen the Properties panel to see it. Click on **New** there as well. The texture Type will say "Clouds."

Step 28: Change the **Type** to **Image or Movie**.

Step 29: Click on **Open** (not New!) in the Image dialog area and find the **ship.png** file that you just exported from GIMP. **Highlight** the file and click on **Open Image**. The texture panel should look like Figure 8.15.

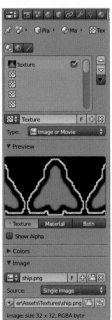

➤ **FIGURE 8.15** Texture panel showing spaceship.

Step 30: Scroll down to the lower part of the texture panel and find the **Mapping** section. Change the **Coordinates** property from Generated to **UV**.

You're probably wondering why spaceship still isn't showing up on the Plane object. This is normal because you're still not quite done yet with this rather complex procedure.

Step 31: Go into **Edit Mode** by hitting the **Tab** key on your keyboard or by clicking on Object Mode and selecting Edit Mode. Take a look at Figure 8.16.

▼ **FIGURE 8.16** Creating a new panel in Blender.

Find the diagonal lines depicted at the bottom left corner of Figure 8.16. These lines indicate that you can grab them with the mouse and drag them to make a new panel. Your mouse icon will change to a cross when you're hovering above those lines.

Step 32: Create a second panel by **dragging** the **diagonal lines up and to the right**. Aim to have two equal size panels as shown in Figure 8.17.

You created this second panel so you could load the UV/Image editor.

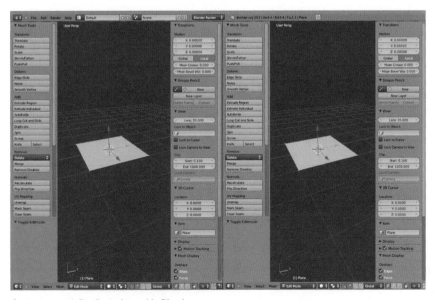

▲ **FIGURE 8.17** Duplicated panel in Blender.

Step 33: Click on the **editor type** icon at the bottom left of the **panel on the right**, and select **UV/Image Editor**.

You are now ready to load the spaceship into the editor.

Step 34: Click on **Image – Open Image** and load the same **ship.png** file as before from the Assets/Textures folder of the Unity project. You should now see a small spaceship in the middle of the Image Editor panel.

Step 35: Zoom in on the image in the UV/Image Editor by **scrolling the mouse wheel**. The result will be Figure 8.18.

▼ **FIGURE 8.18** ship.png displayed in Blender image editor.

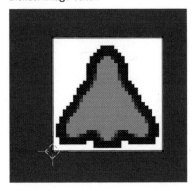

Finally, here are the steps that bring the image on top of the Plane object.

Step 36: Hover the mouse over the left panel, and press **a** once or twice to select all four vertices.

Step 37: Press **7** in the numeric keypad to get the Top perspective view.

Step 38: Click on the sphere to the right of the Edit Mode icon and select **Texture** as the **Viewport Shading**.

Step 39: Do **Mesh – UV Unwrap… – Project from View (Bounds)**.

If nothing went wrong along the way, you should now see the spaceship in both panels as shown in Figure 8.19.

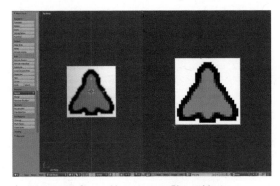

▲ **FIGURE 8.19** Spaceship texture on Plane object.

As a final test, render the Blender scene.

Step 40: Render – Render Image (or press **F12**). You now see the spaceship from a 3D perspective using the Blender camera. You won't be using that perspective in this project but rather a 2D top-down view.

Step 41: Render – Show/Hide Render View (or press **F11**).

Step 42: Save your work by clicking on **File – Save As…** and put the .blend file into the **Assets** directory of the Unity project with the name **ship2dquad.blend**.

Step 43: Exit Blender.

You're now ready to look at the ship2dquad.blend file in Unity and see if it works!

Step 44: Run Unity and click on the **Assets** folder.

The Project panel now looks like Figure 8.20.

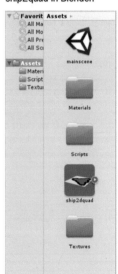

▼ **FIGURE 8.20** Project panel after creating ship2quad in Blender.

Step 45: Click on **ship2quad** in the Assets panel and look at the Inspector panel. Click on the **Animations** box, **uncheck Import Animation,** and then click on **Apply**. You are going to animate the ship directly in Unity rather than using the imported animation from Blender. Blender's default animation is to have the object stationary at the origin, which would make for a pretty poor game.

Now you're ready put the ship into the Hierarchy.

Step 46: Drag the **ship2dquad** asset into the **Hierarchy** panel.

Step 47: Set **Position** to **(0, 0, 5)**, **Rotation** to **(0, 0, 0)**. Your Unity window should now look like Figure 8.21.

It worked, sort of. The spaceship is a bit too large, but at least you can see the spaceship. You needed to change the x-rotation from -90 to 0. The z position was increased so that the spaceship is displayed on top of the starfield.

You probably noticed that the spaceship is surrounded by a white square. That's because the alpha transparency is broken. Here's how to fix it.

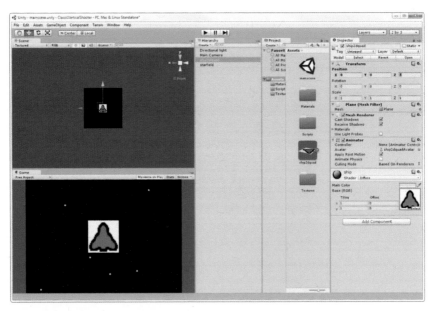

▲ FIGURE 8.21 Spaceship displayed in Unity.

Step 48: Double-click on the **Materials** folder. Click on the **ship** material.

Look at the Inspector panel. The Shader is set to the default "Diffuse." That's the wrong shader if you want alpha to work. Shaders are powerful, advanced programs that control how your graphics will be displayed. You won't be writing any shaders in this book, but you do have access to Unity's useful assortment of built-in shaders.

Step 49: Set the **Shader** to **Transparent – Diffuse**. As soon as you make that change, the white box surrounding the ship disappears!

There's one more cleanup step you should do.

Step 50: Click on the **ship** texture in the **Textures** folder and change the **Filter Mode** to **Point** instead of Bilinear. Change **Wrap Mode** to **Clamp**. Then click on **Apply**.

These changes make the texture appear pristine rather than filtered, which is the preferred look when displaying classic 2D sprites. Feel free to disagree and use the bilinear filter instead. This is basically a cosmetic adjustment.

Step 51: That was a lot of steps. **Save** your work, then **exit** Unity.

In the next section, you'll continue with your development of the sprites in this game.

VERSION 0.03: SPRITES

You just made a single 2D sprite for your spaceship, which was a good first step in learning how to deal with sprites. Next, you'll create your second sprite, the shots, and you'll learn how to dynamically create and destroy them. This is necessary so that when a shot hits something the shot disappears, and when the player hits a "Fire" button a shot is created.

You'll start by drawing your shot in GIMP. This is similar to drawing the spaceship. You'll be able to reuse the Blender work, so overall it'll go much faster this time.

Step 1: Open GIMP and create a **new image** with a **width** of **8 pixels** and **height** of **16 pixels**.

Step 2: Select the **pencil tool** and set the **size** to **1**. Zoom in on the image, make the **foreground color yellow** and **draw an arrow** pointing up as displayed in Figure 8.22.

▼ **FIGURE 8.22**
Arrow skeleton.

Step 3: Add the alpha by doing **Colors – Color to Alpha...** and then add a **white border** at the top and **fins** at the bottom as shown in Figure 8.23.

You're getting a taste of how all graphics were created in the early days of video games. That's right, the artist, or possibly even the programmer, drew every piece of graphics one pixel at a time. That was an advance over even earlier days when programmers typed in numbers to create the graphics. Things have come a long way since then.

▼ **FIGURE 8.23**
Arrow with alpha and fins.

Step 4: Save the image to **arrow.xcf** and **export** to **arrow.png**, and put both files into the **Assets/Textures** folder of your Unity project, once again making sure to use compression level 0. You can now go straight into Unity and use this new texture to make an arrow sprite.

Step 5: Open the ClassicVerticalShooter project in Unity. **Zoom** in on the Scene panel to approximately match the Game panel. Notice that you now have a new texture called arrow, plus the xcf file for it in the **Textures** folder.

Step 6: Select and **right-click** the **ship2dquad** object in the Hierarchy and do **Duplicate**.

The scene and game panels don't look any different because the duplicated objects overlap. Next, you'll move one of them to the right so they no longer overlap.

Step 7: In the Scene panel, grab one of the **ship2dquad** objects with the mouse and **move** it **to the right**. **Rename** it to **arrow2dquad**.

Step 8: Drag the **arrow texture** on top of **arrow2dquad**. Your game panel should now look like Figure 8.24.

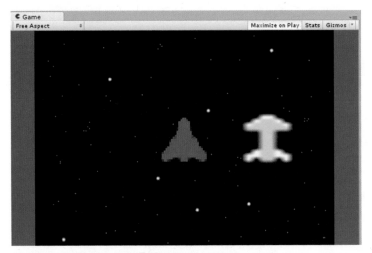

▲ FIGURE 8.24 The arrow's first appearance in Unity.

Note that a new arrow material has been automatically created in the Materials folder. The arrow object itself is distorted and too large.

Step 9: Set the **Scale** of **arrow2dquad** to (**0.05, 0.2, 1**). This rescaling brings back the 4 to 1 aspect ratio of the arrow texture. It's about time to rescale and move the ship as well.

Step 10: Set the **Scale** of the **ship2dquad** to **(0.4, 0.4, 1)** and the **Position** to **(0, -2.8, 5)**. The -2.8 was determined by trial and error. Make sure that the Main Camera is at (0, 0, 10), or you might be placing the ship off-screen. Our goal is to have the ship near the bottom edge of the Game panel.

Of course, the arrow shouldn't be just sitting out there in space. It should be shooting out of the front of the spaceship. To make that happen, you need to create a *prefab*. Prefabs are a great feature of Unity. They are templates that enable users to easily make linked copies (also called instances) of objects. You're going to make a Prefabs folder to store them.

Step 11: Create a **Folder** named **Prefabs** at the top level of the Assets folder. You should now have a Materials, Prefabs, Scripts, and Textures folder in the Assets folder.

Step 12: Drag the **arrow2dquad** into the **Prefabs** folder and rename it **arrowprefab**.

Dragging objects from the Hierarchy back to the Assets folder automatically creates a prefab. Try it out.

Step 13: Drag the **arrowprefab** into the **Scene**.

Step 14: Repeat the previous step a few times. The Game panel should now have a few arrows in it as displayed in Figure 8.25.

▼ **FIGURE 8.25** Testing the arrow prefab.

Step 15: Run the game, then **stop** running it.

Step 16: Delete all **arrowprefabs** in the **Hierarchy** panel.

You only need to keep the prefab itself in the Prefabs folder. You're now ready to use the prefab in your scripting.

Step 17: Save the **scene** and **project**.

Next, you'll create the code to control the ship.

Step 18: Select the **Scripts** folder and create a new **JavaScript** with name **ship-script**. Enter the following code:

```
#pragma strict

var shipSpeed: float;

function Start () {
    transform.position.y = -2.8;
}



function Update () {
    if (Input.GetKey ("right"))
    {
        transform.Translate(-shipSpeed * Time.deltaTime,0,0);
    }
    if (Input.GetKey ("left"))
    {
        transform.Translate(shipSpeed * Time.deltaTime,0,0);
    }
}
```

Step 19: **Save** the code and drag it onto the **ship2dquad** object.

Step 20: Set the **Ship Speed** to **5** in the Inspector panel and **test** out the code.

You're now controlling the ship with the arrow keys on the keyboard. You could also add mouse control as was done in the brick game, but that might make the game too easy, so that option will be left for later experimentation.

Next, you'll add a boundary check to make sure the ship doesn't disappear.

Step 21: Add the screenBoundary variable below the shipSpeed variable declaration as follows:

```
var screenBoundary: float;
```

Step 22: At the end of the Update function, add the following lines:

```
if (transform.position.x <  -screenBoundary)
    transform.position.x = -screenBoundary;
if (transform.position.x >  screenBoundary)
    transform.position.x = screenBoundary;
```

Step 23: Save the new version of **shipscript** and set the **screen Boundary** to 3 in the Inspector.

Step 24: Try out the game and test to see what happens at both edges of the screen, and adjust the Screen Boundary accordingly so the ship can move close to the edge. The ship should act like it's hitting an invisible wall. You should be able to move the ship closer to the edge, so try 4 for the Screen Boundary.

You are taking tiny steps here, adding small improvements, and immediately testing them.

Next, you'll add code to shoot arrows.

Step 25: Create a new JavaScript in the **Scripts** folder and rename it to **shotscript**. Open the script and enter the following code:

```
#pragma strict

var shotSpeed : float;



function Start () {
}

function Update () {
    transform.Translate(0, shotSpeed * Time.deltaTime, 0);
}
```

Step 26: Save the file in Monodevelop.

Step 27: Select arrowprefab in the Prefabs folder, scroll down in the inspector if necessary to reveal the "Add Component" box. Do **Add Componenet – Scripts – Shotscript**. Then set the **Shot Speed** to 4 in the Inspector.

You just created a script for the arrows, but you have no arrows in your scene right now to test. Just drag an arrow back into the scene, and test out the shot code as follows:

Step 28: Drag an **arrowprefab** into the **Hierarchy** panel and **run** the game. The arrow should fly up and away at a fairly rapid speed.

This is as good a time as any to deal with the arrow after it flies off the top of the screen. You want to destroy the arrow when that happens. This is a one-liner.

Step 29: Stop running the game, then **insert** the following code into the **shotscript** Update function.

```
if (transform.position.y > 6.0)  Destroy(gameObject);
```

Step 30: Save your change and test the code again.

How can you tell if it's working? Running the game looks exactly the same. There are several ways to do this.

Step 31: Change the 6.0 to a 1.0 in **shotscript**. **Test**, and then **undo** the change. You now see how the arrow disappears when it hits a y coordinate of 1.0. This is a reasonable way to test your code, but there is a better way.

Step 32: Turn off Maximize on Play and **run** the game. **Stop** the game and **turn on Maximize on Play**.

When the game is running, look at the Hierarchy panel. You'll see the "arrowprefab" object disappear soon after the arrow disappears from the top of the screen. You can also zoom out in the Scene panel and actually see the arrow disappear above the playfield area. Why is it important to have this cleanup code even though there's no discernible difference when you play the game? You'll be creating many new shots while you're playing the game, and every shot uses up computing resources. It's a good idea to destroy shots that aren't needed any more so that you don't run out of resources, or slow down your game, or both. Practically speaking, it would take many thousands of shots, maybe even millions, before you'd notice a difference. Nevertheless, it's a good habit to clean up after yourself. In the classic era, when memory was relatively expensive, a great deal of effort had to be put into managing memory. Even then, it was common to hear the phrase: memory is cheap. Thankfully, memory is orders of magnitude cheaper thirty years later.

Speaking of cleaning up after yourself:

Step 33: Delete the temporary **arrowprefab** instance in the **Hierarchy**.

CAREFUL: Don't delete the arrowprefab itself in the Prefabs directory!

You're now ready to launch the arrows under player control.

Step 34: In **shipscript**, add the variable "shot" by adding the following line:

```
var shot: GameObject;
```

Step 35: In the Update function, add the following code:

```
if (Input.GetKeyDown("space"))
{
    Instantiate(
        shot,
        Vector3(transform.position.x,transform.position.y,5),
        Quaternion.identity
    );
}
```

What's going on here? The Instantiate function creates a shot at the same position as the ship. The `Quaternion.identity` sets the rotation to be unchanged, which means that the arrow is pointing up.

Step 36: Save the file, then select **ship2dquad** in the Hierarchy.

Step 37: Drag **arrowprefab** from the Assets panel into the **Shot** property of **Shipscript** in the Inspector panel. **Run** the game and **test**. This is pretty easy to test. Pound on the space bar. Move the ship while shooting. If you do this with "Maximize on Play" off your screen should look like Figure 8.26.

Look at all those arrows in the Hierarchy panel. When the game is paused, you can click on each one and look at the properties. This technique can be very helpful when debugging.

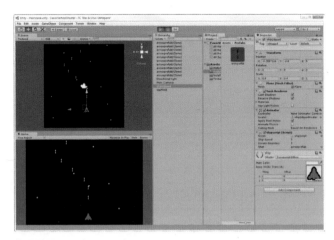

▲ **FIGURE 8.26** Arrows galore.

That was a lot of work, but you're really just getting started.

Step 38: Save your Scene and Project and **exit** Unity.

In this rather lengthy section, you learned about prefabs and how to use them to create and destroy sprites dynamically. In the next section, you'll create sprites for aliens.

VERSION 0.04: ALIENS

Now that you have a spaceship and shots, you need something to shoot at. True to your 2D design for this game, you'll make 2D animated sprites to display the aliens. The design for the aliens is quite simple. They'll be walking left and right in their formation using a four-frame walk animation. You'll be looking at 3D animation tech-niques later on, but for now you'll do animation the old-

▼ **FIGURE 8.27** Alien drawing.

fashioned way: one frame at a time. These animations will be quick and dirty prototype sketches. It's too early in the development process to spend a lot of time polish-ing them.

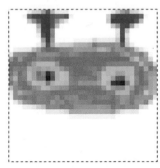

Step 1: Open up GIMP and open up a **new image** with size **32 x 32** pixels. Select a **red brush** of **size 3** and draw a red blob like the head shape in Figure 8.27.

Step 2: Draw yellow and **black eyes** and **blue antennas**.

It's OK if your drawing doesn't match the one from the figure as long as you draw something similar. Keep in mind that the white color will be converted to alpha just as you did earlier for the spaceship and arrow graphics, so don't use white for anything other than the background. Leave some room at the bottom for the legs.

The next step is to duplicate your alien so that you have a comic strip of four copies of the alien. One quick way to do this is as follows:

Step 3: Select all, Edit – Copy, and then **Edit – Paste As – New Pattern…**.

Step 4: File – New for a new image with size **128 x 32** and use the **Bucket Fill Tool** with a **Pattern Fill** using the pattern you just saved. You may need to click on the current pattern used by the Bucket Fill Tool and select the new pattern instead from a large grid of available patterns. The result is Figure 8.28.

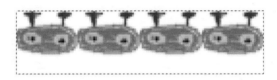

▲ **FIGURE 8.28** Alien strip.

Now, draw the animated legs using a blue brush:

Step 5: Draw the **legs** onto the new image, similar to Figure 8.29.

▲ **FIGURE 8.29** Alien drawing.

You're almost done with the alien.

Step 6: Colors – Color to Alpha, save the file in the **Assets/Textures** directory as **alien.xcf** and then export to **alien.png** using **compression level 0**.

You can safely toss the original image for the alien head.

Let's bring the alien animation into Unity.

Step 7: Run Unity with the **ClassicVerticalShooter** project.

Step 8: Duplicate ship2dquad. Rename the duplicate to "alien" and move it to the top half of the scene panel.

Step 9: Select the alien object and look at it in the Inspector panel. Drag the **alien** texture from the Texture directory on top of the **alien object** in the **Hierarchy** panel. Be careful not to drag it directly on top of the texture in the Inspector as this would overwrite the ship texture for the ship. You should see all four animation frames of the alien in the Game and Scene panels, and the original ship still intact.

Step 10: Select the **Scripts** folder and create a new JavaScript and name it **alien-script**. Enter the following initial code for it:

```
#pragma strict

function Start () {

}


function Update () {


// Simple animation
    var index = Mathf.FloorToInt(Time.time * 12.0) % 4;
    var size = Vector2(0.25,1);
    var offset = Vector2(index / 4.0,0);
    renderer.material.SetTextureScale("_MainTex",size);
    renderer.material.SetTextureOffset("_MainTex",offset);
}
```

Step 11: Save the script file and drag the **alienscript** on top of the **alien object** in the Hierarchy panel.

The alien object now has two scripts showing in the Inspector: Shipscript and Alienscript. We need to remove the old Shipscript.

Step 12: Click on the **gear icon** at the top right of the **Shipscript** section and select **Remove Component**. If you were to forget to do this, the alien would behave like the ship, which is certainly not what you want.

Step 13: Run the game. If everything was done correctly, you should see an animated alien near the top of the screen. You might have noticed that there are some glitches in the graphics. It's not at all obvious why this happened or how to fix it.

The glitches have to do with texture compression.

Step 14: Click on the **alien** Texture in the **Textures** folder.

The format is set to compressed. This saves memory on your graphics card, but it can cause the graphics to be displayed with compression artifacts.

Step 15: Select the **16 bits Format** instead, and while you're there, select a **Filter Mode** of **Point**. Then, click on **Apply** and **run** the game again. The graphics should now look pretty much the same as in GIMP. You selected 16 bits instead of Truecolor because this saves some memory and yet the display of this particular animation has no perceptible quality loss. Feel free to go back to GIMP and improve the graphics, save and export, and then test again in Unity.

Just as you did with the arrow object, you're going to make a prefab so you can easily create multiple aliens using a script.

Step 16: Select the **Prefabs** folder in the **Assets** panel and drag the **alien** object into it. **Rename** the alien prefab to **alienprefab**.

You're including "prefab" in the name of this prefab to more easily distinguish it from other objects, such as the alien texture.

Recall that dragging an object into the Assets folder automatically turns it into a prefab. If you like, test the prefab by making a few test instances in the Scene. Run the game to check out the test prefabs. When you're done testing, delete them all.

Step 17: Delete any **alien objects** in the **Hierarchy** panel, including the original alien and any objects with the name alienprefab.

You've encountered this before and it bears repeating. *Be sure to only delete Hierarchy objects and keep the prefab itself in the Assets/Prefabs folder.*

You're now ready to build your grid of aliens. This is done using a technique similar to your creation of the bricks in the Classic Brick Game.

Step 18: GameObject – Create Empty with name **alienfactory**. Assign to it the new JavaScript with name **alienfactoryscript** and the following code:

```
#pragma strict

var alien: GameObject;

function MakeAliens () {

    var al: GameObject;

    for(var i=0; i<15; i++)
    for(var j=0; j<6; j++)
    {
        al = Instantiate(
            alien,
            Vector3((i - 7) * 0.4, (j - 1) * 0.6, 5),
            Quaternion.identity);
    }
}

function Start() {
    MakeAliens();
}

function Update () {
}
```

Step 19: Save your files.

Step 20: Assign alienprefab to **Alien** in the Inspector for **alienfactory**, and try out the game.

Those aliens are too big, so you should make them smaller. It doesn't work to change the scale of alienfactory, because that's just an empty object. You need to do that for the alienprefab instead.

Step 21: Change the **Scale** of **alienprefab** to **(0.18, 0.18, 1)**.

You needed to stop running the game, do the change, and then start the game again to try it out. While it's true that it's possible to change properties of game objects while running the game, this doesn't apply to prefabs. Also, because you want this change to be permanent, you needed to stop running the game anyhow before making that edit. The game screen should now look like Figure 8.30.

▲ **FIGURE 8.30** A grid of aliens.

You're making some good progress. As you know, those shots from the spaceship aren't doing any damage to those pesky aliens. It's time to add collision detection between arrows and aliens.

In previous projects, it was OK to just detect collisions with any other type of object. But here you want to detect only objects of a specific type. For this you're going to use the "tag" feature of Unity.

Step 22: Add the following code at the end of alienscript:

```
function OnTriggerEnter (other: Collider) {
    if (other.tag == "shot")
    {
        Destroy(gameObject);
        Destroy(other.gameObject);
    }
}
```

This function checks to see if your alien is colliding with a shot. If so, it destroys itself and the shot. In order to make this code work, you'll set up the tags for the shots.

Step 23: Select **arrowprefab** and notice that it is untagged. You can see this by looking at the Tag property at the top of the Inspector panel. As you might guess, tags are a way to group objects together and, thus, making some scripting tasks easier. Before you can tag your arrowprefab with the "shot" tag, you need to create the "shot" tag.

Step 24: Click on **Untagged**. This activates the drop-down menu next to the Tag property.

Step 25: Choose **Add Tag** at the very bottom. This activates the TagManager. That's where you create or otherwise manage the tags for your project.

Step 26: Click on the **small triangle** next to **Tags**.

Step 27: Click on **Element 0**.

Step 28: Click in the **right half of the blue bar** for Element 0. Enter the text **shot**.

▼ **FIGURE 8.31** The shot tag.

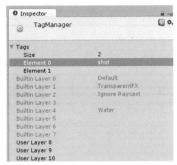

You have just created a new tag as shown in Figure 8.31. This was a little bit strange because the blue bar for Element 0 had no indication that there was a text input box available for it.

Step 29: Close the Tag manager by clicking on **arrowprefab** again, and now select the **shot tag** from the drop-down menu next to the Tag property.

If you're expecting your collision detection to work now, you're mistaken. You still have to carefully add some physics and collider components to your prefabs to make this work.

Step 30: Make sure that the **arrowprefab** is still selected and do **Component – Physics – Rigidbody. Uncheck** the **Use Gravity** box because the game is in outer space after all. Now do **Component – Physics – Box Collider, check Is Trigger**, and make the **Size (0.1, 1, 10)**.

You put a box collider around your sprite and made it very narrow in the x direction and full size in the y direction. The 10 in the z direction is somewhat arbitrary. It's there to make sure that the arrow collides with anything that overlaps with it in the x and y direction.

Step 31: Next select the **alienprefab** and add a **box collider** for it as well, but no rigid body. The **Size** of this box collider is **(2, 1, 10)** and also **check Is Trigger**.

Step 32: Test it, save and exit. Finally! You can shoot the aliens. It took much more of an effort this time, but you once again added just enough features to make the game playable. You're getting a good feel for what it might be like to play the final game, even though those aliens are just sitting there.

In the next section, you'll turn things around and introduce enemy shots.

VERSION 0.05: ALIEN SHOTS

It wouldn't be fair to just shoot at the aliens without having them shoot back. So let's create alien shots. This is somewhat familiar territory because you just did something similar in the previous section.

Step 1: Open GIMP and load **arrow.xcf** from **File – Open Recent** or, if it's been a while, from the **Textures** folder in your Unity project.

Step 2: Click on the **Flip Tool** in the tool grid and click on the **Vertical** radio button for the **Flip Type** in the **Tool Options** dialog.

Step 3: Zoom in by 16 (press the "5" key) to see the arrow and then click on it to make it point down instead of up. Then **make some minor changes** to it using the **pencil tool**. Feel free to get creative. When you're done, you should see a downward pointing arrow somewhat like Figure 8.32.

▼ FIGURE 8.32 Alien shot.

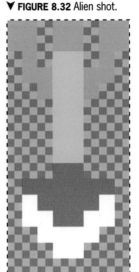

Step 4: Save as **ashot.xcf** and **export ashot.png** using **compression level 0**.

Step 5: Run Unity and load the **ClassicVerticalShooter** project, if necessary.

Once again, you'll bring in your new graphics into Unity, just as you did for the arrow.

Step 6: Duplicate ship2dquad, rename it to "ashot" and move it off to the side in the Scene panel by dragging it with the mouse.

Step 7: Drag the **ashot texture** (not the xcf file!) on top of the **ashot object** in the Hierarchy (not the texture in the Inspector panel!).

The xcf file uses the GIMP icon, the png file uses an icon that looks like the contents of the file.

You'll see the alien shot as a rather large object in the scene. Leave it at that size while making the following adjustments to it.

Step 8: Click on the **ashot** texture and select a **Wrap Mode** of **Clamp**, **Filter Mode** of **Point**, and **Format** of **16 bits**, followed by **Apply**. The rather fuzzy alien shot now looks clean and pristine. Your Scene should look like Figure 8.33. Feel free to use different settings here, if you prefer. Also, you might review these settings for the arrow texture and adjust them to your liking.

Step 9: Change the **Scale** of **ashot** to (**0.05, 0.2, 1**) to match the scale of the arrow.

Step 10: Remove the **shipscript** component from **ashot**. Now you're ready to turn this into a prefab. Click on the **Prefabs** folder and drag **ashot** into it.

▲ **FIGURE 8.33** The alien shot in the Unity scene.

Rename it to **ashotprefab**. Now, once again, it's time to write a script for the alien shots.

Step 11: Create a **new script**, call it **ashotscript**, assign it to **ashotprefab**, and enter the following code for it:

```
#pragma strict

var ashotSpeed : float;


function Start () {

}

function Update () {
    transform.Translate(0, ashotSpeed * Time.deltaTime, 0);
    if (transform.position.y < -8.0)
        Destroy(gameObject);
}
```

This code simply moves the alien shot down the screen and destroys the shot if it falls off the bottom of the screen.

Step 12: Save your script code and set the **ashotspeed** to -5 for the **ashotprefab**.

Step 13: Test it. Here's one way to test this. Drag a couple of ashotprefabs into the Scene panel and run the game. The shots should fly down the screen and disappear at the bottom. To verify that the "Destroy" is working, run the game without the "Maximize on Play" enabled, and monitor the Hierarchy. Because all those aliens are clogging up the Hierarchy display, you can temporarily remove them by commenting out the `MakeAliens()` call in alienfactoryscript as follows:

```
function Start() {
// MakeAliens();
}
```

Just be sure to remove those slashes and bring back the aliens when you're done debugging.

This kind of testing, where you modify the source code in order to test, is called "white box testing." If you don't modify anything, and don't even look at the source code while testing, you're doing "black box testing."

Now it's time to make those aliens shoot at you.

Step 14: Add the following code to the Update function in **alienscript**:

```
// shoot sometimes

if (Mathf.FloorToInt(Random.value * 10000.0) % 2000 == 0)
{
    Instantiate(
        ashot,
        Vector3(transform.position.x,transform.position.y,5),
        Quaternion.identity
    );
}
```

Step 15: Insert the variable **ashot** at the **beginning** of the script like this:

```
var ashot: GameObject;
```

Step 16: Save the script file, select **alienprefab**, and **drag ashotprefab** to the **Ashot property** in the Inspector.

Step 17: Run the game. You'll be getting shot at, but of course, you don't have the collision detect working yet so the alien shots go right through you without damage.

You'll do the collision handling pretty much the same way as for arrows hitting aliens.

Step 18: Add the following OnTriggerEnter function to **shipscript**:

```
function OnTriggerEnter (other: Collider) {
    if (other.tag == "ashot")
        {
            Destroy(gameObject);
            Destroy(other.gameObject);
        }
}
```

Once again you'll be using tags here. This time you'll have the tag "ashot" assigned to the ashotprefab.

Step 19: Save the **shipscript** file and select **ashotprefab**.

Step 20: Click on **Untagged** in the Inspector panel.

Step 21: Select Add Tag from the drop-down menu, type in the tag **ashot** for Element 1, click on **ashotprefab**, and select **ashot** as the tag for this prefab.

Just as you had to do for the arrow prefab, it's necessary to add box collider and rigidbody components.

Step 22: Component – Physics – Rigidbody and **uncheck Use Gravity**.

Step 23: Component – Physics – Box Collider and set the **Size** to (**0.1, 0.7, 10**). **Check** the **Is Trigger** Box.

You also need to have a box collider for your ship.

Step 24: Select **ship2dquad** in the Hierarchy panel, do **Component – Physics – Box Collider**, and change the **Size** to (**1, 1, 10**).

You're finally ready to test the collision code.

Step 25: Run the game and watch what happens when an alien shot hits the ship. Both the shot and the ship disappear. It's game over. This is a bit severe. Just one life!

You've "found the fun" just now. That's right, this game is fun just the way it is. Try to kill all the aliens. It's not exactly easy. If you think it's too easy, you can change shot speed or the rate the aliens are firing at you to make the game harder.

Step 26: Save your progress, take a **break**, you **deserve** it.

In the next section, you'll put some structure to the game and add multiple lives.

VERSION 0.06: SCORING AND LIVES

As the name implies, in this section you'll add scoring and lives. You'll use a technique called "finite state machines" or FSM for short. This is a common coding technique that goes way back to the early days of game development, and yet is still used today. It's somewhat surprising how few of the old techniques have become obsolete many decades later.

Before you get into finite state machines, you'll put in a simple display of scoring and lives, just as in your previous projects.

Step 1: Create an **empty GameObject** named **Scoring. Assign** the new JavaScript named **scoring** with the following code:

```
#pragma strict

static var score: int;
static var lives: int;

function InitializeGame () {
    score = 0;
    lives = 3;
```

```
    }

function Start () {
    InitializeGame();
}

function OnGUI () {
    GUI.Box (Rect (10,10,90,30), "Score:     "+score);
    GUI.Box (Rect (Screen.width - 100,10,90,30),"Lives:     "+lives);
}
```

Step 2: Deselect "Maximize on Play", run the game, **pause** it, and compare it to Figure 8.34.

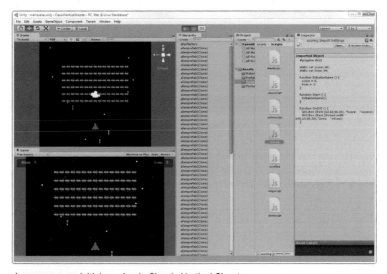

▲ **FIGURE 8.34** Initial scoring in Classic Vertical Shooter.

You're displaying the score and the lives, though they still aren't functional. Also, take a look at the Scripts folder. You now have seven scripts: alienfactory, alienscript, ashotscript, scroring, scrollme, shipscript, and shotscript. If you're seeing something else in the Scripts folder, chances are your scripts are residing at the top level of Assets. This would be a good time to move any stray scripts into the Scripts folder.

In the next step, you'll get the scoring working.

Step 3: Add the following line in **alienscript** at the correct spot:

```
scoring.score += 10;
```

Can you guess where to put that line? Think about it before reading on. Usually the scoring code gets put where the action happens that you're trying to reward, in this case the destruction of the alien. Thus, the correct spot is in the `OnTrigger-Enter` function, anywhere inside the curly brackets after the if statement, because that's where you're destroying the alien and the shot too.

Note that the "scoring" in that line isn't capitalized. It's a reference to the scoring script, which isn't capitalized.

You could, of course, get much fancier with the scoring, but for now it's a good start. Next, you'll create finite state machine to handle the various states of the game.

Step 4: Create an **empty GameObject**, name **GameState**, script name **GameSta-teScript assigned** to GameState, and enter the following code:

```
#pragma strict

static var state: int;

public enum GameState
{
    PressStart = 1,
    StartingPlay = 2,
    GamePlay = 3,
    Dying = 4,
    GameOver = 5,
    NextLevel = 6
}
```

```
function Start () {
    state = GameState.PressStart;
}

function Update () {
}
```

The enum statement defines the various states that your game can be in. Examine them one by one:

- PressStart is the state where a press start message is displayed. During this state, the game waits for the player to hit a key to start the game. When that happens, the game enters the StartingPlay state.
- StartingPlay is the state where the game is initialized and there are no user inputs being accepted yet. When the initializations are done, the game enters the GamePlay state.
- GamePlay is the main state where the player is playing the game. If at any time the player gets hit by a shot, you go to the Dying state. If all aliens get killed, you go to NextLevel.
- Dying is a state where the ship enters a death sequence, the aliens celebrate, etc. At the end of the death sequence, if there are no lives left, you go to GameOver, or else to StartingPlay.
- GameOver is the state where a "GAME OVER" message is displayed. The message will time out and you go to PressStart next.
- NextLevel is the state where a new wave of aliens is created, presumably harder.

It's now your job to start to implement all these states according to this informal description.

Step 5: Run the game, then **stop running** the game.

The first step is, what else, to test the code to make sure it compiles and doesn't break anything. The GameState object doesn't do anything except initialize the "state" variable.

Then, implement the first state, `PressStart`, as follows

Step 6: In the **scoring** script, **insert** the following lines into the `OnGUI` function:

```
if (GameStateScript.state == GameState.PressStart)
{
    if (GUI.Button (Rect (Screen.width/2 - 150,
                         Screen.height/2 - 50,
                         300, 50),"Click Me to Start"))
    {
    GameStateScript.state = GameState.StartingPlay;
    }
}

// for debugging
GUI.Box (Rect (Screen.width/2 - 30,10,90,30),
    "State: "+GameStateScript.state);
```

This creates the "Click Me" button in the middle of the screen. It doesn't work quite how you want yet, and it's ugly, but at least you can look at it. You added a debug output box to display the current game state. Unfortunately, the game state needs to be a static variable, and static variables can't easily be displayed in the Inspector, so you're using a GUI box to display the current state instead. When the game is released, you'll disable this debug display.

Displaying property values using the application is a time-honored tradition and goes way back to the old days of developing code using punch cards and line printers. It's still a useful method to use as an alternative to other debugging methods.

Now you'll make the button look better.

Step 7: Save your work and open GIMP.

You're going to make a custom button to replace the default button in Unity.

Step 8: Create a new image of size **128 x 128**.

Once again, you're using powers of 2 for your size.

Step 9: Zoom in by a factor of 2.

Step 10: Choose the **Rectangle Select Tool**.

Step 11: Check the **rounded corners checkbox** and choose a **Radius** of **25**.

Step 12: Uncheck the **expand from center** check box.

Step 13: Draw a **rounded rectangle** leaving a small uniform margin.

Step 14: Choose a **light green color** and use the **Bucket Fill** tool to fill the rectangle.

Your image should look like Figure 8.35.

Step 15: Do a **Select – All** to get ready for the next step.

Step 16: Filters – Artistic – Cartoon... with **Mask radius 10** and **Percent Black 0**.

Step 17: Colors – Color to Alpha, and then **save** the file as **roundbox.xcf** and **export** to **roundbox.png** in the Textures folder of our Unity project with **compression 0**.

Your image should look like Figure 8.36.

Step 18: Quit GIMP and go back to Unity.

You'll notice a new Texture called roundbox in the Textures folder.

Step 19: Select the **roundbox** Texture and change the **Texture Type** to **GUI**, the **Filter Mode** to **Point** and the **Format** to **16 bits**. Click on **Apply**. You're now ready to use the texture for your GUI box.

Step 20: Open the **scoring** script and add the following line at the top:

```
public var customButton: GUIStyle;
```

Step 21: Add a customButton argument to the GUI.Button statement like this:

▼ **FIGURE 8.35** Box with rounded corners in GIMP.

▼ **FIGURE 8.36** Round cornered box with alpha.

```
if (GameStateScript.state == GameState.PressStart)
{
    if (GUI.Button (Rect (Screen.width/2 - 150,
                        Screen.height/2 - 50,
                        300, 50),
                        "Click Me To Start",
                        customButton))
    {
        GameStateScript.state = GameState.StartingPlay;
    }
}
```

The only change was to add a comma and `customButton` at the end of the GUI. Button function call.

Step 22: Save the script and then select the **Scoring** object in the Hierarchy panel.

Step 23: You'll now see an innocent looking Custom Button property in the Inspector. Click on it and take a look at Figure 8.37.

You'll be trying to match those properties shown in Figure 8.37. This will require quite a few steps.

Step 24: Expand the **Normal** property and drag the **roundbox** Texture into the **Background** property.

Step 25: Just below it change the **Text Color** to a **bright Red**.

Step 26: Expand **Border** and change the **four Border values** to **30**.

Step 27: Expand **Overflow** and change the **four Overflow values** to **10**.

▼ **FIGURE 8.37** Custom Button properties in Unity.

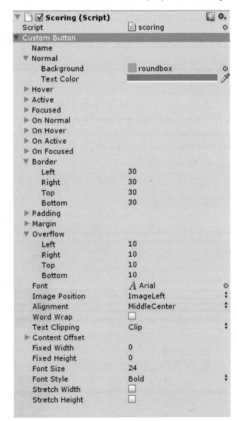

Step 28: Use the **Arial Font** and change the **Alignment** to **Middle Center**.

Step 29: Set the **Font Size** to **24** and the **Font Style** to **Bold**.

Step 30: Run the game and notice the somewhat different look of the button as shown in Figure 8.38.

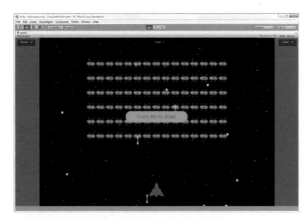

▲ **FIGURE 8.38** Custom Button properties in Unity.

Feel free to experiment with the various settings for the Custom Button. The tricky part is setting the Border and Overflow values to match the rounded corners in the roundbox Texture. The Unity documentation has more details about the various settings and their effects.

Now that the button graphics look better, it's time to fix the next big problem, which is that the game is active during the PressStart state. This is pretty easy to fix. First, look at alienfactoryscript. The aliens are getting initialized in the Start function, which is not where you want it.

Step 31: In **alienfactoryscript**, delete the call to MakeAliens in the Start function. The Start function now looks like this:

```
function Start() {
}
```

Now, when you run the game, the aliens are gone. You'll get them back as follows.

Step 32: Open up **shipscript** and add the following variable declaration at the top:

```
var alienfactory: alienfactoryscript;
```

Step 33: Change the name of the Update function to ShipControl, and insert the following new Update function below the end of ShipControl:

```
function Update () {
    if (GameStateScript.state == GameState.GamePlay)
    {
        ShipControl();
    }

    if (GameStateScript.state == GameState.StartingPlay)
    {
        alienfactory.MakeAliens();
        GameStateScript.state = GameState.GamePlay;
    }
}
```

Step 34: Save the file, select **ship2dquad**, and assign **alienfactory** to the new Alienfactory variable in the **Shipscript (Script)** section in the Inspector panel. Do this by dragging alienfactory from the Hierarchy into the Alienfactory property in the Inspector.

It's instructive to follow the new logic in the Update function. You are only allowing the player to control the ship during the GamePlay state, and you initialize the aliens during the StartingPlay state, immediately followed by a transition to the GamePlay state.

If you test the game right now, you can click on the "Click me to Start" button and play the game after that.

Your next step is to make the lives counter work.

Step 35: Enter the new OnTriggerEnter function for **shipscript**:

```
function OnTriggerEnter (other: Collider) {
    if (other.tag == "ashot")
    {
```

```
    scoring.lives--;
    if (scoring.lives == 0)
    {
        Destroy(other.gameObject);
        GameStateScript.state = GameState.GameOver;
    }
  }
}
```

Instead of destroying the ship every time it gets hit by an alien shot, you now decrease the lives counter. When the lives counter reaches zero, rather than destroying the ship, you change state to GameOver.

Step 36: Save the file and now **add** the following **code fragment** to the OnGUI function in the scoring script:

```
if (GameStateScript.state == GameState.GameOver)
{
    if (GUI.Button (Rect (Screen.width/2 - 200,
                          Screen.height/2 - 50,
                          400, 50),"Game Over, Try again",
                          customButton))
    {
        InitializeGame();
        GameStateScript.state = GameState.PressStart;
    }
}
```

The game structure almost works now, but there's a tricky bug. At the end of the game, you need to clean up after yourself and delete all the leftover aliens.

Step 37: Add the following code to the Update function in alienscript:

```
if (GameStateScript.state == GameState.GameOver)
{
    Destroy(gameObject);
}
```

This code is particularly interesting. It basically orders all aliens to destroy themselves when the game state is GameOver. Now save all your script files and try out the game. It still has some problems, but it's basically playable.

Make the following minor adjustment. You're killing off the left over aliens too soon. If you wait until you enter the PressStart state, it'll look a little better.

Step 38: Replace the `GameOver` with a `PressStart` as follows:

```
if (GameStateScript.state == GameState.PressStart)
{
    Destroy(gameObject);
}
```

Now the aliens disappear after you click on the "Game Over" message.

Your next goal is to have the ship disappear and reappear depending on the game state. First, fix the bug where the lives counter reaches -1. It's bad enough that you can have zero lives left, but you don't even want to think about what it would mean to have negative lives.

Step 39: In shipscript, add the following line at the beginning of `OnTriggerEnter`:

```
if (GameStateScript.state == GameState.GamePlay)
```

This assures that you have no ship-vs.-alien shot collisions except during gameplay.

You're now ready to add the death sequence for the ship. Currently, when the ship gets hit, it either has no reaction or, if you're on the last life, it just freezes and it's game over. What you really want is some kind of animation that shows the ship got hit, have the ship disappear for a while, and then you either go into the game over state or you try again with another ship. Here is where the "Dying" state gets used.

Step 40: Add a `deathtimer` variable to **shipscript** as follows:

```
var deathtimer: float;
```

Step 41: Add the following code fragment to the `Update` function:

```
if (GameStateScript.state == GameState.Dying)
{
    transform.Rotate(0, 0, Time.deltaTime * 400.0);
    deathtimer -= 0.1;
    if (deathtimer < 5.0)
    {
        renderer.enabled = false;
    }
    if (deathtimer < 0)
    {
        GameStateScript.state = GameState.GamePlay;
            transform.position.x = 0.0;
            transform.rotation.z = 0.0;
            renderer.enabled = true;
    }
}
```

Step 42: Change the `OnTriggerEnter` funtion as follows:

```
function OnTriggerEnter (other: Collider) {
    if (GameStateScript.state == GameState.GamePlay)
    if (other.tag == "ashot")
    {
        scoring.lives--;
        deathtimer = 10.0;
        GameStateScript.state = GameState.Dying;
        if (scoring.lives == 0)
        {
            Destroy(other.gameObject);
            GameStateScript.state = GameState.GameOver;
        }
    }
}
```

The only change in the `OnTriggerEnter` function was to initialize the death-timer and to change the state to `Dying`. Notice that when the lives counter hits zero, you bypass the `Dying` state and go directly to GameOver. This isn't quite what you want but it's good enough for now.

When you test this code, the ship does a rotation animation when hit, disappears, and then reappears, sometimes with disastrous consequences because it might get resurrected right on top of an alien shot! The fix for this is to have the aliens stop shooting when the ship is in its death sequence.

Step 43: Add the following line in **alienscript**:

```
if (GameStateScript.state == GameState.GamePlay)
```

right after the "shoot sometimes" comment and before the Instantiate section.

Now clean up what's happening with the ship right before Game Over. When you detect a collision with an alien shot, you go into the `Dying` state, regardless of how many lives are left.

This has the effect of simplifying the `OnTriggerEnter` function.

Step 44: In **shipscript**, **replace** the `OnTriggerEnter` function with the following code:

```
function OnTriggerEnter (other: Collider) {
   if (GameStateScript.state == GameState.GamePlay)
   if (other.tag == "ashot")
   {
      scoring.lives--;
      deathtimer = 10.0;
      GameStateScript.state = GameState.Dying;
      Destroy(other.gameObject);
   }
}
```

Step 45: Also in **shipscript**, **edit** the `Dying` section at the bottom of the **Update** function to look like this:

```
if (GameStateScript.state == GameState.Dying)
{
```

```
transform.Rotate(0, 0, Time.deltaTime * 400.0);
deathtimer -= 0.1;
if (deathtimer < 5.0)
{
   renderer.enabled = false;
}

if (deathtimer < 0)
{
   GameStateScript.state = GameState.GamePlay;
   transform.position.x = 0.0;
   transform.rotation.z = 0.0;
   renderer.enabled = true;

   if (scoring.lives == 0)
   {
      GameStateScript.state = GameState.GameOver;
   }
}
}
```

Step 46: Save your files, test, and exit Unity.

In this section, you developed a finite state machine to handle the basic structure of your game. In the next section, you'll implement a death animation for the aliens by creating a small finite state machine for each alien.

VERSION 0.07: ALIEN DEATH SEQUENCE

Your next goal is to have the aliens go through a death animation when they get hit by an arrow, and then disappear. This is pretty similar to what you just did with the player character, so it will seem like familiar territory. The main difference is that you are now dealing with an entire array of aliens.

You're going to need a state variable and a timer, so add them to alienscript. Here is the new version of alienscript.

Step 1: Run Unity, take a look at the code below and then **edit alienscript** to match. There are some underlines to the left of the new lines to help you in your editing.

```
#pragma strict

var ashot: GameObject;
var state: int;
var timer: float;

function Start () {
}

function Update () {

// Simple animation
var index = Mathf.FloorToInt(Time.time * 12.0) % 4;
var size = Vector2(0.25,1);
var offset = Vector2(index / 4.0,0);
renderer.material.SetTextureScale("_MainTex",size);
renderer.material.SetTextureOffset("_MainTex",offset);

// shoot sometimes

if (GameStateScript.state == GameState.GamePlay)
if ( Mathf.FloorToInt(Random.value * 10000.0) % 2000 == 0)
{
    Instantiate(
        ashot,
        Vector3(
            transform.position.x,
            transform.position.y,
            5),
        Quaternion.identity
    );
}
```

```
    // if it's dying go through the death sequence
    if (state == 1)
    {
        transform.Rotate(0, 0, Time.deltaTime * 400.0);
        transform.Translate(
            0.3  * Time.deltaTime,
            3.0  * Time.deltaTime,
            0, Space.World);
        transform.localScale = transform.localScale * 0.99;
        timer -= 0.1;
        if (timer < 0)
            Destroy(gameObject);
    }

    if (GameStateScript.state == GameState.PressStart)
      {
        Destroy(gameObject);
      }

    }


    function OnTriggerEnter (other: Collider) {

        if (other.tag == "shot")
        {
            scoring.score += 10;
            state = 1;
            timer = 5.0;
            Destroy(other.gameObject);
        }
    }
```

Don't forget to delete the "Destroy(gameObject)" line at the end of OnTrigger-Enter!

Step 2: We also need to initialize the alien state to 0 in **alienfactoryscript** as follows:

```
#pragma strict

var alien: GameObject;

function MakeAliens () {

   var al: GameObject;

   for(var i=0; i<15; i++)
   for(var j=0; j<6; j++)
   {
      al = Instantiate(
         alien,
         Vector3(
            (i - 7) * 0.5,
            (j - 1) * 0.6,
            5
         ),
         Quaternion.identity
      );

___   var alscript : alienscript;
___   alscript = al.GetComponent(alienscript);
___   alscript.state = 0;
   }

}

function Start() {
}

function Update () {
}
```

That looks like a lot of code, but most of it got entered earlier in this chapter. This is a good time to review it, try to understand it, and to make sure your old code didn't get changed somehow. The new code has to do with the state and timer variables. The initialization in alienfactoryscript is just three lines. The alienscript changes are more substantial, but also straightforward.

The strangest thing is the line with the 0.99 in it. That line makes your object smaller by 1 percent. The effect is that the aliens appear to shrink as they spin off the top of the screen.

Notice that you have two state variables affecting the aliens, the game state and the alien state. The alien state is very simple. If it's 0, it's alive and kicking, if it's 1, it's dying.

Those constants in the code, numbers such as 0.99, 400.0, 3.0, and 0.3, are commonly called "fudge factors." Yes, really. It's fun to change the numbers and watch the effect on the death sequence in the aliens. It's a good idea, in general, to replace the fudge factors by more meaningful variables and to document the effects, especially in production code. Sometimes though, it makes the code easier to deal with and to understand if the fudge factors are "hardwired" into the code, such as in the current version of alienscript.

Step 3: Test, save, and exit.

The game is starting to look pretty good, but you still don't have any sound! The next section addresses this.

VERSION 0.08: SOUND

Designing the sound for a game can be a full-time job for several people in a major AAA title. For you, it's a small section in a large chapter. The classic approach to sound effects in games is to just throw some simple effects in there without too much planning, experiment a little bit, and don't worry about being realistic.

The vacuum of outer space is completely silent. This hasn't stopped countless sci-fi movies from adding sound effect to their space battles. You're going to keep things extremely simple and just do two sound effects and no music in this game. You need a sound effect for when the arrow gets launched, and another for when aliens get hit. Most space shooters use some kind of laser "bleep" for shots and an explosion sound for aliens getting hit, but, of course, there are exceptions. Let's go into Audacity and get started.

Step 1: Start **Audacity**.

Step 2: Tracks – Add New – Stereo Track.

Step 3: Generate – Chirp with the settings **Frequency Start 440, End 1320, Amplitude Start 0.8, End 0.1, Interpolation Linear** and **Duration 1 second**.

Step 4: Apply the **Wahwah** effect with settings **LFO Frequency (Hz): 1.5, LFO Start Phase (deg.): 0, Depth (%) 70, Resonance 2.5** and **Wah Frequency Offset (%) 30**.

Your wave forms should look like Figure 8.39.

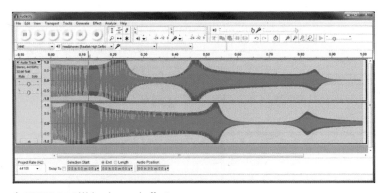

▲ **FIGURE 8.39** Wahwah sound effect.

That sounds pretty weird. You want your sound effect to be shorter.

Step 5: Select everything after 0.30 and **delete** it. **Save** the project to **cshot.aup** and **export** to **cshot.wav** in the Assets folder of your Unity project. **Exit** Audacity.

Next, you'll make a simple explosion sound.

Step 6: Start Audacity, **Add** a **new stereo track, Generate – Noise** with **Noise type: Pink, Amplitude 0.7** and **Duration of 1 second**. Do **Effect – FadeOut** and the **Effect – WahWah** with the same settings as the cshot sound effect.

The wave forms should look like Figure 8.40.

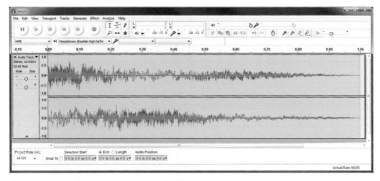

▲ **FIGURE 8.40** Alien explosion sound effect.

This sound effect is even stranger, just what you want. Of course, feel free to make your own different and bizarre sound effects. The only thing that really matters is that they are about 0.3 seconds and 1 second in duration, and even that can be changed quite a bit.

Step 7: Save this "explosion" sound effect to **cexplo.aup** and **export** to cexplo.wav, both in the Assets folder of your Unity project.

Was there any method to this madness? Not really. Just as in the old days when technology was much more primitive, game designers simply fiddled with the numbers until they liked what they heard. Today, many independent game developers still make sound effects this way, mainly because it's cheap and fun.

Now put the sounds into your game.

Step 8: Open Unity and load the **ClassicVerticalShooter** project, if necessary.

Step 9: Create a **Sounds** folder in the Assets panel, and **move all six sound files** into it. Your Project panel should look similar to Figure 8.41.

The exact layout depends on some of your custom settings in Unity. Make sure that your two .wav files are located in the Sounds folder. Try previewing them in the Inspector, if you wish.

▼ **FIGURE 8.41** Project panel with sound effects.

Step 10: Open **shipscript** and add the following variable:

```
var ShotSound : AudioClip;
```

Step 11: In the section where you test for the "space" key, right after the Instantiate, add

```
audio.PlayOneShot(ShotSound);
```

Step 12: Save the file.

Step 13: Select ship2quad in the Hierarchy panel and do **Component – Audio – Audio Source**.

Step 14: Uncheck the **Play on Awake** checkmark.

Step 15: Drag the **cshot** sound from the Project panel to the Shot Sound property. Remember that you want the wav file, the one with the wave form in the icon.

Step 16: Also **drag** the same **cshot** sound into the **Audio Clip** property in **Audio Source** in the Inspector panel.

If everything worked, your cshot sound will play every time you fire a shot with the space bar. One fun slider to play with is the Pitch in the Audio Source section.

Step 17: Set the **Pitch** in the Audio Source section to **1.4**.

That was pretty much the same procedure you used in your previous projects. Now you'd think that doing the explosion sound would be easy and more of the same. Well, not so fast.

First, look at alienscript.

Step 18: In **alienscript**, add the following line to the variables section at the top:

```
var ExplosionSound : AudioClip;
```

Step 19: Immediately after the statement that adds 10 points to the score, **insert** this code:

```
audio.PlayClipAtPoint(ExplosionSound,transform.position);
```

This is necessary because you don't have an AudioSource available, so you use this function instead which does the creation and cleanup of the AudioSource for you.

Now you're stuck because there's no alien object to select to be your audio source! Never fear, Unity can handle this as follows:

Step 20: Open up alienfactoryscript. In the variables section add

```
var ExploSound: AudioClip;
```

Step 21: Immediately after `alscript.state = 0` add the following:

```
alscript.ExplosionSound = ExploSound;
```

Step 22: Save the new version of alienfactoryscript.

Step 23: Select the **alienfactory** object and assign the **cexplo** sound to the **Explo Sound** property in the Inspector. Amazingly, that's all there is to it.

Step 24: Save the Scene in Unity, **test**, and **exit** Unity.

Additional sound effects are certainly possible for this game. Feel free to add your own sounds for aliens shooting, game over, and maybe even a speech sound for starting the game. Check out the exercises at the end of this chapter for more possibilities for sound.

In the next section you'll put in level handling.

VERSION 0.09: LEVELS

So far one of the truly defining features of classic gaming has been ignored: difficulty ramping implemented as levels. A large majority of video games increase the difficulty of the game depending on the progress of the players. This is only logical. The players would get bored if the games didn't continue to challenge them as they got farther into the game.

In your vertical shooter, you'll increase the difficulty with each wave of aliens. You'll keep it simple and increase the rate of shots getting fired. In preparation for this, you need to think about how to test this. It'll be a lot simpler if there are fewer aliens.

Step 1: Run Unity and in **alienfactoryscript** change the **15** and the **6** to **2** and **2** and **save** the file.

You should now see just four aliens instead of 90.

The next thing to think about is how to detect when you have no more aliens on the screen. That's going to be your trigger for starting the next level. To do this you create a variable to count how many aliens exist at any given moment.

Step 2: Declare the aliencounter variable in the scoring script as follows:

```
static var score: int;
static var lives: int;
static var aliencounter: int;
```

You're declaring it in scoring rather than in alienscript because it's a single global variable, and that's a good place for it. The initialization needs to happen when you create the aliens, which is in alienfactoryscript.

Step 3: In the `MakeAliens` function, at the beginning, just before the double loop, **add** the line

```
scoring.aliencounter = 0;
```

Step 4: Inside the double loop, **insert** the following line:

```
scoring.aliencounter++;
```

Step 5: Save the file in MonoDevelop.

To see that it's working, change your debug display.

Step 6: In the **scoring** script, change the debug display code as follows:

```
// for debugging
GUI.Box (Rect (Screen.width/2 - 60,10,120,30),
"Aliencounter: "+scoring.aliencounter);
```

The box is now a little wider to accommodate the longer label.

Step 7: Save all your changes in MonoDevelop and **run** the game. You should see an aliencounter of 4 displayed at the top center of the game screen. Next, make the counter decrease when aliens get destroyed. This is easy to do in alienscript.

Step 8: In **alienscript**, insert the line immediately after the line where the alien gets destroyed:

```
scoring.aliencounter--;
```

Step 9: Put in **curly braces** surrounding the Destroy statement and the line you just inserted. Your code should now look like this:

```
if (timer < 0)
{
    Destroy(gameObject);
    scoring.aliencounter--;
}
```

Here is what you did: you added a line to decrement the aliencounter immediately after the line where an alien is destroyed. You also had to add braces to group the two lines together, otherwise the aliencounter would get decremented even when the timer is greater than or equal to 0.

Step 10: Save your work and **try it out**.

The aliencounter variable should now decrement whenever an alien disappears. What's next? How about another small change with big consequences!

Step 11: Add the following

```
if (scoring.aliencounter == 0)
{
    GameStateScript.state = GameState.StartingPlay;
    scoring.level++;
}
```

immediately after the aliencounter decrement in alienscript.

Step 12: At the beginning of scoring, insert the new level variable as follows:

```
static var score: int;
static var lives: int;
static var level: int;
static var aliencounter: int;
```

Step 13: Initialize `level` in the `InitializeGame` function:

```
function InitializeGame() {
    score = 0;
    lives = 3;
    level = 0;
}
```

Step 14: You also want to display the level, so change the debug display to this:

```
// for debugging
    GUI.Box (Rect (Screen.width/2 - 60,10,120,30),
        "Level: "+scoring.level);
```

Step 15: Now **save** all your changed script files and try out the game.

Your level should be displayed and it should increment every time you clobber those four aliens. Also, merely by transitioning to the `StartingPlay` state in Step 11, you automatically get a new batch of aliens via the `Update` function in shipscript.

Now do some cleanup. You started with level 0, but that was a mistake. People want to start at level 1.

Step 16: Change the initialization of `level` to **1** in the **scoring** script.

Step 17: The comment "// for debugging" is incorrect at the bottom of the **scoring** script, so replace it with "// level display". Save your changes and test again.

In the old days, many decades ago, programmers were encouraged to put a lot of comments into their code. Years of experience have taught us that comments are often incorrect, especially when the code gets reworked and changed a lot. The modern bias is to write code so well and so clearly that comments become mostly unnecessary.

You can never test enough, and this is a great example. You have a pretty serious bug. If you wish, you can try to duplicate it by dying right as you shoot the last alien. Guess what, your ship never comes back even though you get advanced to the next level. It takes some patience to do this, or you can increase the shot rate of the aliens to make testing easier.

What's going on here? Well, the player is still in the death sequence when we're changing state, which doesn't work. To fix it, do the following:

Step 18: Take the following code section from alienscript:

```
if (scoring.aliencounter == 0)
{
    GameStateScript.state = GameState.StartingPlay;
    scoring.level++;
}
```

and move it to the Update function in shipscript, immediately after the call to ShipControl. Use cutting and pasting to do this edit fairly quickly. The beginning of that Update function should now look like this:

```
if (GameStateScript.state == GameState.GamePlay)
{
    ShipControl();
    if (scoring.aliencounter == 0)
    {
        GameStateScript.state = GameState.StartingPlay;
        scoring.level++;
    }
}
```

The effect of this change to your code is that you're only advancing to the next level during GamePlay, not during the Dying state.

Step 19: Save your changes and test again, making sure that you can die and advance to the next level after the death sequence completes.

This was a nasty and subtle bug that can only be revealed by thorough testing. You're lucky that it was found now, rather than after release.

Finally, you're able to make use of the level variable and increase the difficulty of the game depending on the level. A simple start is to change the firing rate of the aliens depending on the level.

Step 20: Add the following statement at the beginning of alienscript:

```
static var levelarr = [50, 30, 20, 10];
```

This creates an array of tuning numbers for the first four levels of the game.

Step 21: Replace the "shoot sometimes" section with:

```
// shoot sometimes

var levindex: int;
levindex = scoring.level - 1;
if (levindex > 3) levindex = 3;
if (levindex < 0) levindex = 0;

if (GameStateScript.state == GameState.GamePlay)
if (Mathf.FloorToInt(Random.value * 10000.0) %
    (levelarr[levindex] * scoring.aliencounter) == 0)
{
    Instantiate(
    ashot,
    Vector3(
       transform.position.x,
       transform.position.y,
       5),
    Quaternion.identity);
}
```

This code looks at the array levelarr and, depending on which level we're at, shoots alien shots at that level's shooting rate.

Additional difficulty ramping possibilities are explored in the exercises at the end of the chapter.

Step 21: Save your edits, **test** the game.

Wow, this game is difficult at level 4, and you haven't even brought back the original 90 aliens.

Step 22: In **alienfactoryscript**, bring back the **15** and **6** in the loop statements. Test and **tune**. **Save** and **exit**.

You have a pretty good game here with a world of potential for expansion and enhancements. The time has come to release it. Figure 8.42 shows a screenshot.

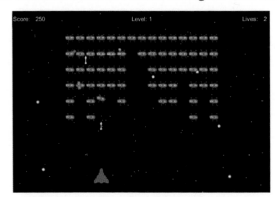

▲ **FIGURE 8.42** Screen shot of released classic vertical shooter.

VERSION 1.00: RELEASE AND POSTMORTEM

You've reached an important milestone. You now know enough basic game development techniques to make some interesting 2D and 3D games. You know how to make graphics, animations, sounds, collisions, and basic game logic.

The game is ready for release the way it is, but, of course, there's always room for improvement. The biggest and most obvious problem is that you're not matching the initial design sketch very well. There are several missing elements such as the barriers. This is perfectly OK. What matters is that the game is fun and makes sense. It's up to you to take it from here and add the missing elements, or to invent your own enhancements. Check out the exercises for additional development practice and ideas for where to take the game from here.

The best part of this game is that it's really fun to play, and you have a mechanism in place to tune the difficulty ramping. It's still a very small game by today's standards, but it wouldn't be that difficult to make it larger. The colors are vivid and the sound effects are weird and fit the game well.

The development of the game was a valuable learning experience. You used all of your tools for the first time, and saw how the different parts fit together and interact. You also did much more programming this time around, but it was all fairly easy. The built-in functions of Unity do all the heavy lifting, so the only thing left for you to do is to script the sequence of events.

On the negative side, it all seemed just a little more difficult than it should have been. This is the nature of technical work. As great and useful as the tools are, there are still hoops to jump through and hurdles to overcome to make it all happen the way you want. It seemed tedious to have to type all that code. There really ought to be an easier way, but the sad reality is that real game development can be tedious at times, especially when you're doing something new.

The single most important lesson from this chapter is simply this: Take tiny steps, test each step along the way whenever possible, and then fix any problems and bugs right away.

All in all, it felt good to create this game. If you did all the steps in this chapter and finished with a playable game, congratulations! Now keep going, because this is just the beginning.

EXERCISES

1. Make the starfield scroll horizontally instead of vertically. Then, make the starfield scroll in different directions depending on the level of the game.
2. Create a second starfield in GIMP and use alpha to make the background transparent. Display the second starfield on top of the original starfield and scroll it at a different vertical rate.
3. Draw a more detailed starship in GIMP using a 64 x 64 texture. Give it a different color scheme. Integrate the new starship into your game by using a variable named "shiptype" and setting it to 1 for the original ship, 2 for the new ship. At the beginning of the game, allow the user to choose which ship to use by pressing a key on the keyboard. Integrate a text display that explains which keys to use for which ship type.

4. Use GIMP to draw an animated arrow with 4 frames using the same technique you used to animate the aliens. Replace the arrow in the game with the animated arrow and animate it in Unity.

5. Rearrange the aliens into a grid of 12 by 4 aliens. Change the layout of the aliens so they cover the entire top half of the screen.

6. Change the "shoot sometimes" code to something less random. Add a shot timer to each alien and have each alien shoot after the timer expires. Then reset the timer based on a random range of values.

7. Create a sound effect for the loss of a life by the ship using Audacity and make it work in the game.

8. Use a recording device to record your own voice saying "Game Over." Use Audacity to edit the sound and integrate the sound into the game using Unity.

9. Make the aliens move left and right, similar to the movement in *Space Invaders*.

10. Add barriers at the bottom of the screen and have them block shots both by you and by the aliens. Have the barriers show destruction every time they get hit by somebody. When they get destroyed, have them disappear from the screen entirely. Optional: Animate the barriers so that they move horizontally.

11. Make the scoring more fair by increasing the score value of the aliens depending on the level. Change the graphics of the aliens depending on the level.

12. Create two more alien types by drawing them in GIMP and putting them into the game. Arrange the different alien types row by row, so that the top two rows have different aliens than the next two rows, etc. Make the new aliens more valuable by increasing the score awarded for hitting them.

13. Create a flying saucer at the top of the screen, have it move left to right. Make it difficult to hit, and make it worth 1000 points when the player shoots it.

14. Show the high score on top of the screen at all times. Optional: Save the high score in a file every time it changes, and load it from that file when the game starts.

CHAPTER 9 — *Scramble*

IN THIS CHAPTER

Scramble is one of the first scrolling arcade shooters, developed by Konami and distributed by Stern in the United States in 1981. It introduced millions of players to forced scrolling backgrounds, checkpoints, and the concept of level design.

SCROLLING SHOOTER

Scramble was, in its day, one of the major arcade games. The game is still a lot of fun today, decades later, and well worth a closer look. In *Scramble*, the player moves a spaceship along in a forced scroll, shoots aliens while trying to stay alive, and explores new levels on the way to the goal of destroying a well-fortified base.

Figure 9.1 shows the basic screen layout of *Scramble*.

Movement is always to the right, and the screen scrolls at a constant speed. The player character can move anywhere within the confines of the camera view. Controlling the movement of the spaceship is critical. If the ship touches the ground or any other solid object, the player loses a life.

▼ **FIGURE 9.1** *Scramble* screen layout.

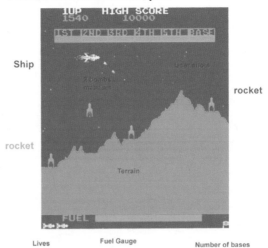

Ship — rocket — rocket — Terrain — Lives — Fuel Gauge — Number of bases

There are two weapons, a laser to the right and a bomb to the right and down. Each weapon is controlled by its own button. An eight-way arcade joystick controls movement.

EXPERTS RULE

Scramble uses the idea of a *checkpoint*. Checkpoints are invisible spots in the terrain. When a player dies, he continues the game from the closest checkpoint, provided the player has previously crossed that checkpoint. This feature can be generalized to the following rule:

Classic Game Design Rule 6: Experts Rule: Keep experts interested.

It's boring to repeat the same levels over and over, especially for experts. This realization has led to several advances in game design such as checkpoint systems, level-select, and secret warps. But it all boils down to keeping players interested in the game, regardless of their skill level or familiarity with the game. *Scramble* ramps difficulty in a subtle way for the benefit of experts. After the base is destroyed, the six levels repeat, but the rate of fuel consumption is increased. After the third base, the game stops ramping difficulty. The designers decided that the game was difficult enough at that point. They were correct, in a way, except that many top experts had no difficulty playing the game all day long.

In the early '80s, Atari coin-op used the phrase "lunatic fringe" for the players who could play arcade games for hours on a single quarter. The feeling was that there weren't very many players like that so they didn't really matter. Later on, arcade game designers realized that the top experts do matter because they would tie up machines for too long. This led to the invention of *level-select*, first used in *Tempest*. Level-select allows a player to select a starting level at the beginning of the game, and, at the end of a game the player could start another game at the beginning of the most recently completed level group. Level groups were designed to be long enough to stop beginners from getting through them, but short enough to allow experts to zip through.

Some years later, level-select was replaced with add-a-coin, a feature that contributed to the demise of the entire coin-op industry! The add-a-coin feature simply allowed people to add a coin at the end of an arcade game and keep playing at essentially the same point of the game. This encouraged players to put a lot of coins into a new game to see how far they could go. Eventually, they would run out of time and money and go home. The next time, in order to get to the same spot in the game, they would have to put in a lot of quarters again, so usually there wouldn't be a next time.

Level-select, also used in Atari's *Millipede*, led to a better experience for the players. They would put in a few quarters to reach a point where they were challenged but not frustrated. The starting level would stabilize and players would then play many games at that stabilized starting level.

Why did add-a-coin lead to the demise of coin-op? It's simple. Games that incorporated add-a-coin would make good money in the first week or two at a location, but then the earnings would drop dramatically. Needless to say, this was not good business. Of course, the rise of home consoles is generally seen as the real culprit, but add-a-coin didn't help.

SCRAMBLE SEQUELS

Konami's official sequel to *Scramble* is *Super Cobra* (1981), a very similar game when compared to *Scramble*. The player character in *Super Cobra* is a helicopter and there's more of the same design elements. There are eleven sections per level instead of six in *Scramble*, and there's a larger variety of enemies, including tanks that move. In general, the game is more difficult than *Scramble*, and there's more territory to explore, but the controls are the same, and the quest for fuel still dominates the gameplay.

Later on, *Gradius*, *Parodius*, and *Xevious*®, while not officially sequels of *Scramble*, share significant design elements with *Scramble*. The arcade shooter genre was eventually replaced by first-person shooters as the favorite for hard-core gamers, but there's a little bit of *Scramble* in every modern FPS.

The forced scrolling mechanic lives on as a popular control mechanism in plat-formers. While it's true that platformers mostly allow the player to control scrolling, it's a nice change of pace to include a few forced scrolling levels, for example, the underwater levels in the *Super Mario Bros.*® series.

Years later, the concept of a *rail shooter* emerged, which is basically any shoot-ing game or level in a shooting game where your main path is on a rail, though your specific movement might be controllable within the confines of the main path. There are too many games in this genre to mention here, but they all can trace their origins to the early forced scrollers.

In the next chapter, you'll be designing and developing a side scrolling game inspired by the scrollers of the '80s but implemented using Unity's 3D engine.

CHAPTER 10 Classic Scrolling Shooter

DESIGNING A SCROLLING SHOOTER

In the fourth classic project, you'll make a scrolling shooter in the spirit of *Scramble*. In the early '80s, scrolling shooters typically would scroll in a horizontal direction with the playfield scrolling to the left, which makes the player character appear to be moving to the right. Soon thereafter vertical scrolling shooters would become commonplace with the playfield scrolling down, making the player character appear to be moving up. Regardless of the scroll direction, this really opened up great possibilities and challenges. The big design issues with these types of games revolve around the backgrounds, the enemies, the weapons, and the player controls.

Once again, you'll start by making a simple sketch of the game screen. Take a look at Figure 10.1. It shows a spaceship flying along an alien planet getting attacked by rockets launched from the ground and flying enemies above ground. The spaceship has bombs and horizontal shots as weapons to fight back against its enemies.

Sometimes it's easier to just use GIMP instead of paper to make the sketch. To put all

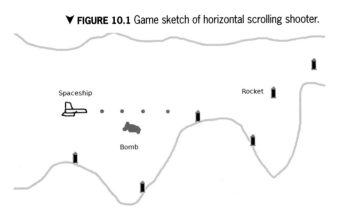

▼ **FIGURE 10.1** Game sketch of horizontal scrolling shooter.

Spaceship

Rocket

Bomb

those identical rockets into your sketch, you can make a separate image and save it as a custom brush. This is enough of a concept to get you started, even though the sketch doesn't show everything, such as scoring for instance.

You could choose to use the same 2D techniques as in Chapter 8 to make this game, but here is a great opportunity to move to 3D, especially because both Blender and Unity are designed to make 3D games. In the early '80s, real-time 3D was just getting invented and very costly, so for most arcade game developers that wouldn't have been a practical option.

It's important to distinguish between a 3D tool chain and 3D gameplay. Our tool chain fully embraces 3D technology including 3D models, a perspective view, and 3D lighting. Contrast that with the gameplay, which is firmly rooted in 2D. Over the years, this way of developing classic games and their sequels has become very popular with game developers.

The basic idea for using 3D technology on a 2D game is simple: Make a 3D game but give the player 2D controls. Usually this is done by limiting the location of the player character to a 2D plane and putting the camera at a fixed distance from that plane. The camera looks in a direction that's perpendicular to that plane. That's the setup you used in your Classic Paddle Game. This time around you're going to move the camera which will result in a scrolling effect.

The advantages of using 3D tech vs. 2D tech are numerous. First and foremost is that 3D technology is more easily ported among the various platforms. It is resolution independent, and can be adjusted to handle the graphics capabilities of high-end gaming PCs, low-end phones, and anything in between. Another huge advantage is this: most developers use 3D tech for their 3D games already, so for them it's less of a learning curve to adapt that technology for 2D gameplay.

There are, however, some real disadvantages to 3D tech as well. The graphic look may appear to be less clean, memory usage might be larger, and the graphics processing power needed to adequately display your scenes may not be available on some of the target game systems. Still, the advantages usually outweigh the disadvantages, especially when targeting consoles or PCs. The choice of 2D vs. 3D is ultimately up to the designer. It's time to get started. As always, you'll build the playfield first.

VERSION 0.01: THE PLAYFIELD

The plan for this section is to create the playfield in Blender, but first you'll create the Unity project and set up the folder structure.

Step 1: Start up Unity and create a project with the name **ClassicScrollingShooter**. There's no need to import any of the packages just yet.

Step 2: Create the following folders in the Assets panel: **Materials**, **Models**, **Scripts**, **Sounds**. One fast way to do this is to click on the Assets folder, right-click in the Assets panel, and select **Create – Folder** from the pop-up menu. Then you rename the New Folder and repeat. The Models folder will be used to store our various Blender files. The other folders contain the usual assets.

Step 3: Save the scene **mainscene**. **Save** the project as well. Exit Unity.

Next, you'll use Blender to make the terrain for your game. The terrain will consist of a 3D mesh, built using some very powerful features of Blender.

The following steps will be used to create a section of terrain in Blender. The plan is to create a 2D grid, shape it, and then extrude it into the third dimension.

Step 4: Start Blender.

Step 5: Delete the default cube.

Step 6: Add – Mesh – Grid.

Step 7: Press the **t** key **twice** to turn the Tools panel on and off. That shows you where the Tools panel is, on the left side. At the bottom of the Tools panel you'll see text entry boxes for X Subdivisions and Y Subdivisions for the Grid object.

Step 8: Enter **100** for **X Subdivisions**, 3 for **Y Subdivisions**.

Step 9: Right-click on the new grid, then type **5** and **7** into the numeric keypad. You should now see the Top Ortho view of the Grid object. The text "Top Ortho" is displayed in the top-left corner of the 3D View. On the numeric keypad, the "5" key switches between the *orthgraphic* and *perspective* views, the "7" key selects the *top view*, the "1" selects the *front view*, and the "3" key selects the *right view*. These are the bread and butter keys in Blender to get to a known view. You can also zoom in and out with the plus and minus keys.

Step 10: Use the **<Tab>** key to enter **Edit mode**. The <Tab> key toggles between the two major modes of Blender, Edit mode and Object mode. In Edit mode, you have the ability to edit the currently selected object at a low level. In Object mode, you work with multiple objects, create new objects, delete objects, etc.

Step 11: Use the Scroll Wheel on your mouse to **zoom in** on the grid. Your Blender Screen should look like Figure 10.2.

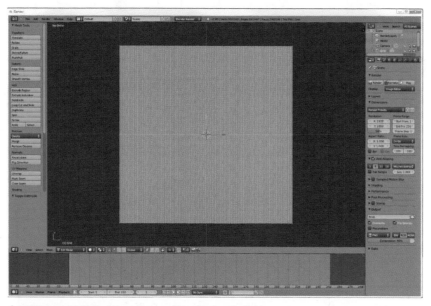

▲ **FIGURE 10.2** Initial grid used by scrolling shooter playfield.

Next, you'll delete the unnecessary lower half of the Grid object.

Step 12: Press **a** to deselect everything. The "a" key flips between selecting and deselecting every part of the Grid object. As you know by now, the orange color indicates items that are selected. The "a" key is very useful and worth remembering.

Step 13: Press **b** to enter Box mode. Draw a box around all of the vertices of the bottom edge of the square. Your screen should now look like Figure 10.3.

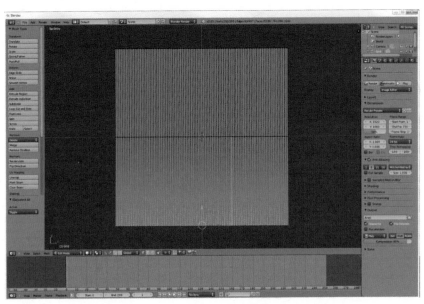

▲ **FIGURE 10.3** Using Box mode to select the bottom edge of the square.

Box mode lets you select everything inside a box. Your goal is to delete all those vertices, so do this:

Step 14: Press **x** and select **Vertices** to delete all the vertices of the bottom edge.

It's time to save your work. You're going to experiment with this piece of geometry and put the result into Unity to see what it looks like there. Then you'll get back to this point and start over.

Step 15: Save the file in **Assets/Models** using the name **BasicGrid.blend**.

Next, we'll enable Proportional Editing to make the top edge look like terrain. Look at Figure 10.4 to help find the icon and Figure 10.5 to see the goal, and then do this:

Step 16: Click on the **Proportional editing** icon below the 3D view and **select Enable**.

Proportional editing is a feature in Blender which, when enabled, causes nearby vertices, edges, and faces to be affected when you edit something. You'll see this effect in the next two steps.

▼ **FIGURE 10.4** Proportional editing icon, circular shape in the middle.

Step 17: Press **b** to enter Box mode. Using the mouse and the **left mouse button**, **select** a few vertices from the middle of the **top edge**.

Step 18: Press **g** to grab the vertices, press **y** to restrict the movement to the y axis.

Step 19: Scroll the mouse **wheel** to adjust the size of the circle. The circle indicates the area of influence for proportional editing and needs to be smaller.

Step 20: Move the **mouse down** a short distance, and then **left-click** to finalize the new vertex positions.

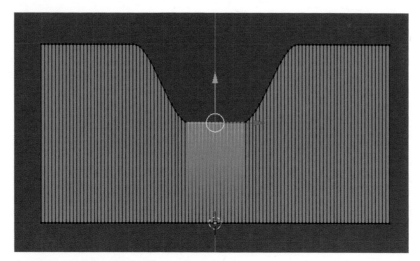

▲ **FIGURE 10.5** Proportional editing result.

That was a lot of steps for doing basically one thing. Your result may look different than the figure, but you're just testing so you don't need to match the figure exactly.

Step 21: Press **a** to deselect the vertices.

Step 22: Repeat Steps 17-21 a few times using different selections of vertices.

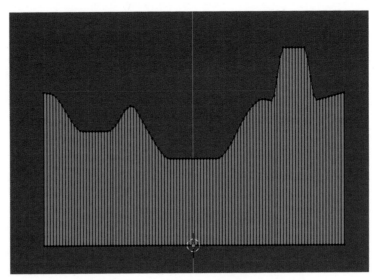

▲ **FIGURE 10.6** Distorted grid, the result of multiple proportional edits.

You'll end up with something like Figure 10.6. The next steps turn the distorted grid into a piece of terrain.

Step 23: Press **a** to select all vertices. If you forgot to do Step 21, you'll need to type "a" a second time.

Step 24: Press **1** on your numeric keypad to get a front view.

Step 25: Press **e** to start extruding.

Step 26: Type **0.2** and **<Enter>** to set the amount of extrusion. The user interface for this step is a little unusual for Blender neophytes, because you're typing in numbers and they magically show up below the 3D panel at the lower left. When you're extruding, or doing similar operations, you have a choice of setting the parameter of the operation with the mouse or by typing in numbers.

Step 27: Press **5** on the numeric keypad to get to Front Perspective view.

For this next step, you'll take a closer look at the effect of the extrusion.

Step 28: Press and hold the **middle mouse button**, and while holding that button **move the mouse** to rotate the view to match Figure 10.7. Alternatively, you can type the "6" and "8" keys on the numeric keypad to rotate the view in discrete steps. The "2" and "4" keys can be used to rotate the view back if you went too far.

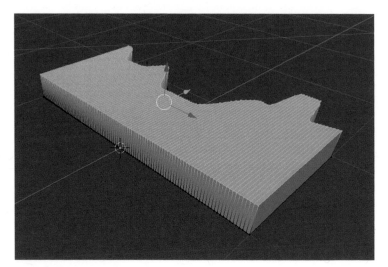

▲ **FIGURE 10.7** Extrusion.

Step 29: Press **5** and **7** on the numeric keypad to get back to the Top Ortho view.

Now, we'll set up a color for the terrain.

Step 30: Toggle into **Object mode** by hitting the **<Tab>** key.

Step 31: In the Properties panel, select the **Material** icon. Recall that the Material icon looks like an orange sphere, and it's the eighth icon in a horizontal layout of icons near the top right of the Blender window. If your Properties panel isn't wide enough to see the Material icon, make that panel wider by dragging the border between the Properties panel and the 3D View to the left.

Step 32: Create a new material by clicking on the **New** box with the **plus sign**.

Step 33: Set the **diffuse color** by left clicking on the box below **Diffuse**. Select a **purple** color on the pop-up color wheel. This will be the color of your terrain, as shown in Figure 10.8.

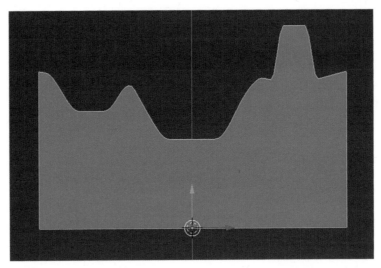

▲ **FIGURE 10.8** Purple terrain piece.

Step 34: File – Save As… in the **Assets/Models** folder using the name **GridTest**.

Next you're going to look at your piece of terrain in Unity. You can leave Blender open because we're going back to it in a few steps. Or, you can close it now and load the GridTest file at that time.

Step 35: In Unity, find **GridTest** in the Models folder and drag it into the **Hierarchy** (not the Scene panel) panel. This is a common situation. We want the object to be placed exactly at (0, 0, 0). This is easier to do by just dragging it into the Hierarchy panel, rather than the Scene panel. Notice that the Rotation of GridTest is –90, so make it 0 instead in the following step.

Step 36: Select GridTest and in the Inspector, enter **0** for **Rotation X**.

Step 37: Use a **Front Perspective** view by manipulating the Scene Gizmo in the Scene panel.

Remember that clicking on the Gizmo text toggles Perspective and Ortho view in the Scene panel in Unity. This is the equivalent of the "5" key in Blender.

Step 38: Press **f** to focus on **GridTest**. Your Scene and Game panels should now look like Figure 10.9.

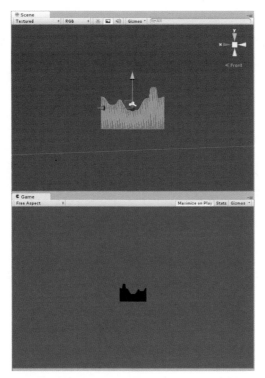

▲ **FIGURE 10.9** GridTest in Unity.

Next you'll make some adjustments to the imported object to make it look better.

Step 39: Select **GridTest** in the **Assets/Models** folder. If you have more than one GridTest, select the one with the cube icon.

Step 40: Click on Animations in the Inspector and **uncheck Import Animation**, then click on **Apply**.

Step 41: Click on **Model** and in the Normals & Tangents Section, set **Normals** to **Calculate** and the click on **Apply**. Our terrain looks crisper. Here you used a built-in feature of Unity which calculates the normals of your mesh rather than importing them from Blender. The normals affect the lighting of meshes and Unity lets you adjust them using the Smoothing Angle slider. For this mesh, it is not necessary to adjust the Smoothing Angle.

Step 42: Save the scene and project in Unity.

You're not done with the playfield yet, but this test is a start. You'll complete the construction of your playfield later by making several different terrain pieces and then stringing them along to form a much longer playfield. Rather than spending time creating the playfield in its entirety, you'd like to have some basic gameplay first. So you'll move on to the next gameplay element. In the next section, you'll be modeling the scrolling spaceship.

VERSION 0.02: SPACESHIP
PART 1: MODELING *

In this section, you'll be using Blender to make the mesh for the scrolling ship. In the next section, Version 0.03, you'll use Blender's texture painting mode to paint the ship, and after that you'll bring it into Unity. Feel free to skip this section and load the .blend file from the DVD instead.

The ship starts out as a cube and you'll do some 3D editing to turn it into a spaceship.

Step 1: In Blender, select **File – New**, accept the "Reload Start-Up File" prompt (if necessary), and immediately do **File – Save As...** with the name **ScrollingShip** in the Assets/Models folder. Your 3D View panel should show the default starting cube of Blender. If necessary, do **File – Load Factory Settings** and then redo Step 1 if you don't have a default cube.

Step 2: Right-click on the starting cube, toggle into Edit mode (with **<Tab>**), and click on **Subdivide** in the Tool panel (on the left). You should now see the cube cut into eight smaller cubes.

Step 3: Type **7** and **5** in the numeric keypad to get into the Top Ortho view.

Step 4: Type **a** to deselect everything.

Step 5: Type **z** to toggle into wireframe mode.

Step 6: Type **b** to box-select the bottom three vertices and delete them.

Step 7: Type **z** and **5** to get to solid perspective mode. Then **hold** the **middle mouse button** and **move** the **mouse**. Then **let go** of the **middle mouse button** when you get a good view of the mesh. If you don't have a middle mouse button, you can type 2 2 2 4 4 on the numeric keypad to rotate the view using your keyboard instead. Your screen should look similar to Figure 10.10.

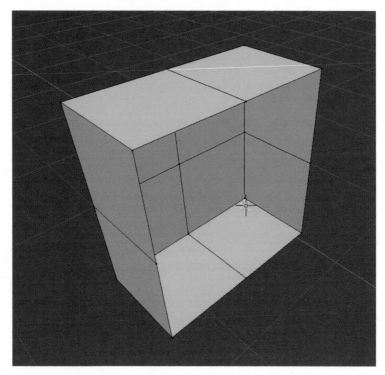

▲ **FIGURE 10.10** Half of a cube.

Step 8: Type **z** to toggle back into wireframe viewport shading.

Step 9: Type **a** to select everything, click on **Subdivide** again, and set the **Number of Cuts** to **2** in the Tool panel. You just created the basic framework for the spaceship, even though it doesn't look like it just yet.

Step 10: Click on the **Object Modifiers icon** (the sixth icon that looks like a wrench) in the Properties panel on the right and click on **Add Modifier – Mirror**. This didn't appear to do anything yet, but watch what happens next.

Step 11: In the **Axis** section in the Properties panel, **check Y** and **uncheck X**. You are now using the Mirror modifier along the Y axis. The half of the cube you deleted is now a mirror of the other half.

Step 12: Type **a** twice to make sure everything is selected.

Step 13: Type **s x 3.0 <Enter>** to scale the mesh by a factor of 3 along the x axis.

Step 14: Type **7** and **5** on the numeric keypad to get to Top Ortho view. Depending on your screen dimensions, you may need to zoom out a little using the mouse wheel, or the plus and minus keys on your numeric keypad, so you can see the entire mesh.

Step 15: Type **a** to deselect everything, and then type **b** and use box select to select the right three vertices. Your screen mesh should look like Figure 10.11.

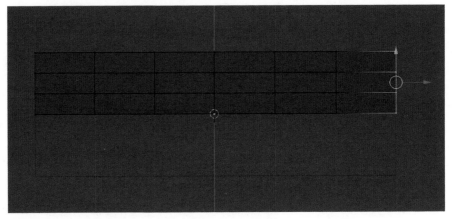

▲ **FIGURE 10.11** Stretched and mirrored cube, Top Ortho view.

Step 16: Type **1** on the numeric keypad to get to the Front Ortho view.

Step 17: Type **s z 0.3 <Enter>** to scale the front of our scrolling ship, restricted to the z axis.

Step 18: Type **z** to get Solid Viewport shading, **5** to use perspective view. **Spin and Zoom** the view of the scene until you have the front of the ship facing you, as shown in Figure 10.12.

To do the spin, type 8, and then 6 several times, or use the mouse with the middle mouse button as before. You may need to zoom out to see the entire mesh.

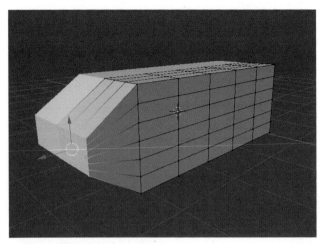

▲ **FIGURE 10.12** Front of the ship.

Step 19: Use **Face Select mode** by clicking on the Face Select icon.

The Face Select icon is indicated in Figure 10.13. Notice that the faces now have dots in the center of them. Those are just face indicators that only appear during Edit mode and don't get rendered in the game.

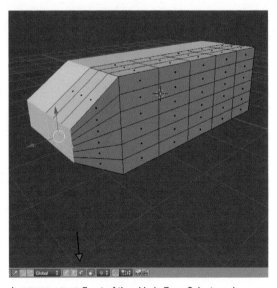

▲ **FIGURE 10.13** Front of the ship in Face Select mode.

You are now going to select two adjacent faces. After that you'll extrude them. Extruding is a common 3D modeling technique. It means you're going to pull on that face away from the rest of the mesh. Take a look at Figure 10.14 to see your goal. In the following steps, you'll select a few faces on the fuselage of your ship and extrude them to form wings.

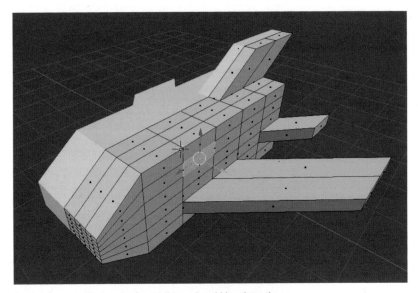

▲ **FIGURE 10.14** The result of extruding and grabbing three times.

Step 20: Type **a** to deselect the faces at the nose of the fuselage.

Step 21: Right-click on a side face, then **<Shift>-right-click** on an adjacent face farther away from the front. These are the faces where the main wing attaches to the fuselage.

Use Figure 10.14 to help locate these particular faces.

Step 22: Type **e** and move the mouse to pull the two faces away from the ship, creating a wing. **Left-click** to stop the extrusion.

Amazingly, the wing on the other side of the ship is also there because you still have the Mirror Modifier active. To get a better view, use the 8 and the 2 keys on your numeric keypad.

Step 23: Type **g x** and move the mouse to pull the wings away from the front somewhat. **Left-click** to stop the move. The letter g stands for "grabbing." This is also a very popular modeling command in Blender.

Step 24: Right-click on a single side face near the back of the fuselage, and make a wing out of it just like you did in the previous two steps.

Step 25: Right-click and Shift-right-click on two faces on the top of the fuselage, extrude, and slant back as in the previous steps. Your goal is to create something similar to Figure 10.14.

Step 26: Add Modifier – Subdivision Surface in the Object Modifiers panel. You now have two modifiers active, the Mirror and the Subsurf modifiers. The Object Modifiers panel shows all the currently active modifiers.

Step 27: Render – Render Image.

Your render should look like Figure 10.15. Those are professional looking wings, and it didn't take much effort at all. When you're done admiring the render, do **Render – Show/Hide Render View** to exit the render view.

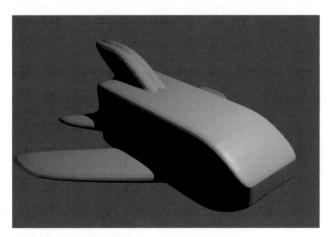

▲ **FIGURE 10.15** Blender render of spaceship mesh.

Step 28: File – Save. The name of your model should still be **ScrollingShip**.

The mesh for the spaceship is now complete, so it's time to give it a good texture. In the next section, we'll use Blender's texture paint mode to do that.

VERSION 0.03: SPACESHIP PART 2: TEXTURING

Most 3D creation tools such as Blender have a great feature that allows the user to paint directly onto the 3D model using the mouse. The beginning of this section is optional, so if you wish, you can skip to Step 24 and use the unpainted version of ScrollingShip instead. You can also copy the textured version of ScrollingShip from this book's DVD, but that would be cheating. Even if you're not an artist, it can be very educational for you to go through these steps and learn a little bit about the world of 3D modeling and texturing.

Step 1: Load the saved work from the previous section, if necessary.

Step 2: Do the **Split Area** command as described below. This is a simple step but it requires some explanation for the uninitiated. Carefully move the mouse to the top edge of the 3D view until the mouse icon turns into a vertical double arrow. Then, right-click to bring up the "Area Options" menu. Click on the "Split Area" menu item, move the mouse horizontally to select a balanced split, and left-click to complete the split. Your screen should now look similar to Figure 10.16.

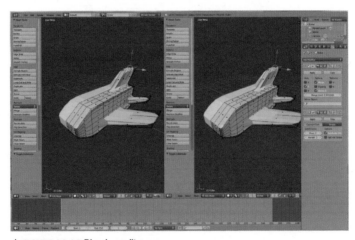

▲ **FIGURE 10.16** Blender split area.

Alternatively, you could have split the area by dragging the lower-left corner of the area like you did previously.

Step 3: In the right panel, select the **UV/Image Editor** type. You select the Editor type by clicking on the shaded cube icon. There are two of these cube icons on your screen, one for each of the split areas. They are located in the bottom-left corner of each area.

You should now see one scrollingship on the left and a grid in the UV/Image Editor. In case you're curious, the UV has nothing to do with ultraviolet rays. It's a naming convention for texture coordinates.

Step 4: Hover the mouse over the spaceship, and type **a** to deselect the currently selected faces, if necessary. Then type **a** again to select all faces. Your goal is to have all the faces appear orange. Some of the faces are partially obscured because of the subdivision modifier. You should verify that you are still in Edit mode and Face Select mode. If you're new to Blender, take the mouse and hover over the icons at the bottom of the 3D view to see the names. You'll eventually find the "Mode" box and the Vertex Select, Edge Select, and Face Select icons. You can also tell that you're in Face Select mode because the faces have dots in the center.

Step 5: In the Properties panel on the right, select the **Textures icon** (the ninth icon). In the Mapping Section for the Coordinates property, **change Generated to UV**.

Step 6: Again in the Texture panel, just above the Mapping section, change the Type from **None** to **Image or Movie**. You are telling Blender to use an image for texturing rather than a default solid texture.

Step 7: In the UV/Image Editor window, do **Image – New Image**.

Step 8: Give it the name **shiptexture** and **click** on **OK**.

Step 9: View – View All. Your screen should now look like Figure 10.17.

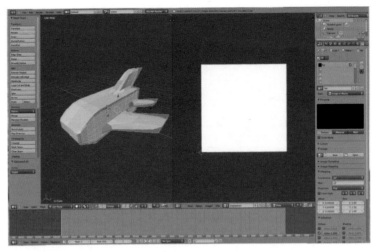

▲ **FIGURE 10.17** Image editor setup in Blender.

Step 10: Click on **Image** again, and select **Save as Image**. Save the image using the name shiptexture.png in the **Assets/Models** folder.

Step 11: In the 3D view (on the left), do **Mesh - Uv Unwrap... - Smart UV Project** followed by **OK**. *This is the crucial step that allows texture painting to work.* The spaceship mesh has been cut into pieces and projected onto our texture. It should look like Figure 10.18.

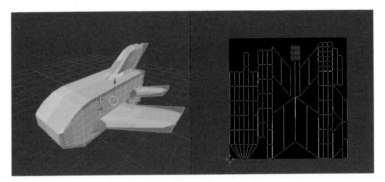

▲ **FIGURE 10.18** Smart UV project in Blender.

Next, you need to enable texture painting, but first change the color of your texture to white as described in the next steps. You won't see the white color until after Step 13.

Step 12: In the Image panel on the right, do **Image – Invert – Invert Image Colors**.

Step 13: Image – Save Image. Image – Reload Image. The shiptexture file is now entirely white. The mesh display is just an overlay and not part of the texture itself.

Step 14: Change **Edit** mode to **Texture Paint** in the 3D View.

Step 15: Change **View** to **Paint** in the UV/Image editor, using the Editing context selector at the right.

Step 16: Select a **red color** in the **color dialog** at the top left.

Step 17: Draw a red stripe across the main wing.

Step 18: Continue to select some different colors, change the Radius and Strength, if you wish, and decorate the scrollingship. You can rotate the ship while you're doing this using the middle mouse button or the numpad keys.

Notice that the Mirror Modifier is still in effect even for texture painting. You can paint in the image editor as well as directly on the 3D model.

Step 19: Select the **Object Modifiers** icon (the wrench), and look for the Subsurf Subdivisions section. **Change** the **View** property from **1** to **2**. You can compare your creation with Figure 10.19.

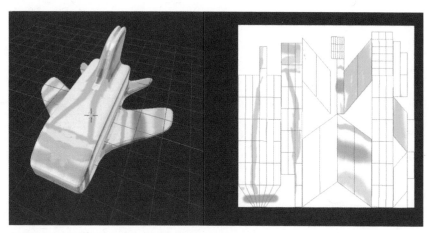

▲ **FIGURE 10.19** Texture painting in Blender.

There are just a few more steps to finalize your vehicle. If you do a Blender render right now the texture won't show up. That's because the texture file from texture painting hasn't yet been associated with the texture used by the 3D object. The next two steps fix this issue.

Step 20: In the UV/Image Editor, click on **Image – Save Image**.

Step 21: Select the **Textures** icon. In the Textures panel below, find the Image section, and click on the **Open** box. Use the **shiptexture.png** file that you just saved in the Assets/Models folder.

Step 22: Do a Blender **render** and verify that your texture is displayed just like inside the 3D view in Blender itself.

Step 23: File – Save.

You just finished making a textured spaceship. Next, you'll look at it in Unity. Fortunately, this part is going to be very easy.

Step 24: Go to Unity.

Step 25: Select the **ScrollingShip** asset in the Models folder (the one with the cube icon).

There might be one or more ScrollingShip assets with white icons there as well. You can ignore them, as they are just the backup files used by Blender.

Step 26: Change the **Normals** from Import to **Calculate** and then click on **Apply**. This step has only a minimal effect because of the smooth nature of this model.

Step 27: Drag the **ScrollingShip** into the **Hierarchy** panel.

The ship is much too large in relation to the playfield. There's a simple remedy:

Step 28: Change the **Scale** from 1 to **0.02** for X, Y, and Z.

Step 29: Change the **Position** to **(0, 1, 0)**.

Step 30: Save the scene and Project.

You just learned a useful technique for texturing 3D models. The scrolling spaceship looks much more interesting as a result. Next, you'll make the spaceship fly.

VERSION 0.04: SPACESHIP CONTROL

Controlling the ship can be implemented in a number of ways. You're going to opt for a very simple solution, constant speed in the left-right direction and user control in the up-down direction. First, though, you need to set up the camera and lighting so you can see what you're doing.

Step 1: Select **Main Camera**, and set **Position** to **(0, 1, 1.3)**, **Rotation** to **(0, -180, 0)**.

Step 2: In the Scene panel, use **Front Perspective View**.

Step 3: Select GridTest, focus using the **f** key, and use the mouse scroll wheel or the up and down arrow keys on your keyboard to **zoom** in on GridTest.

The Scene and Game panels should look like Figure 10.20.

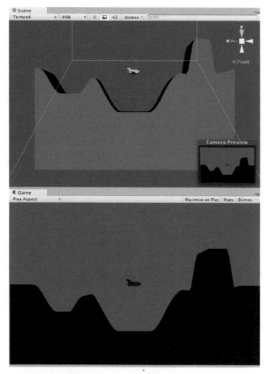

▲ **FIGURE 10.20** Initial camera setup.

Next, you're going to put in better lighting.

Step 4: GameObject – Create Other – Directional Light.

Step 5: Rotation (30, 0, 45) and **Position (0, 0, 0)**. The position has no effect on the game itself with a directional light, but it does determine the location of the associated gizmo. The next step will allow you to control the size of the gizmo.

Step 6: Click on **Gizmos** in the **Scene** panel and adjust the size by sliding the **size slider**.

This step is cosmetic, but it allows you to control the appearance of gizmos in the Scene panel. It's useful to know about this to avoid clutter and giant gizmos.

Speaking of cosmetic changes, this next one is truly remarkable and really improves the appearance of your game. You're going to add a *skybox*. Skyboxes are a common and easy technique for making 3D games look realistic. Rather than creating and rendering individual objects that are far away, such as clouds, mountains, or thousands of trees, a few large textures are displayed in the background. It's called a box because the texture is pasted on the inside of a very large box so that no matter where the camera is pointing, there's always a visible background texture.

Step 7: Assets – Import Package – Skyboxes and import all the skyboxes. You didn't really need to import all of them, but because you're just learning about them, it's a good idea to take a look at all of them.

Step 8: Edit – Render Settings.

Step 9: Click on the **bullseye icon** on the right of **Skybox Material**, and select the **DawnDusk Skybox**. The icons in the skybox selector can also be scaled using a slider at the top, just like the gizmos. Feel free to choose one of the other skyboxes instead. It's fun to try them all. With the DawnDusk skybox, the Game panel should now look like Figure 10.21.

▼ **FIGURE 10.21** The DawnDusk skybox.

As an optional experiment, it's instructive to see how the skybox works by spinning the camera around. Just select the Main Camera and use the Rotation Gizmo, the third icon at the top left of the Unity window. You may wish to save your scene before doing this so you easily get back to where you started.

Now that your scene is looking presentable, it's time to make the scrolling ship move.

Step 10: Assign the following code to **ScrollingShip**, with the name **scrollingship**, and put the **scrollingship** script into the **Scripts** folder.

```
#pragma strict

function Update ()
{
    transform.Translate(-0.3 * Time.deltaTime, 0, 0);
}
```

If you run the game now, the ship scrolls off the screen, never to be seen again. It's time to have the camera follow the moving ship.

Step 11: Create the script **camera** in the Scripts folder and assign it to **Main Camera**. Use the following code:

```
#pragma strict

function Update () {

    var player : GameObject = GameObject.Find("ScrollingShip");
    var xpos : float = player.transform.position.x;

    transform.position =
        new Vector3(
        xpos,
        transform.position.y,
        transform.position.z
        );
}
```

When you run the game now, the camera follows the moving ship. The code takes the current x-coordinate from the ship and uses that as the x-coordinate of the camera.

Next, you'll add some simple up and down controls to the ship.

Step 12: Insert the following code into the Update function of scrollingship.js:

```
if (Input.GetKey ("w"))
{
   transform.Translate (0,0, 0.8 * Time.deltaTime);
}
if (Input.GetKey ("s"))
{
   transform.Translate (0,0,-0.8 * Time.deltaTime);
}
```

This code moves the ship up or down depending on key presses by the player.

In the following section, you'll replace GridTest with a much larger playfield.

VERSION 0.05: LEVEL 1

The playfield is due for an expansion. You're going to go back to Blender and make several grid pieces similar to GridTest. Then, you'll assemble copies of them into a long strip, and join them all together into a single mesh consisting of several thousand faces.

As a historical note, this method of making a playfield would have been very foreign to game developers in the eighties. Instead, playfields were created using stamps. Each stamp was an 8 x 8 or 16 x 16 square. The stamps were laboriously drawn pixel by pixel, often with a limited color palette. The stamps would then be assembled using a stamp map. In a way, we're doing a similar thing here, just using 3D faces instead of pixels.

Step 1: In Blender, do **File – Open Recent – BasicGrid.blend**.

Step 2: Zoom out using the **Mouse scroll wheel** or the **numpad minus** key.

Step 3: Type the **<Tab>** key to enter Object mode.

Step 4: Type **a** to deselect everything.

Step 5: Right-click on the Grid object to select it.

Step 6: Type **<Shift> d** and then **y**, move the mouse up, and left-click to place the new copy of the Grid object.

Step 7: Repeat Step 6 six more times until you have a total of eight Grid objects, stacked vertically, as shown in Figure 10.22.

In the next step, you'll be using proportional editing as described in the very beginning of this chapter. Don't do the extrusion step yet because we'll be doing that later. Try the different falloff types, such as Smooth, Random, and Root. The falloff types are set in a menu immediately to the right of the proportional editing mode icon.

▼ **FIGURE 10.22** Setting up Grid pieces.

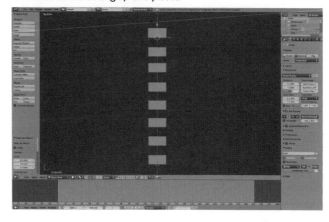

Step 8: Use Proportional Editing to create a collection of Grid pieces similar to Figure 10.23.

You'll need to go into Object mode, select the piece that you're editing with a right-click, and then go back to Edit mode for each of the pieces.

Step 9: Save the file with the name **GridPieces.blend**. Now that you have a collection of playfield pieces, you'll assemble them.

▶ **FIGURE 10.23** Completed Grid pieces.

Step 10: Use **<Shift>-D** to make copies of the pieces and assemble them like in Figure 10.24.

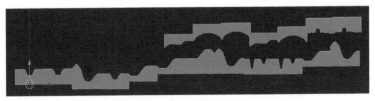

▲ **FIGURE 10.24** Playfield layout.

Step 11: Delete the original pieces in the vertical stack.

Step 12: In Object mode, **select** all pieces of the playfield, and do **Object - Join**.

Step 13: Select the playfield, go into **Edit** mode, and **select** all vertices using **a**.

Step 14: Type **1** to go into Front Ortho view.

Step 15: Type **e 0.3 <Enter>** to extrude by 0.3 units.

Step 16: Type **7** to go into Top Ortho view.

Step 17: File – Save As… using the name level_1.blend.

You just completed making the mesh for the Level 1 playfield.

Step 18: In Unity, select **Level_1**.

Step 19: In the Inspector, set **Normals** to **Calculate**.

Step 20: In Animations, **disable Import Animation**.

Step 21: Drag **Level_1** into the **Hierarchy panel**.

Step 22: Set **Position** to **(0, 0, 0)** and **Rotation** to **(0, 0, 0)**.

Step 23: Set **Main Color** to a **purple** shade.

Step 24: In the Hierarchy, **delete GridTest**.

As always, you'll do some testing of the new playfield.

Step 25: Select Level_1 in the Hierarchy panel, and focus on it in the Scene panel using the **f** key. Use the mouse scroll wheel to zoom in on the playfield.

Step 26: Select ScrollingShip in the Hierarchy panel.

Step 27: Save. Your screen should now look like Figure 10.25.

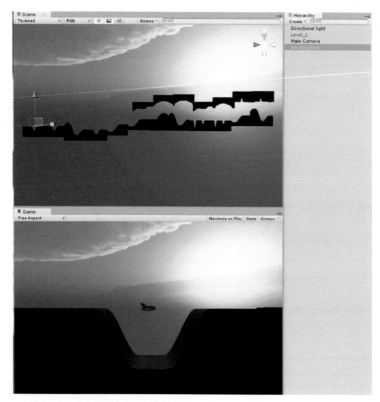

▲ **FIGURE 10.25** Scrolling playfield in Unity.

This playfield is relatively small, but it's large enough for development purposes. If you play the game now, you'll see that you have a problem with the camera not moving up and down with the ship. This will be fixed in the next section.

VERSION 0.06: ROCKETS

You need something for our scrolling ship to shoot at, and later on, you'll be making shots to be launched by the ship. In this section, you'll create the rockets that rise up as defensive weapons for the playfield. First though, you'll improve the camera so you can have a better view of what's happening.

Step 1: In camera.js, replace the Update function with the following code:

```
function Update () {
    var player : GameObject = GameObject.Find("ScrollingShip");

    var xpos : float = player.transform.position.x;
    var ypos : float = player.transform.position.y;

    var new_ypos = transform.position.y;
    if (new_ypos < ypos - 0.5) new_ypos = ypos - 0.5;
    if (new_ypos > ypos + 0.5) new_ypos = ypos + 0.5;


    transform.position =
        new Vector3(
        xpos - 0.7,
        new_ypos,
        transform.position.z
        );
}
```

This code puts the camera to the left of center, and follows the ship up and down if the ship y position is more than 0.5 units away from the camera y position. Give it a try and move the ship up and down using the w and s keys.

Next you'll build a rocket mesh in Blender.

Step 2: In Blender, **File – New**, delete the default cube, and save the file with the name as **rocket.blend**.

Step 3: Add – Mesh – Cylinder with **24** Vertices and Depth of **8**. The settings for the cylinder are in the Tool panel on the bottom left.

Step 4: Type g z 4 <Enter>. This moves the cylinder up so that the base is at an elevation of 0. The 4 is half the height of the cylinder.

Step 5: Press **<Tab>** to enter Edit mode and zoom out so you can see the entire cylinder.

Step 6: Click on **Loop Cut and Slide** in the Mesh Tools panel, move the mouse over the cylinder, **scroll** the mouse wheel until you see **four rings**, then left-click, **slide** the rings down a little, then **right-click**. The cylinder should now look like Figure 10.26.

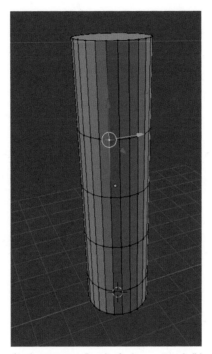

▲ **FIGURE 10.26** Result of a loop cut and slide.

This was a relatively quick way to chop up the cylinder into a mesh that you can now turn into a rocket.

Step 7: Type **7** and **5** on the numeric keyboard to get to Front Ortho view.

Step 8: Use **Wireframe** Viewport Shading.

Step 9: Deselect everything using the **a** key.

Step 10: Use **b** to select the top vertices of the cylinder, then type **s 0.3 <Enter>**.

Step 11: Repeat Steps 9 and 10 for the next two rings with a scale factor of 0.5.

You just created the basic shape for the rocket. Next, you'll add the fins.

Step 12: Use **Solid Viewport shading**.

Step 13: Use **Face Select** mode.

Step 14: Right-click on the face immediately to the left of center at the bottom.

Step 15: Type e 1.0 <Enter>.

Step 16: Type **numpad 6** six times.

Step 17: Repeat Steps 14-16 three times.

Step 18: Type **numpad 7**. You're now looking at the rocket from the top with the four fins clearly visible as shown in Figure 10.27.

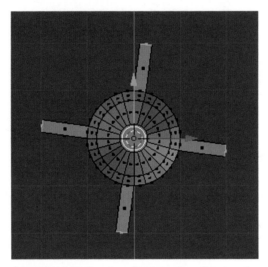

▲ **FIGURE 10.27** Top view of rocket in Face Select mode.

You'll do just one last tweak to the model in the following steps.

Step 19: Type **numpad 1**.

Step 20: Type **numpad 6** repeatedly to spin the rocket. While doing so, select all four outer faces of the fins using **right-click** for the first one and **<Shift>-right-click** for the other three.

Step 21: Hold the **middle mouse button** and **move** the **mouse** to look at the rocket as shown in Figure 10.28. Alternately, use the numpad 2-4-6-8 buttons to adjust your view.

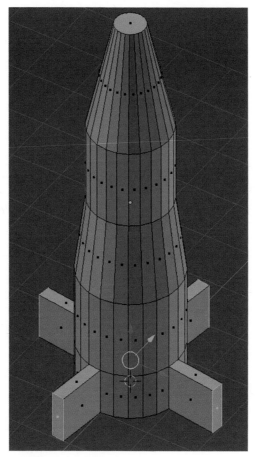

▲ **FIGURE 10.28** Orange highlights on four outer faces of rocket fins.

Step 22: Type **g z -1 <Enter>**.

Step 23: Type **g z 1 <Enter>**.

Step 24: Type **numpad 1**.

Step 25: File-Save. The rocket mesh is now complete. This is what's called a low-poly model. Modern games use thousands of polygons to make very detailed meshes for game objects. In these classic game projects, you're going to be content with relatively simple meshes.

Step 26: In Unity, select the rocket model in the Models folder.

Step 27: Turn off Animations, set Normals to Calculate.

Step 28: Drag the rocket model into the Hierarchy panel and select the rocket.

Step 29: Set **Position** to **(0, 1, 0)**, **Scale (0.02, 0.02, 0.02)**.

Step 30: In the Scene panel, select the Front Ortho view using the View Gizmo.

Step 31: Focus on the rocket using the **f** key.

Step 32: Zoom out using the mouse wheel, select the four arrow Move icon at the top left next to the hand icon, and drag the rocket up and down with the yellow arrow to line it up with the playfield. The Scene panel should now look similar to Figure 10.29.

▼ **FIGURE 10.29** Rocket on the playfield.

The Game panel doesn't look quite right because the playfield isn't centered correctly. You'll fix that in the next step.

Step 33: Select Level_1 and set the **Z Position** to **-0.15**.

The rocket needs its own material, so you'll use the usual method to create one.

Step 34: In the **Materials folder**, create a new Material with name **RocketMat**, set the Main Color to a **bright red**, select the **Specular Shader**, and **drag** the material onto the **rocket** object in the Hierarchy.

The playfield needs a material, too.

Step 35: Do the previous step with Material name **LevelMat**, a **purple** color, and **Level_1**.

When you play the game with the new material for Level_1, you'll see a nice improvement in the graphic look because of the specular shader.

The rocket is just sitting there, and there's only one rocket. In the next section, you'll create many duplicates of the rocket and make them fly.

VERSION 0.07: FLYING ROCKETS

The plan for this section is to make a prefab out of the rocket, place many rockets on the playfield, and add code that makes them fly. After all of that, you'll start with collision detection between rockets and the scrolling spaceship.

There's no Prefabs folder yet, so it's time to make one.

Step 1: Create a folder in the Project panel and rename it to **Prefabs**.

Step 2: Drag the rocket object from the Hierarchy to the Prefabs folder. This is the quick and easy way of creating a prefab. You can now remove the original rocket.

Step 3: Delete the rocket object in the Hierarchy panel. Then drag the rocket from the Prefabs folder back into the Hierarchy panel. This step doesn't appear to change anything, but it does have an important side effect. The rocket in the Hierarchy is now an instance of the rocket prefab in the Prefabs folder. This allows you to make wholesale changes to all rockets by just changing the prefab.

In the next few steps, you'll make copies of the rocket and put them on the playfield.

Step 4: Select the **rocket** in the Hierarchy panel.

Step 5: Edit – Duplicate.

Step 6: Select the Move icon (the one next to the hand icon) and grab the red arrow handle on the rocket to move it to the right a little.

Step 7: Zoom out, using the mouse scroll wheel, if necessary, and move the duplicate rocket to the next valley.

Step 8: Continue to duplicate and place rockets until you have five rockets set up similar to Figure 10.30.

▼ **FIGURE 10.30** The first five rockets.

Step 9: Play the game and make sure you can see all five rockets along the way.

Step 10: Stop playing the game.

Those rockets need to start flying, so you'll write a short script to make that happen. As an optional exercise, try to write a script that makes all the rockets fly straight up. Then compare it to the published version in the next step.

Step 11: Create the script **rocket.js** with the following code:

```
#pragma strict

public var rocketspeed : float;

function Update () {
    transform.Translate (0, 0, rocketspeed * Time.deltaTime);
}
```

Step 12: Select the rocket prefab and use the Add Component box to add the rocket.js component to it.

Step 13: Set rocketspeed in the rocket prefab to 0.5. If you play the game right now, you'll see the rockets taking off. You have the basic motion working, but it would be wrong to have the rockets launch all at once at the beginning of the game. The following new code for rocket.js fixes that.

Step 14: Replace the contents of rocket.js with the following code:

```
#pragma strict

public var rocketspeed : float;

function Update () {
    var player : GameObject = GameObject.Find("ScrollingShip");
    if (player.transform.position.x - transform.position.x < 0.5)
        transform.Translate (0,0,rocketspeed * Time.deltaTime);
}
```

The if-statement checks that the ScrollingShip object is within 0.5 units to the left of the rocket before the rocket starts to move.

Step 15: Pick the second rocket from the left and change its rocketspeed to 1.0. Test this.

This shows the power of prefabs. You can override the rocketspeed property of an individual rocket, which is still inheriting the other properties of the prefab rocket.

Next, you'll add a particle system to simulate the exhaust of the rocket. Unity makes this easy.

Step 16: Click on GameObject – Create Other – Particle System.

Step 17: Change the **Position** to **(0, 1, 0)**. You now have a particle system with the default settings located at (0, 1, 0). You now need to change the settings to simulate a rocket exhaust pointing down.

Step 18: Set **Duration 1.0**, **Start Lifetime 0.7**, **Start Speed -0.1**, **Start Size 0.05**, **uncheck Shape**, set the **Start Color** to a **bright orange**. Your new particle system settings are shown in Figure 10.31.

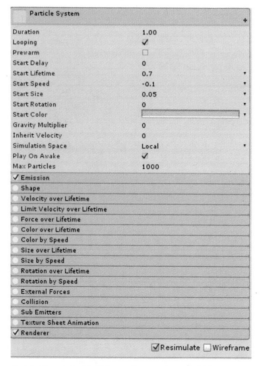

▲ **FIGURE 10.31** Particle system settings in Unity.

Feel free to experiment with the Particle settings. Particle systems are cosmetic special effects and usually don't affect gameplay directly.

The next steps line up our particle system with the left-most rocket.

Step 19: Select the left-most rocket, and Control-select the Particle System so that both the rocket and the Particle System are selected. Focus on both using the **f** key in the Scene panel.

Step 20: Select the Particle System and move it to the bottom of the rocket in the Scene panel.

Step 21: In the Hierarchy panel, drag the Particle System on top of the rocket.

Test the game to see that the first rocket now flies with an orange exhaust trailing after it. Unfortunately, the Prefab for the rocket doesn't have the Particle System, so you need to rebuild it. There might be a simpler way to do this, but sometimes it's more practical to just do something that you know is going to work, rather than to worry about the best possible way of doing something.

Step 22: Delete the **other four rockets**.

Step 23: Delete the **rocket prefab**.

Step 24: Select the one remaining **rocket** (the one with the Particle System) and **drag** it to the **Prefabs** folder.

Step 25: Delete the last remaining **rocket** in the Hierarchy.

Step 26: Drag the Prefab **rocket** from the Prefabs folder to the Hierarchy.

Step 27: Repeat Steps 4 through 10 to place four new rockets onto the Playfield.

NOTE

Later on, we'll place many more rockets in our playfield, but as you just saw, it pays to keep things small and simple at first, just in case you need to make drastic changes.

Next, you'll add collision detection between the ship and the rockets. What should happen when a rocket collides with the ship? For now, you'll simply destroy the ship and the rocket. As in previous projects, you'll be using tags.

Step 28: Insert the following code into rocket.js:

```
function OnTriggerEnter (other: Collider) {
    if (other.tag == "scrollingship")
    {
        Destroy(gameObject);
        Destroy(other.gameObject);
    }
}
```

To enable this code to work you need to put in colliders and tags.

Step 29: Tag the ScrollingShip with scrollingship.

Step 30: Add a box collider component to scrollingship, and check Is Trigger.

Step 31: Add a rigidbody component to the rocket prefab, and uncheck Use Gravity.

Step 32: Add a box collider component to the rocket prefab, and check Is Trigger.

Step 33: If necessary, move the ship away from the first rocket so they don't collide right away.

Step 34: Test the game.

Step 35: Save.

You now have something resembling gameplay. The player needs to avoid the rockets or else it's game over. The rockets are flying and have a particle system that displays their exhaust.

In the next section you'll make the game more interesting by adding shots.

VERSION 0.08: SHOTS

In this section, you're going to add horizontal shots that have the ability to destroy rockets and flying saucers. The scrolling ship shoots under player control. When the player hits the space bar a single shot is released. You could use Blender to make the shot models, but it's not really necessary. You use Unity to create shots as long and skinny boxes. Before you go ahead with the shots, you'll do a couple of cosmetic changes. In game development it's very common to be working on one thing only to discover that there's a simple change on something entirely different that will yield an improvement.

Step 1: Select the ScrollingShip and in the Inspector panel, change the Shader for shiptexture to Specular. This small change makes the scrolling ship look more realistic.

Step 2: Change the X Position of the Main Camera to –0.2 and the X Position of ScrollingShip to 0.5. This change initializes the Main Camera to the correct position so that there's no jarring motion at the beginning of the game. The difference between the ScrollingShip and the Main Camera should be 0.7 right at the beginning of the game since the Main Camera X position is computed to be at an offset of 0.7 during gameplay.

Step 3: Change the Directional light Y Rotation to 100. This has a dramatic effect on the lighting. Try it out and compare your screen with Figure 10.32.

▲ **FIGURE 10.32** Improved lighting and shading for scrolling ship.

It's time to get started with actually making the shots.

Step 4: GameObject – Create Other – Capsule.

Step 5: Rename to shipshot.

Step 6: Position (0, 1, 0), Rotation (0,0, 90), Scale (0.01, 0.05, 0.05).

Step 7: In the **Materials Folder**, create a **red, specular** Material, name **ShotMat**.

Step 8: Assign **ShotMat** to **shipshot**. So far all you have is a shot floating in space, not doing anything.

Step 9: Create a JavaScript with name shipshot.js, and enter the following code for it:

```
#pragma strict

public var shotspeed : float = 1.0;

function Update () {
    transform.Translate (0, shotspeed * Time.deltaTime,0);
}
```

Step 10: Assign shipshot.js to shipshot. The shot is moving, but not colliding with anything, so add collision with the terrain.

Step 11: Create the **terrain** tag and tag **Level_1** with it.

Step 12: Add a **Mesh Collider** to **Level_1**.

Step 13: Add a **RigidBody** component to **shipshot**, and **uncheck Use Gravity** for it.

Step 14: Check Is Trigger for the **Capsule Collider** of **shipshot**.

Step 15: Add the following code to **shipshot.js**:

```
function OnTriggerEnter (other: Collider) {
    if (other.tag == "terrain")
    {
        Destroy(gameObject);
    }
}
```

You did this so that when a shot hits terrain it gets destroyed, just as you would expect.

Step 16: Test this as follows: turn off Maximize on Play, select shipshot in the Hierarchy, and watch when the shot gets destroyed.

You're ready to launch shots from the ship.

One way to help with testing this is to use the step button. Here's how that works. Press play and quickly press pause after that. With the game paused, click on the step icon. You can also use the keyboard shortcut for it. The shortcuts for Play, Pause, and Step can be found in the Edit drop-down menu.

Step 17: Make **shipshot** into a Prefab by dragging it into the **Prefabs** folder. Then **delete shipshot** in the **Hierarchy** panel.

Step 18: Replace the contents of scrollingship.js with the following code:

```
#pragma strict

public var shotprefab: GameObject;

function Update ()
{
    if (Input.GetKey ("w"))
    {
        transform.Translate (0,0, 0.8 * Time.deltaTime);
    }
    if (Input.GetKey ("s"))
    {
        transform.Translate (0,0,-0.8 * Time.deltaTime);
    }
    transform.Translate(-0.3 * Time.deltaTime, 0, 0);


    if (Input.GetKeyDown ("space"))
    {
        Instantiate(shotprefab,
                    Vector3(transform.position.x,
                    transform.position.y,
                    0.0),
        Quaternion.AngleAxis(90,Vector3.forward));
    }
```

The contents of this code are discussed below, but first, go ahead and test it.

Step 19: Select **ScrollingShip,** and assign the **shipshot** Prefab to **Shotprefab** in the ScrollingShip section of the Inspector by dragging or by using the bullseye icon.

Step 20: Play the game and press the space bar repeatedly to launch the shots.

The shots don't do any damage yet. That will happen soon enough. Meanwhile, take a look at the code in scrollingship.js. The Instantiate statement creates a shot every time the player presses the space bar. The initial location of the shot is the same as that of the ship, except that you're hardwiring the z coordinate to zero. The initial launch angle is set in the Quaternion statement. You can change the angle by adjusting the first parameter, currently set to 90. Experiment with different values for the angle to get a sense of how that works.

You're finally ready to shoot at the rockets. All you're missing is the following step.

Step 21: Create a shipshot tag and assign it to the shipshot prefab.

Step 22: Add the following code to the end of the `OnTriggerEnter` function in rocket.js:

```
if (other.tag == "shipshot")
{
    Destroy(gameObject);
    Destroy(other.gameObject);
}
```

This is basically the same code as for colliding rockets with the scrolling ship. You can now test this and try shoot down the rockets.

Testing reveals a common problem in scrolling shooters: the shots keep going forever and may destroy rockets at an unrealistic distance away from the ship. The next step addresses this.

Step 23: In shipshot.js, replace the Update function with the following:

```
function Update () {
    transform.Translate (0, shotspeed * Time.deltaTime,0);

    var player : GameObject = GameObject.Find("ScrollingShip");
    if (player.transform.position.x - transform.position.x > 3.0)
        Destroy(gameObject);


}
```

This is fairly straightforward. The code checks to see if the shipshot is over 3 units away from the ship, and destroys the shot if it is.

Step 24: Test and **save**.

This game is still too easy. In the next section, you'll add some true enemies, flying saucers.

VERSION 0.09: FLYING SAUCERS

In Blender, it's incredibly easy to make flying saucers. After making the 3D model for flying saucers, we'll animate the motion in Unity, have them shoot at the scrolling ship, and do the usual collision detection setup and scripting.

Step 1: In Blender, **select File – New** and **OK**.

Step 2: Delete the **startup cube**.

Step 3: Add – Mesh – UV Sphere.

Step 4: Type **Numpad 1**, **Numpad 5**, **<Tab>**, and **View – View Selected**.

Step 5: Use Wireframe Viewport Shading.

Step 6: Type **a** to deselect all, then **b** and select the bottom half of the sphere.

Step 7: Type **s <Shift> z 2 <Enter>**.

Step 8: Type **s z 0.3 <Enter>**.

Step 9: Type **g z 0.4 <Enter>**.

Step 10: Use **Solid Viewport Shading**.

You should now be looking at a flying saucer mesh as shown in Figure 10.33.

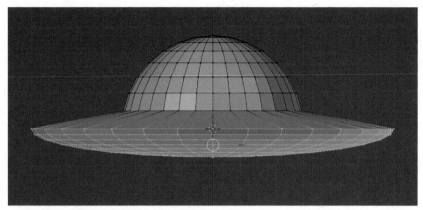

▲ **FIGURE 10.33** Simple flying saucer model in Blender.

Step 11: Save the blend file in Assets/Models as saucer.blend.

An advancing Blender user such as yourself could do these last 10 steps in about a minute or two. The keyboard shortcuts in Blender are a great way to become extremely fast at creating 3D models.

Step 12: In Unity, create a new Material in the Materials folder, call it SaucerMat.

Step 13: For SaucerMat, select a Specular shader, and a light grey Main Color.

Step 14: Select the saucer model in the Models directory, disable Import Animation, set Normals to Calculate, and Apply.

Step 15: Drag the saucer model into the Hierarchy.

Step 16: Select **Position (0, 1, 0)**, **Scale (0.04, 0.04, 0.04)**.

Step 17: Assign **SaucerMat** to the **saucer** object.

Step 18: Drag saucer into the Prefabs folder.

Step 19: Delete the original saucer object in the Hierarchy panel.

You now have a flying saucer prefab, though it still needs some work. The following steps implement collisions of saucers vs. ship shots and saucers vs. ship.

Step 20: Add a **Rigidbody** component to the **saucer prefab**. **Uncheck Use Gravity**.

Step 21: Add a **Box Collider** component to the **saucer prefab**. **Check Is Trigger**.

Step 22: Change the **Size** of the box collider to **(2, 2, 1.2)**. You reduced the size of the box collider to surround just the main hemisphere of the saucer. When in doubt, it's good to have colliders be smaller than the actual meshes, though the collider setting usually gets finalized during extensive testing.

It would be tempting to just use a mesh collider for the saucer, but that would be less efficient and it doesn't take into account that you might want the saucer to survive a glancing hit.

Step 23: Create **saucer.js** and assign it to the **saucer prefab**. Use the following code:

```
#pragma strict

public var radius: float = 0.2;
private var centerx: float;
private var centery: float;
private var saucertime: float;


function Start () {
    saucertime = 0;
    centerx = transform.position.x;
    centery = transform.position.y;
}

function Update () {
  saucertime += Time.deltaTime;
  transform.position.x =
      centerx + radius * Mathf.Sin(saucertime * 4.0);
  transform.position.y =
      centery + radius * Mathf.Cos(saucertime * 4.0);
}
```

```
function OnTriggerEnter (other: Collider) {
    if (other.tag == "scrollingship")
    {
        Destroy(gameObject);
        Destroy(other.gameObject);
    }


    if (other.tag == "shipshot")
    {
        Destroy(gameObject);
        Destroy(other.gameObject);
    }
}
```

This code makes the saucers move in a circular path using built-in trig functions. You're also doing collisions with shipshots and the scrollingship in the usual manner.

Step 24: Test this by shooting saucers and crashing the ship into a saucer. You're continuing to follow the philosophy of testing your changes right away.

Next you'll create shots for the flying saucers, and then you'll have the saucers shoot them. The saucer shots will be the same as the ship shots, only they'll fly to the left and they'll have slightly different collision detect code.

Step 25: Drag a shipshot from the Prefabs into the Hierarchy panel.

Step 26: Rename the shipshot object in the Hierarchy panel to saucershot.

Step 27: Remove the Shipshot (Script) component from saucershot.

Step 28: Open shipshot.js by double-clicking on it in the Scripts folder.

Step 29: In Monodevelop, do a Save As with the name saucershot.js.

Step 30: In saucershot.js, change the initial value of shotspeed from 1.0 to –1.0.

The Update needs to be changed as well, because the code that destroys the shot if it's too far away from ScrollingShip no longer makes sense for alien shots.

Step 31: Assign saucershot.js to the saucershot object in the Hierarchy.

Step 32: Test this by watching the saucershot fly to the left when you play the game.

Step 33: Drag saucershot into the **Prefabs** folder. **Delete** the saucershot object in the Hierarchy panel.

Step 34: In saucer.js, add the following code section at the end of the Update function:

```
var player : GameObject = GameObject.Find("ScrollingShip");
   if (player.transform.position.x - transform.position.x < 3.0)
   {

   if (saucertime > 3.14159 / 2)
   {
      Instantiate(saucershot,
            Vector3(transform.position.x,
                    transform.position.y,
                    0.0),
         Quaternion.AngleAxis(90,Vector3.forward));
      saucertime = 0.0;
   }
   }
```

Step 35: In saucer.js, add the following line of code near the beginning of the file:

```
public var saucershot: GameObject;
```

Step 36: In the **saucer prefab,** click on the bullseye icon for Saucershot and assign the saucershot prefab. You need to give the saucershot its own tag.

Step 37: Select the saucershot prefab, create a saucershot tag, and use it to tag the saucershot prefab. In theory, those saucers should now be shooting at you.

Step 38: Test by observing that the saucers are periodically shooting to the left.

The saucershots don't harm the ScrollingShip at all. Both the saucershot prefab and the scrollingship are set up for collision detection, so all that's missing is a bit of code.

Step 39: In saucershot.js, add the following code to the `OnTriggerEnter` function:

```
if (other.tag == "scrollingship")
{
    Destroy(gameObject);
    Destroy(other.gameObject);
}
```

Step 40: Test this by seeing if the saucershots destroy the scrollingship.

Step 41: Save. It's time to take inventory of where you are. You have all the graphical elements, except for the bombs. There's some basic gameplay and control. The main things that are missing are scoring, audio, and populating the level with rockets and saucers. There are also bound to be additional changes to the code as you get more experience with playing the game. In the next section, you'll do some level design.

VERSION 0.10: LEVEL DESIGN

For a change of pace, you'll do something that's technically easy, but artistically it isn't easy at all. Where are you going to put the rockets and saucers? It's really up to you, the designer.

Unity does double duty as both a development environment and a level editor. For large, complex games developers often build stand-alone level editor applications, but this won't be necessary for you in this game. You simply use your rocket and saucer prefabs and place instances into the scene wherever you want. It's up to you where to locate the saucers and rockets. However, as you do this, you're going to discover some things that will motivate you to make some changes to the code.

Step 1: Duplicate and drag five more rockets into the scene and test.

This is just a warm-up exercise to get you started.

Step 2: Select one of the rockets, and rotate it using the rotate icon. Test it to see if it works.

You may wish to compare your Unity screen with Figure 10.34.

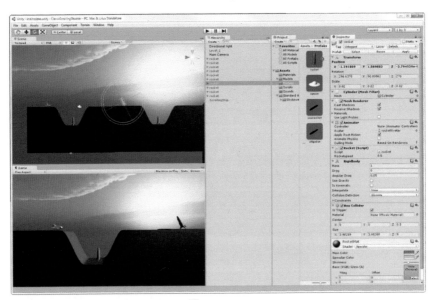

▲ **FIGURE 10.34** Rotated rockets.

Step 3: Test to see if the rocket collides with the terrain. Apparently you didn't put in collisions between rockets and terrain.

Step 4: In rocket.js, add the following code to the `OnTriggerEnter` function:

```
if (other.tag == "terrain")
{
    Destroy(gameObject);
}
```

Step 5: Test. Well, probably you're going to see a very serious problem now. Any rocket that gets initialized too close to the terrain gets immediately destroyed. How are you going to fix this? There's an old joke. A man goes into the doctor's office and says that it hurts when he raises his arm. The doctor's advice: don't raise your arm. So, you could just avoid the problem by never placing the rockets too close to the terrain. There's a better way to fix this, though. Let's put in a timer and only do the rocket vs. terrain collision detect after about a second after launch.

Step 6: Update rocket.js to match the following code:

```
public var rocketspeed : float;
private var flighttimer: float = 0.0;


function Update () {
   var player : GameObject = GameObject.Find("ScrollingShip");
   if (player.transform.position.x - transform.position.x < 0.5)
   {
      transform.Translate (0,0,rocketspeed * Time.deltaTime);
      flighttimer += Time.deltaTime;
   }
}


function OnTriggerEnter (other: Collider) {
   if (other.tag == "scrollingship")
   {
      Destroy(gameObject);
      Destroy(other.gameObject);
   }

   if (other.tag == "shipshot")
   {
      Destroy(gameObject);
      Destroy(other.gameObject);
   }

   if (flighttimer > 1.0)
   if (other.tag == "terrain")
   {
      Destroy(gameObject);
   }
}
```

You've added a private timer variable, initialized it to zero, and you only update it when the rocket is moving. In the `OnTriggerEnter` function, you check to see if the rocket has been flying for a while, and only then do you do the terrain collision.

You might have noticed that the rockets fly forever if there's nothing in the way. This can't be good, so let's add some code to limit the life of rockets.

Step 7: Add the following code to the `Update` function in rocket.js:

```
if (flighttimer > 5.0) Destroy(gameObject);
```

Step 8: Test this by watching what happens to a rocket after five seconds of flight. There's another rather obvious problem. You don't have collision detect between ScrollingShip and the terrain. This is a case where it's not obvious what to do. Should the ship crash and burn when it hits the playfield? Maybe it should just bounce, or take some minor damage.

You're going to follow the traditional route and destroy the ship whenever it touches terrain. While you're at it, we shouldn't let the ship fly over the tunnel that you created, so you also should limit the flight of the ship in the vertical direction.

Step 9: Add the following code to scrollingship.js:

```
function OnTriggerEnter (other: Collider) {
    if (other.tag == "terrain")
    {
        Destroy(gameObject);
    }
}
```

Step 10: Test crashing the ship into terrain. Nothing happens. The first thing to check is to see if ScrollingShip has a trigger. It looks like you didn't check the Is Trigger checkbox, not to mention that ScrollingShip doesn't have a Rigidbody component. The next step fixes that.

Step 11: Check the **Is Trigger checkbox** for the Box Collider for ScrollingShip. Then add a Rigidbody component to ScrollingShip and as usual, uncheck the Use Gravity checkbox.

Step 12: Test crashing the ship into terrain again. It should work this time, sort of. There's a scary error message at the bottom of the screen as shown in Figure 10.35.

To get more information about this error message, open the Console Window.

Step 13: Window – Console. This shows you have a problem in the camera script at line 29 (your line number may be slightly different). When you look at camera. js you'll see the problem. The code is trying to find the ScrollingShip object, but you just destroyed it! This is an old bug, and it's been in this game for a while. The fix is simple. You need to stop updating the camera position when the ScrollingShip cannot be found.

▼ **FIGURE 10.35** Exception error message.

Step 14: Change the **Update** function in camera.js to the following code:

```
function Update () {

    var player : GameObject = GameObject.Find("ScrollingShip");

    if (player)
    {
        var xpos : float = player.transform.position.x;
        var ypos : float = player.transform.position.y;

        var new_ypos = transform.position.y;
        if (new_ypos < ypos - 0.5) new_ypos = ypos - 0.5;
        if (new_ypos > ypos + 0.5) new_ypos = ypos + 0.5;

        transform.position =
            new Vector3(
            xpos - 0.7,
```

```
        new_ypos,
        transform.position.z
        );
    }
}
```

This takes very little editing, just three lines of code are new. The Find function returns "null" when it can't find the object. The new if-statement checks to see if the player variable is null.

Step 15: Test it again. This is one of the most important lessons in this book. If you think you fixed something, test it again to make sure you really fixed it! It's still not fixed. You now look at the Console window again, and see that you have the same bug in rocket.js.

Step 16: In rocket.js, replace the Update function with this code:

```
function Update () {
    var player : GameObject = GameObject.Find("ScrollingShip");

    if (player)
    if (player.transform.position.x - transform.position.x < 0.5)
    {
        transform.Translate (0,0,rocketspeed * Time.deltaTime);
        flighttimer += Time.deltaTime;
    }

    if (flighttimer > 5.0) Destroy(gameObject);
}
```

The fix is the same as before, this time requiring just one new line of code.

Step 17: Test it again. You should no longer have any error messages. You may need to first clear the console window of error messages, or to use the "Clear on Play" button in the Console window to verify this. Just to be sure, though, review the rest of the code.

Step 18: Review the rest of the code for similar bugs. Amazingly, shipshot.js, saucer.js, and saucershot.js have the same bug.

Step 19: Fix the bugs in shipshot.js, saucer.js, and saucershot.js. They are all one line fixes just as you did in Step 16. Was it worth it to fix it? Yes! If you want your code to be of a high quality and free of bugs, there's no substitute for squashing all error messages.

Step 20: Continue to duplicate rockets into the playfield until you have at least twenty rockets, and then test the game.

It's starting to be fun to play this game. You do have another gameplay problem. The player has the ability to just fly up and avoid all the obstacles. The following step keeps the player from doing that.

Step 21: Add the following line of code to scrollingship.js at the beginning of the Update function:

```
if (transform.position.y < 3.5)
```

The official technical term for code such as this is a "horrible hack." The word goes back to the early days of coding when hacking was considered a good thing, and being called a hacker was the ultimate compliment. A horrible hack is bad code that works, typed in at the last possible moment when you're working on a deadline. Why is this code bad? Well, it's that 3.5 in there. The 3.5 is a "magic number." This code will always keep the ScrollingShip below an elevation of 3.5, regardless of the level design. Sometimes, at the end of a project, you do what you have to do to get the thing done quickly.

Step 22: Put at least ten saucers toward the end of the level.

Step 23: Test the game. Is it fun? In a word, yes! Compare your layout with the one in Figure 10.36.

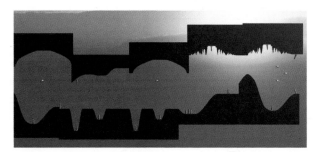

▲ **FIGURE 10.36** Level layout.

Step 24: Save. You're done with basic gameplay. Let's add audio.

VERSION 0.11: AUDIO

Most of today's games have background music, or at least some kind of a background soundtrack. The very early classic games relied entirely on game-triggered sound effects to provide audio. In this section, you'll take it one step further and create a simple background soundtrack using Audacity and the looping feature in Unity.

Step 1: Open Audacity.

Step 2: Generate – Risset Drum....

Use the default settings, which are 100.0, 2.0, 500.0, 400.0, 25, and 0.8.

Step 3: Effect – PaulStretch.

Again, use the default settings of 10 and 0.25.

Step 4: View – Zoom Out.

Step 5: Drag the mouse in the track to make a selection from time 0 to about 2.5 seconds.

Step 6: View – Zoom to Selection.

Step 7: Effect – Fade In, Effect – Fade Out, Effect – Normalize.

Step 8: Transport – Loop Play.

This is the effect you want, a rumbling, pulsating sound effect.

Step 9: Press the **Stop** icon.

Step 10: File – Save Project with the name rumble.aup in the Sounds folder of our game.

Step 11: File – Export Selection … and use the name rumble.wav.

Step 12: Back in Unity, **uncheck 3D Sound** for the rumble asset.

Step 13: Drag the **rumble** sound to the **Main Camera**, and **check** the **Loop** box in the Inspector.

Step 14: Test it by playing the game. If you play the game now, you should hear the rumble effect looping in the background.

Step 15: Select the Sounds folder in the Assets panel.

Step 16: Assets – Import New Asset..., and then navigate to cexplo.wav from the previous project. Repeat for cshot.wav. These two sound effects may not be perfect but they'll be good placeholders for now. You'll start with the obvious first sound, the shot sound.

Step 17: Select **ScrollingShip**, and add an **Audio Source** component. **Uncheck Play on Awake**.

Step 18: In **scrollingship.js**, make the following changes. In the variables section at the top, insert the line:

```
public var ShotSound: AudioClip;
```

In the GetKeyDown("space") section of the Update function, insert the line

```
audio.PlayOneShot(ShotSound);
```

Step 19: In the Inspector for **ScrollingShip**, assign **cshot** to **Shot Sound**.

Step 20: Test.

Step 21: In **shipshot.js**, make the following changes.

In the variables section at the top, insert the line

```
public var shotexplo: AudioClip;
```

In the OnTriggerEnter function, insert the line

```
audio.PlayClipAtPoint(shotexplo,transform.position);
```

immediately before the Destroy statement.

This is similar to the technique you used in the last project. It's necessary to use the PlayClipAtPoint function because the PlayOneShot function needs the object to be alive while playing the sound, and as you can see, the shot is about to be destroyed.

Step 22: Repeat Step 21 to add the **cexplo** sound effect for **all the collision events in rocket.js and saucer.js**.

Step 23: Save. In the next section, you'll wrap things up by adding scoring.

VERSION 0.12: SCORING

You're going to keep the scoring as simple as possible. The player gets one life, there's just one level, ending and game over messages, and scores added when the shots hit rockets and saucers.

Step 1: Select GameObject – Create Empty and rename it to **scoring**.

Step 2: Create a script with name **scoring**, assign it to the **scoring** object, and use the following code:

```
#pragma strict

static var score: int;

function Start () {
   score = 0;
}

function OnGUI () {
   GUI.Box (Rect (10,10,120,30), "Score:    "+score);

   var player : GameObject = GameObject.Find("ScrollingShip");
   if (!player)
   {
   GUI.Button (Rect (Screen.width/2 - 200,
                     Screen.height/2 - 50,
                     400, 50),"Game Over");
   }

   if (player)
   if (player.transform.position.x < -25.0)
   {
   GUI.Button (Rect (Screen.width/2 - 200,
                     Screen.height/2 - 50,
                     400, 50),"The End");
   }
}
```

We put in two buttons to make a minimal attempt at game structure. The "Game Over" message tells the player to stop playing. The only way to play another game is to exit the program and try again. The "The End" button is the reward for surviving the entire level.

Step 3: Add the following line to saucer.js in the `OnTriggerEnter` function in the shipshot section:

```
scoring.score += 900;
```

Step 4: Repeat Step 3 for rocket.js and a score of 400.

Step 5: Test and **save**. More interesting scoring and game structures are possible. The exercises explore them.

VERSION 1.00: RELEASE AND POSTMORTEM

Our fourth classic project turned into quite a game. It's not ready for a commercial release, but it's a great start. There's a lot of fun to be had playing the game the way it is, but of course the best part is this: because you built it from scratch, you can now make changes and improve it (or make it worse) with just a few clicks of the mouse and a few lines of code.

This project shows how to make a 2D game using 3D tools. The development of the game went very smoothly. There were a few bugs along the way, but that's always going to happen in game development. The worst problem is obvious: the game isn't finished yet. It would really help to build several levels with graphic and gameplay variety. To only give the player one life also seems very harsh. The bomb weapon from the original design was dropped from production, no pun intended. There was also an issue with the rocket prefab where you had to toss the prefab and all the instances and start over in order to put in the rocket exhaust particle system. It can happen in game development that you have to throw out your precious creations and rebuild them. There's no sense in getting upset over something like that. It's part of the process. In short, the game is looking great and you learned a great deal. In the exercises, you are going to explore some new directions for the game.

EXERCISES

1. Use Blender to build a new scrolling ship with the wings near the top of the fuselage. Use texture painting to give it a polkadot texture. Put the new ship into the game.

2. Take the ship from Exercise 1, or the original from the game, load it into Blender, and modify the mesh by extruding a few faces on the back of the ship to create an exhaust. Scale the exhaust faces to make them slightly larger.

3. Build a new and different level using the techniques of Section 0.06. Save it as Level_2.blend. Create a new Scene in Unity and use Level_2 as your playfield in that scene.

4. Create a bomb in Blender using the same techniques that were used to make the rocket. Integrate the bomb into the game and launch the bomb from the scrolling ship using the "b" key. Use Gravity to have the bomb fall to the ground, and have the bomb collide with terrain and with rockets.

5. Create two new sound effects by experimenting in Audacity. Export the sound effects into the Sounds folder and use them in the game.

6. Create level and lives displays in scoring.js. Initialize the level to 1 and lives to 3.

7. Use a state machine similar to the one in the Classic Vertical Shooter to implement Game Over and Press Start. When the scrolling ship collides with something, instead of going to Game Over, decrease the lives counter and restart the current level.

8. At the end of level 1, go on to level 2 from Exercise 3 and have the ending of the game at the end of level 2 instead.

9. Instead of having an ending, go back to level 1 after level 2. Increase the difficulty of the game by making the rockets tougher to avoid and by having the saucers shoot more frequently.

10. Make the saucer shots home in on the scrolling ship on higher levels.

11. Create a Particle System for an exhaust of the Scrolling Ship.

11 *Pac-Man*

Pac-Man (Namco, 1980) changed everything. It introduced a completely new game mechanic, was almost entirely nonviolent, and really brought video games to a worldwide mass audience, including women, adults, seniors, and children. *Pac-Man* was created by Namco in Japan and first released in 1980. Official credits weren't given in those early days of game development, but Toru Iwatami is now recognized as the person most responsible for creating this iconic and hugely influential game. Figure 11.1 shows a level diagram of the first maze.

▼ **FIGURE 11.1** *Pac-Man* maze.

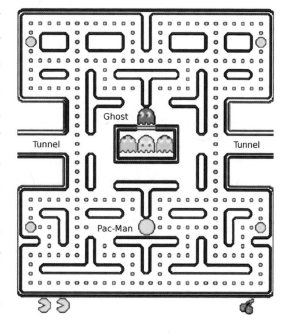

Ghost

Tunnel   Tunnel

Pac-Man

THE FIRST MAZE GAME

Was *Pac-Man* really the first maze game? The answer depends on how you define maze game. Sega's *Head On* from 1979 has some similarities to *Pac-Man* but it's a bit of a stretch to put the two games into the same category. *Pac-Man* is definitely the first well-known arcade maze game. The gameplay is deceptively simple, requiring no buttons and just a single joystick to control the main character. It's instructive to look at gameplay footage of the original arcade *Pac-Man*. Countless videos of this can be found on the web and it's worth looking at one or two before reading the rest of this chapter.

In *Pac-Man*, the player moves the character around the maze to avoid the four enemies. Three brilliant and novel design elements in the game are the tunnels, the power pellets, and the bonus fruits. The tunnels make it easier for the player to escape when he's cornered. The power pellets let the player fight back instead of getting chased all the time. The bonus items, mostly fruits such as cherries and apples, are optional rewards that appear at a fixed spot for a limited time, tempting the players to risk their lives to get a few extra points. The bonus fruits aren't really essential to the game, but they add color, and having an extra reward out there to lure greedy players is a fun way to add depth to most any arcade game.

CUTSCENES

Pac-Man isn't just a maze game. It also introduced cutscenes as a way to advance the story in video games. They are noninteractive and, in arcade games, they are necessarily brief. Today's much longer cutscenes need to be skippable, but in these early arcade cutscenes the players had no choice but to watch them in their entirety. The real hidden purpose of cutscenes to an arcade gamer is to provide a short period of rest between intense periods of gameplay action. You might get bored when watching the same cutscene too many times, but getting a few seconds of respite is always appreciated. It only took a few years for the game industry to respond by going hog-wild with cutscenes, eventually culminating in million dollar budgets that sometimes eclipsed the budgets for the rest of the game, or so it seemed.

Cutscenes have even been used as an anti-piracy measure. The short but plentiful cutscenes in 1996's *Gubble*™ were used as uncompressed filler on the CD-ROM to make the game artificially large, thus harder to pirate and download using a slow Internet connection.

PAC-MAN FEVER

Pac-Man had a huge cultural impact, especially in the United States. Soon after the release of the game itself, there appeared an animated television series, t-shirts, and the hit pop-song "Pac-Man Fever." Amazingly Ken Uston's strategy guide, *Mastering Pac-Man*, sold over a million copies in the '80s. Video games had reached mainstream popular culture, virtually overnight.

ENDING RULE

Our next classic game design rule is somewhat of an oddity, because most classic games, and all games featured in this book, including *Pac-Man*, break it!

Classic Game Design Rule 7: Ending Rule: Make an ending.

Just about all classic coin-op games in the classic era don't have a designed ending. The strange thing is that due to programming limitations, a few of the games had what's now called a "kill screen," including *Pac-Man*. Kill screens kill the player off due to a programming or design bug, effectively ending the game. If you haven't seen the *Pac-Man* kill screen, go and search for it online to take a look.

The main point is that the designers of that era simply didn't bother to design an ending for their games, which was a mistake. This was a great example of industry-wide group-think, where everybody thought it was OK to have the games go on "forever." Even stranger was the general feeling that games without an ending were the "standard" way of designing arcade games. It was something that arcade players had come to expect, mainly due to the publicity surrounding marathon gaming sessions on *Asteroids* and *Missile Command*. There was a certain mystique surrounding people who had "mastered" a particular game, and thus could play it as long as they wanted, effectively "owning" the machine. The downside of not having an ending is clear. The top scores become more a measure of endurance than skill, violating the Score Rule. Experts lose interest when the game just goes on and on the same way, breaking the Experts Rule and the Difficulty Ramping Rule as well.

PAC-MAN AI

Here is where it gets really interesting for game designers. Just how do those ghosts decide where to go? In the context of game design, the logic behind character behavior is called artificial intelligence, or AI. First, consider the basics of *Pac-Man* AI. The ghosts go at constant speed and usually don't turn around. They switch between two modes, chase and scatter. When they chase, they use their own individual rules to decide which way to turn at an intersection. When they scatter, they simply aim to go to their individual target location. Each ghost has a target in its own corner.

There remains the question of which way the ghosts should turn when they get to an intersection. If they all turn towards the player, they would all behave the same way and as a result, they could be bunched together like a flock of sheep. If the ghost behavior were truly intelligent, the player would have no chance because the ghosts could simply coordinate their efforts to trap the player. The approach taken by Toru Iwatani is to make all four ghosts aim at different yet sensible target locations.

The exact details of chase mode for the four ghosts can be found online. To summarize, the red ghost always aims at the player, the blue and pink ghosts aim at spots near the player, and the orange ghost only aims for the player when he's far away from the player, otherwise he goes into scatter mode where he aims at his starting position. Of course, when the player has the power pellet the ghosts immediately switch to "run away" mode.

AI programming in *Pac-Man* was done in assembly language, the preferred programming technology of arcade games at the time. Because of this, the artificial intelligence of the ghosts is nothing more than a few carefully crafted assembly language instructions. Modern path finding algorithms have largely supplanted these early AI efforts. The days of writing AI code in assembly are history, but it's still interesting to study the old techniques. They continue to be useful and should be in every game designer's AI arsenal.

PAC-MAN SEQUELS AND MAZE GAMES

In contrast to the earlier arcade mega-hits, for *Pac-Man* the sequels were plentiful and hugely successful, especially in the '80s. Namco's official sequels included *Ms. Pac-Man*, *Super Pac-Man*, *Jr. Pac-Man*, and *Pac-Mania*. The arcade game industry adopted the new maze game category with gusto and released games such as *Mr. Do* (Universal, 1982), *Dig Dug* (Namco, 1982), *Lady Bug*, and *Pepper II*, just to mention a few. The move to 3D maze games started in 1983 with Atari's *Crystal Castles*. A screenshot from *Crystal Castles* is shown in Figure 11.2.

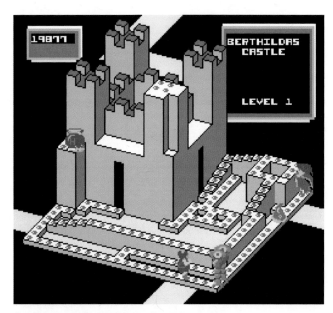

▲ **FIGURE 11.2** *Crystal Castles:* Berthilda's Castle.

Crystal Castles was designed and programmed in 1982 and 1983 by the author of this book, Franz Lanzinger. In this game, the player controls Bentley Bear with a trackball to collect gems from isometric castles. The game achieved some notoriety for being the first coin-op nonracing game with a designed ending.

The ending in *Crystal Castles* illustrates many of the eight rules of classic game design, especially rules five through eight. The unique and strange end maze is shown in Figure 11.3.

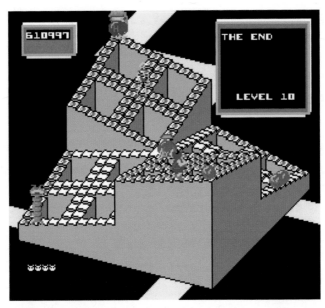

▲ **FIGURE 11.3** *Crystal Castles:* end maze.

After the player completes the end maze, which is easier said than done, there's some surprise bonus scores as shown in Figure 11.4.

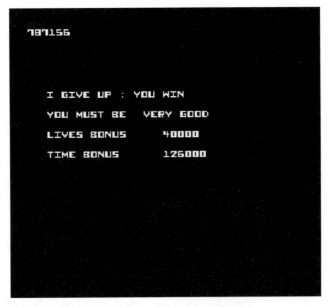

▲ **FIGURE 11.4** *Crystal Castles:* scoring at the end.

A hidden timer is used to calculate the time that it took to get to the end. Then a bonus score is awarded. The faster the player finished the game, the higher the bonus score using a simple linear equation. There's also a bonus for any unused lives at the end. The game selects one of several built-in congratulatory messages based on the lives bonus.

Multiple endings are always problematic, especially in large console games because they imply that players should replay the game over and over if they wish to see all the endings. This can be boring to the players unless the game has good replayability.

Following the score display, there's a short final animation that simply draws random boxes on the screen, as shown in Figure 11.5. This ending had to fit into just a few lines of code, so it reused the existing functions for drawing the mazes.

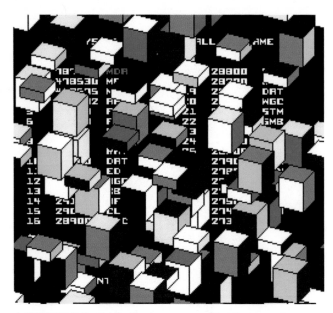

▲ **FIGURE 11.5** *Crystal Castles:* boxes gone wild at the very end.

It is very difficult to get to the ending in Crystal Castles. Only a few of the top players were good enough to get to the end maze, much less finish it. It's even more difficult if not impossible to get to the end when the trackball control is replaced with a joystick.

In 1996, a new independent game development company, Actual Entertainment, was formed by Franz Lanzinger, Mark Robichek, and Eric Ginner to make an unofficial sequel to *Crystal Castles*. The resulting game series, *Gubble*, continues to explore and expand the maze game category. The last maze of the original *Gubble*, right before the ending, is shown in Figure 11.6.

▲ **FIGURE 11.6** *Gubble.*

If you look closely, you'll find the letters "JoeC" as part of the playfield. Many maze games, starting with *Mr. Do*, used this technique to display text, anything from the name of the game itself to initials or even subliminal messages. JoeC stands for Joe Cain, one of the developers of *Gubble*. *Crystal Castles* used this technique in several places, and it even displayed the initials of the current high score holder in this way on the first maze.

Pac-Man is the quintessential classic game. It's simple yet deep. It and its official and unofficial sequels live on decades later. It's fun. Next time you see an original Pac-Man arcade machine, insert a coin, and be amazed at how great it feels to grab a real arcade joystick and be Pac-Man.

CHAPTER

12 Classic Maze Game

It took quite a bit of effort to make the first four classic game projects, so now we're going to make something a little different and smaller, a maze game. Don't forget Rule 1: Keep it simple. It's surprising how much fun the deceptively simple games can be.

DESIGNING A MAZE GAME

You'll start, as always, with the playfield, in this case a maze. You'll be using Blender to make the maze, so there's no need to sketch the maze right now. The main character is going to be a sphere. In order to keep things simple, you don't want to spend a lot of time creating animated characters, but rather just use some built-in shapes and get on with making the game fun. There's a long history of successful classic and modern games that use abstract shapes as characters, so that's reasonable justification for "going abstract" here as well.

Following the classic maze game design pattern, the main character is going to collect things in the maze while trying to avoid enemies, other objects which move around and are trying to attack it. In addition to the main character, you'll need to decide on designs for enemies and things to collect. In keeping with an abstract theme, the enemies are going to be spinning cubes and the things to collect are smaller spheres. It doesn't get much simpler than that. If there's a need for differentiating enemies there's always color, size, and basic animation available.

This isn't going to be a direct *clone* of *Pac-man* or any of the many sequels. Your goal is to make an original game in the same general category as the arcade maze games of the '80s. Cloning famous games can be educational, but it's even more instructive to make an original game where you don't know ahead of time how it's going to turn out.

VERSION 0.01: THE MAZE

Step 1: Start up Unity and create a project with the name **ClassicMazeGame**.

Step 2: Create the following folders in the Assets panel: **Materials**, **Models**, **Prefabs**, **Scripts**, and **Sounds**.

Step 3: Save the scene using the name **mainscene**. **Save** the project as well.

This is the basic setup for starting a new project that was used in some of your previous projects.

Next, you'll use Blender to make the maze.

Step 4: Start Blender.

Step 5: Type s Shift-z 8 <enter>.

This step scales the cube by a factor of 8 in the x and y, but not in the z direction.

Step 6: Select View – View Selected in the 3D View Menu.

Step 7: Press <Tab> to go into edit mode.

Step 8: Type numpad-1 and **numpad-5** to get to Front Ortho view.

Step 9: Type **z** to select **wireframe** viewport shading.

Step 10: Get into Face Select Mode.

Face Select mode is chosen by clicking on the third cube shaped icon at the bottom of the 3D view. The Face Select icon looks like a cube with the front face highlighted in orange.

Step 11: Type a to deselect everything.

Step 12: Type b to get to box mode. Select the top line of the rectangle.

Step 13: Select **Mesh – Edges – Subdivide** and set **Number of Cuts** to **29**.

This step created a 30 x 30 grid on the top of the block.

Step 14: Type numpad-7 to go into Top Ortho view.

Step 15: Type **z a** to exit wireframe mode and deselect everything again. Your screen should now look like Figure 12.1.

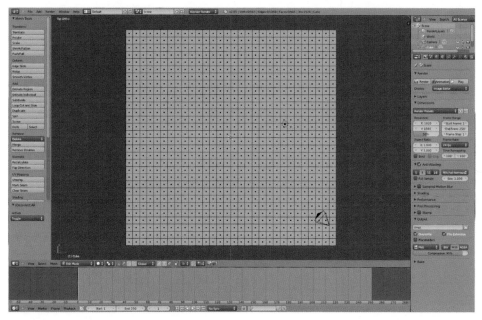

▲ **FIGURE 12.1** Grid for classic maze game.

Step 16: Select File – Save with name **mazegrid.blend** in **Assets/Models**.

You've just created a block with a 30 x 30 grid on top. This prepared you for making a maze by extruding the faces from the grid. First, you'll select the pathways for the maze.

Step 17: Press <Shift>right-click to select a few faces for your pathway. Then use box mode with the **b** key to add groups of faces to your selection. Compare your creation to Figure 12.2. Your selection doesn't need to exactly match that figure, but you should have something similar. You can use Undo while doing this if something doesn't go quite right. You can <Shift>right-click on a selected face to unselect it.

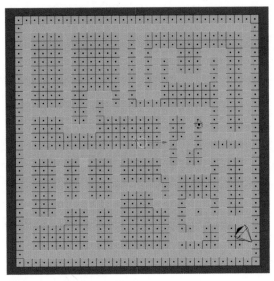

▲ **FIGURE 12.2** Selecting the path.

The next two steps do the extrusion where you take the path and push it into mesh. Think of it as carving a path out of a large block of granite.

Step 18: Type number pad -1 to go back to the Front Ortho view.

In the following step, be sure to type the minus sign in front of the "1".

Step 19: Type e -1 <enter> to extrude the path down into the mesh by 1 unit.

Step 20: Type numpad-8 numpad-8 numpad-4 numpad-4 numpad-5.

Step 21: Use the **numpad-minus** and **numpad-plus** keys to zoom in and out. Alternatively, you can use the mouse scroll wheel. Your screen should now look like Figure 12.3.

This maze is somewhat experimental. You can't expect to make a great maze before having a game to test with. Once you have some basic gameplay, you'll take another shot at making the real maze.

Before you bring this maze into Unity, there's a little bit of housekeeping to do. In order to have a different color or texture for the maze path as opposed to the maze

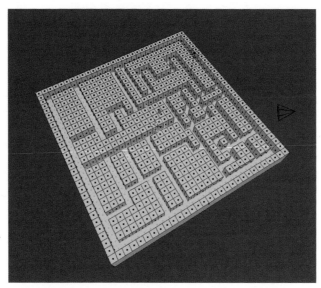

▲ **FIGURE 12.3** Extruded maze path.

walls, it's best to separate the two into different meshes. This may not be the most efficient way of doing things, but it's easy and simple.

Step 22: Type x – faces. Because you still had the path selected, it was easy to delete it. The floor will later be replaced by a single large plane in Unity.

Step 23: Select File – Save As… using the name **maze_proto.blend**.

It's time to go back to Unity and see what this maze looks like there.

Step 24: Run Unity and s**elect maze_proto** in the Models folder in Unity.

Step 25: In the Inspector, click on **Animations**, and **uncheck Import Animation**.

Step 26: Click on **Apply**.

Step 27: Click on **Model**, and use **Calculate** for **Normals** and **Apply**.

Step 28: Drag **maze_proto** from the Assets panel to the **Hierarchy panel**.

Step 29: Set the **Position** to **(0, 0, 0)**, if necessary.

Step 30: Use **Top perspective view** in the Scene panel.

Step 31: Press **f** to focus the Scene panel onto maze_proto.

Step 32: Move the **Main Camera** to **Position (0, 20, 0)**, **Rotation (90, 0, 0)**.

The x rotation of 90 points the camera down, and the y position of 20 moves it up and away from the maze. That's where you want to have the initial position for the camera. Later on, you'll move the camera closer and scroll it to follow the main character around.

Step 33: Use **Front perspective view** in the Scene panel.

Your Unity Scene and Game panels should look like Figure 12.4.

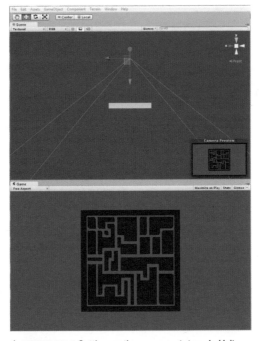

▲ **FIGURE 12.4** Setting up the maze prototype in Unity.

As you can see, the lighting is poor, so it's time to add some simple lighting and a material for the maze.

Step 34: Select GameObject – Create Other – Point Light at **Position (0, 5, 0)**.

Step 35: In the Assets – Materials folder, create a blue specular material, rename it to maze material, and assign it to the maze.

Step 36: Add a **skybox** like you did for the scrolling shooter project. Use the **Sunny1** Skybox. This Skybox is there just for decoration and doesn't affect gameplay. Compare your screen with Figure 12.5.

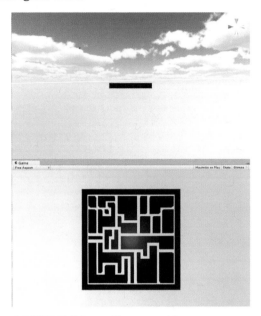

▲ **FIGURE 12.5** Sunny skies surround the maze.

The maze needs a floor, so do the next step to create one.

Step 37: In the Hierarchy Panel, select **Create – Plane**, and rename it to **floor** in the Inspector panel.

Step 38: Change the **Scale** of the floor to **(2, 1, 2)**.

Step 39: Create a **specular material** for the floor, make it **gold**, and name it **floor material**.

The maze is looking kind of dark now, so turn up the range of the light.

Step 40: Set the range of the Point light to 20. There's a lot more to creating good lighting than adjusting the range of the one light. It's fun to put several lights into the scene and to experiment with colors, ranges, and intensities.

Step 41: Save the scene and project. The prototype maze is complete and set up in Unity. You are now ready to create the maze characters.

VERSION 0.02: THE PLAYER

The player will be a sphere. While you might get more control over the mesh by making it in Blender, the built-in sphere in Unity is fine, so go ahead and use that.

Step 1: In the Hierarchy panel, create a Sphere and rename it to **player**.

Step 2: Create a **green player material** and assign it to the **player**.

Step 3: Change the **Position** to **(0, 2, 0)**, **Scale (0.4, 0.4, 0.4)**. You just placed the player hovering above the maze for now.

Step 4: Add Component – Physics – Rigidbody.

Step 5: Create a **player.js** JavaScript and assign it to **player**. Use the following code:

```
#pragma strict

var factor:float = 10;
function Update ()
{
   if (Input.GetKey ("right"))
   {
      rigidbody.AddForce(Vector3.right * factor);
   }
   if (Input.GetKey ("left"))
   {
      rigidbody.AddForce(Vector3.left * factor);
   }
   if (Input.GetKey ("down"))
   {
      rigidbody.AddForce(Vector3.back * factor);
   }
   if (Input.GetKey ("up"))
   {
      rigidbody.AddForce(Vector3.forward * factor);
   }
}
```

This code lets you control the player with the four arrow keys on your keyboard. To test this out, do the following steps:

Step 6: Disable the **Mesh Renderer** for **maze_proto** by unchecking the box next to "Mesh Renderer" in the Inspector panel.

Step 7: Run the game. Your game panel should look like Figure 12.6. Press the four arrow keys and test that you can control the player.

▲ **FIGURE 12.6** Testing the player control.

Step 8: Stop running the game.

Step 9: Enable the **Mesh Renderer** for **maze_proto**.

Step 10: Add Component – Physics – Mesh Collider.

Step 11: Run the game. This time you turned on the renderer for maze_proto and added a mesh collider component. This allows you to move the ball around in the maze. If the player starts out on top of a blue wall, slowly move it into a maze path and it will drop down.

Step 12: Stop running the game.

In the next step, you'll initialize the player in the maze rather than floating above it.

Step 13: Change the Position of the **player** so that the player is initialized in the maze, if necessary. Use a y position of 0.5. Depending on your maze, you may need to adjust the x and z position. A good y position is 0.5. You can use the Scene panel with at Top Iso view and move the player around with the mouse until the player gets initialized where you want. For the maze from the book, the new initial position is (0, 0.5, 0.8). When you're done making this adjustment, don't forget to test.

Step 14: Test the player control one more time.

Step 15: Save. It was relatively easy to put in the player. In the next section, you'll create the enemies.

VERSION 0.03: NASTY ENEMIES

The enemies are going to be cubes, but you're going to use a sphere collider for them. This makes the cubes appear to be tumbling around.

Step 1: In the Hierarchy panel, create a cube, rename it **nasty enemy**.

Step 2: Make a **red specular material** for it and name it **nasty enemy material**. As usual, put the material into the Materials folder and don't forget to assign the material to the nasty enemy.

Step 3: Change the **Scale** for the nasty enemy to **(0.4, 0.4, 0.4)** and **place it onto the maze**.

You use the same technique you used for the player. The y position should be 0.3, whereas x and z are adjusted so that the nasty enemy is on a path rather than hidden inside the maze mesh.

Step 4: Add Component – Physics – Rigidbody.

Step 5: Test.

Here is where the real fun begins. The nasty enemy isn't at all nasty yet, but just sits there, but if you crash the player into the nasty enemy it starts to tumble. The tumbling isn't as smooth as you might like, so in the next step you'll use a neat trick to make it tumble more smoothly.

Step 6: Remove the **Box Collider**, and **add** a **Sphere Collider** in **nasty enemy**. To remove the Box Collider, click on the gear icon at the right and select Remove Component.

Step 7: Create a nastyenemy.js JavaScript for nasty enemy and use the following code:

```
#pragma strict

public var factor:float = 5;

function Update ()
{
var dir: Vector3 = Vector3(0,0,0);
var player : GameObject = GameObject.Find("player");

    if (player)
        dir = player.transform.position - transform.position;

    rigidbody.AddForce(dir * factor);
}
```

This code is short and effective. At the bottom of the Update function, you can see an AddForce function call. The variable dir is a vector that stores the 3D direction of the force that's going to be applied. The direction is computed to be a vector from the enemy position to the player position. In other words, this function tells the enemy object to move directly towards the player, and to do so with a force proportional to the distance between them.

Step 8: Test. When you run the game now, the nasty enemy follows the player around like a dog on an elastic leash. Although you're using a modern physics engine to implement it, the resulting movement of the nasty enemy is actually the same as the crystal balls from *Crystal Castles*, written over thirty years ago.

Step 9: Drag nasty enemy into the Prefabs folder.

Step 10: Use the Top Iso view in the Scene panel and drag a few nasty enemy prefabs into the Scene. Check that the y position is 0.3 for all of them.

Step 11: Experiment with different starting positions for the enemies.

Step 12: Create a light blue easy enemy material, and assign it to one of the nasty enemy instances in the Hierarchy. Set the factor to 2 for the easy enemy, and test it.

It's now time to add collision detection for the enemy vs. player. This has to be done a little differently than in the past because you're using the physics engine.

Step 13: Replace the nastyenemy.js file with the following code:

```
#pragma strict

    public var factor:float = 5;

    private var initPosition: Vector3;

    function Start()
    {
        initPosition = transform.position;
    }

    function RestorePosition()
    {
        transform.position = initPosition;
    }

    function Update ()
    {
    var dir: Vector3 = Vector3(0,0,0);
    var player : GameObject = GameObject.Find("player");
        if (player)
            dir = player.transform.position - transform.position;

        rigidbody.AddForce(dir * factor);
    }


    function OnCollisionEnter(collision: Collision)
    {
        if (collision.gameObject.name == "player")
        {
```

```
        collision.gameObject.transform.position.x = 0.0;
        collision.gameObject.transform.position.y = 0.5;
        collision.gameObject.transform.position.z = 0.8;
        RestorePosition();
    }
}
```

This code is fairly straightforward. When the player collides with an enemy, both the player and the enemy is sent back to their starting position. You may need to change the numbers in the code at the end that repositions the player. This is a bit abrupt, but it's good enough for now.

Step 14: Test and **save**.

You now have a pretty good framework for creating a bunch of levels. The enemies aren't exactly smart, but that's OK. It can be fun to try to outwit a bunch of dumb enemies. In the classic era, it wasn't possible to have very sophisticated character movement code and yet it didn't matter because it was still possible to tune and balance these games and end up with something incredibly fun and exciting. In the next section, you'll be adding dots.

VERSION 0.04: DOTS

You still don't have a game. All that's missing is some goal for the player.

Step 1: Create a **Sphere**, **rename** it to **dot**, **Position (0, 0.3, 0)**, **Scale (0.2, 0.2, 0.2)** and put it **on the maze**.

Step 2: Create a **white** material for it.

Step 3: Create a JavaScript **dot.js** and assign it to the dot object. Use the following code:

```
#pragma strict

function OnTriggerEnter (other: Collider) {
    if (other.name == "player")
```

```
{
    Destroy(gameObject);
}
}
```

Step 4: Select the dot object in the Hierarchy and look at the Sphere Collider in the Inspector panel. **Check Is Trigger**.

Step 5: Test that the dot disappears when colliding with the player.

Step 6: Make a dot prefab in the usual manner.

Step 7: Put three dots onto the maze path near the initial player position by dragging two more instances from the prefabs directory into the Hierarchy.

Step 8: Test and **save**. The three dots should disappear when the player runs into them. Later, during development, you'll put many dots out there, but for initial testing and development it's better to just have a few dots. The next section shows how to put in some basic sounds.

VERSION 0.05: AUDIO

The sound design for this game is fairly simple, with one new twist. In the previous projects, the sound effects were typically triggered by collisions. This game doesn't have very many collisions, so how about you put in sound effects for each of the four arrow key controls?

The plan is to first go into Audacity and make four similar sound effects for the four arrow keys, and then a nice happy sound for when the player picks up a dot, a sad sound when the player dies, and a short bonk sound for collisions with walls.

Step 1: Start Audacity.

In the next step, to get the NTSC frames time scale, you'll click on a small arrow next to the Duration display.

Step 2: Select **Generate – Chirp**, set Duration to 5 NTSC frames, Sine Waveform, Frequency 440, 1320. Press Play to test it (the green arrow). Your waveform should be about 0.17 seconds long, just right for a short sound effect. The NTSC frame time scale allows for quick entry of short time durations.

Step 3: Select File – Save Project As … arrowkeys.aup in the Sounds folder in Assets of the ClassicMazeGame project.

Step 4: Select File – Export… arrowup.wav in the same folder.

Step 5: Select **Effect – Change Pitch …** from C down to A (-3 semitones). Press Play to test it.

Step 6: Select File – Export… arrowdown.wav in the same folder.

Step 7: Select **Effect – Change Pitch …** from A up to B (2 semitones). Press Play to test it.

Step 8: Select File – Export… arrowright.wav in the same folder.

Step 9: Select **Effect – Change Pitch …** from B down to E (-7 semitones). Press Play to test it.

Step 10: Select File – Export… arrowleft.wav in the same folder.

The chirp sound effect is a quick way to make the iconic beeps that were so common in classic video games. There are just two more effects for collisions.

Step 11: Select **Generate – Chirp**, Sine Waveform, Frequency 440 – 5000, 15 NTSC frames.

Step 12: Select File – Export… dot.wav in the same folder.

Step 13: Select **Generate – Chirp**, Sawtooth Waveform, Frequency 1000 – 50, 15 NTSC frames.

Step 14: Select File – Export… enemy.wav in the same folder.

There might be a method to this madness. The rising frequency in the chirp makes a happier sound than a falling frequency shift. To get an authentic retro sound, it helps to use Sawtooth and Sine wave forms. Those simple wave forms were easily generated and commonly available in the early sound chips.

Step 15: Get back to Unity and test the sound effects in the Sounds folder.

Step 16: In dot.js, add the following code:

```
public var dotsound: AudioClip;
audio.PlayClipAtPoint(dotsound,transform.position);
```

The first line goes after the pragma, the second line goes before the Destroy function call in the OnTriggerEnter function.

Step 17: For the dot prefab, assign the **dot** sound for the **Dotsound** property in the Inspector using the bullseye icon at the far right and then test the sound in the game.

Step 18: Add the enemy sound in a similar manner to how you added the dot sound, then test it.

Step 19: Add the following code to player.js immediately below the pragma statement:

```
var aleft: AudioClip;
var aright: AudioClip;
var aup: AudioClip;
var adown: AudioClip;
```

Step 20: Add the following code to player.js at the beginning of the Update function:

```
if (Input.GetKeyDown ("right"))
{
    audio.PlayClipAtPoint(aright,transform.position);
}
if (Input.GetKeyDown ("left"))
{
    audio.PlayClipAtPoint(aleft,transform.position);
}
if (Input.GetKeyDown ("down"))
{
    audio.PlayClipAtPoint(adown,transform.position);
}
if (Input.GetKeyDown ("up"))
{
    audio.PlayClipAtPoint(aup,transform.position);
}
```

Step 21: Assign the four arrow sounds to the associated properties for the player.

This code looks similar to the other half of the Update function, but there's an important difference. The `GetKeyDown` function tests for a transition of the key from *not-pressed* to *pressed down*. The `GetKey` function just tests to see if the key is pressed, so it keeps doing the `AddForce` function calls every frame whenever the particular key is pressed.

Step 22: Test and **save**. Much more can be done with sound in this game, of course. The reader is encouraged to experiment with additional sound effects and background sounds.

The next section adds scoring, levels, and difficulty ramping.

VERSION 0.06: SCORING AND LEVELS

Scoring is easy, but adding levels takes a little bit of effort. The tricky part is to restore the dots for the next level. You'll get to that soon, but first set up the scoring framework.

Step 1: Select GameObject – Create Empty, rename it to **scoring**.

Step 2: Create the **scoring.js** script for **scoring** and use the following code:

```
#pragma strict

static var score: int;
static var lives: int;
static var dots: int;
static var totaldots: int;
static var level: int;
static var update: boolean;

function Start () {
    score = 0;
    lives = 3;
    totaldots = 3;   // update this when changing number of dots
```

```
    dots = totaldots;
    level = 1;
    initlevel = false;
}


function Update () {
    if (dots == 0)
    {
        initlevel = true;
        level++;
    }
    if (dots == totaldots) initlevel = false;
}


function OnGUI () {
    GUI.Box (Rect (10,10,90,30), "Score:    "+score);
    GUI.Box (Rect (Screen.width - 100,10,90,30),"Lives:    "+lives);
    GUI.Box (Rect (Screen.width/2 - 100, 10, 200, 30), "Dots: "+dots);
    GUI.Box (Rect (10,Screen.height - 100, 90,30), "Level: "+level);
}
```

Step 3: Replace the code for dots.js with the following:

```
#pragma strict


public var dotsound: AudioClip;


function Start () {
}


function Update () {
    if (scoring.initlevel == true)
        Revive();

}
```

```
function Suspend () {
    gameObject.renderer.enabled = false;
    gameObject.transform.position.y = 20;
}


function Revive () {
    gameObject.renderer.enabled = true;
    gameObject.transform.position.y = 0.3;
    scoring.dots++;
}



function OnTriggerEnter (other: Collider) {
    if (other.name == "player")
    {
        audio.PlayClipAtPoint(dotsound,transform.position);
        Suspend();
        scoring.dots--;
        scoring.score += 10;
    }
}
```

Step 4: Add the following code to player.js:

```
function InitPosition()
{
    transform.position.x = 0;
    transform.position.y = 0.5;
    transform.position.z = 0.8;
    rigidbody.velocity = Vector3(0,0,0);
}


function Start()
{
    InitPosition();
}
```

Step 5: Add the following line to the end of the Update function in player.js:

```
if (scoring.initlevel == true) InitPosition();
```

Step 6: Read the new code, try to understand it and test it. The essential idea behind this code is to suspend the dots instead of destroying them. Their initial position is saved at startup, which allows you to do the restoration. This code also adds level advance when all the dots are collected, and it adds 10 points to the score whenever a dot is collected.

The only essential thing that's missing is the game over screen. We'll do this the cheap and easy way, just like in the last chapter.

Step 7: Add the following code to the OnGUI function in scoring.js:

```
var player : GameObject = GameObject.Find("player");
if (!player)
{
    GUI.Button (Rect (Screen.width/2 - 200,
                      Screen.height/2 - 50,
                      400, 50),"Game Over");
}

if (scoring.level == 3)
{
    GUI.Button (Rect (Screen.width/2 - 200,
                      Screen.height/2 - 50,
                      400, 50),"The End");
}
```

Step 8: Insert the following code at the end of the Update function in player.js:

```
if (scoring.lives == 0) Destroy(gameObject);
if (scoring.level == 3) Destroy(gameObject);
```

This code destroys the player when he's out of lives or when the player reaches the ending. Yes, the ending is hardwired at level 3! That's too soon for the real game, but it's OK for now when you're testing.

Step 9: Insert the following code in nastyenemy.js before the audio call:

```
scoring.lives--;
```

Step 10: Test the ending and the game over screens.

Now a one-liner for adding difficulty ramping.

Step 11: Replace the AddForce line in nastyenemy.js with the following:

```
rigidbody.AddForce(dir * factor * (0.6 + 0.2 * scoring.level));
```

This code ramps the force applied to the enemies, making them more aggressive on higher levels.

Figure 12.7 shows a screen capture when testing the game at level 1.

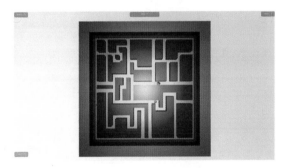

▲ **FIGURE 12.7** Testing the classic maze game.

Step 12: Test and **save**. You now have a framework for making the game into something special, your very own creation. The next and final development section gives you some pointers on where to take things from here.

VERSION 0.07: TUNING

This game just needs a quick tune-up and it's ready to be released. The first step will implement a scrolling camera, very much like you did in the scrolling shooter project.

Step 1: Create a camera.js script for the Main Camera with the following code:

```
#pragma strict

function Update () {
    var player : GameObject = GameObject.Find("player");
```

```
if (player)
{
    transform.position.x = player.transform.position.x;
    transform.position.z = player.transform.position.z;
}
}
```

Step 2: For Main Camera, set the Field of View to 40, and the Position to (0, 10, 0.8).

Step 3: Test it. You can now see that the game looks pretty good this way, but there is a problem with the enemies. They are cutting into the maze walls because of the strange combination of using a sphere collider for a cube. The problem is easily remedied by adjusting the Scale of the object and the radius of the sphere collider.

Step 4: For the nasty enemy prefab, change the Scale to (0.3, 0.3, 0.3) and the Radius of the Sphere Collider to 0.7. Test the effect of this change.

Step 5: Increase the number of dots to at least 20. Modify the code to handle this.

Step 6: Make all the enemies different colors. Your Unity screen should look similar to Figure 12.8.

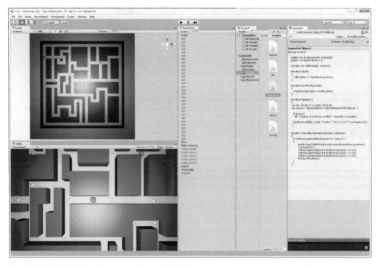

▲ **FIGURE 12.8** Classic maze game in Unity.

Step 7: Test it now. Can you get to the end? The game is quite challenging now. If the game feels too hard to you, make the enemies slower, or change the ramping equation. Compare your game with Figure 12.9.

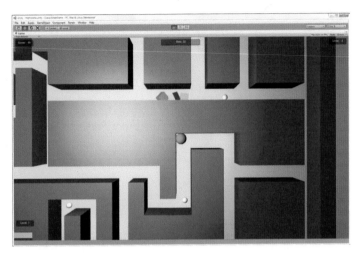

▲ **FIGURE 12.9** Final test of classic maze game.

The game is ready for release, or is it? There's always more to be done. The most obvious next step would be to make new mazes in Blender. Maybe there's a bug or two lurking in the game, ready to be discovered. There's definitely room for exploration with the enemy AI. Check out the exercises at the end of this chapter for more detailed ideas on how to expand the game.

VERSION 1.00: RELEASE AND POSTMORTEM

Finishing a game is just the first step in the release process. For commercial projects, the choice of target platforms, distribution, and marketing are just as critical to a game's success as the game itself. This classic maze game is one of many experimental side projects that all game developers have. As such, it can be released to friends and family. It's great to see their reactions. If you're lucky, they'll inundate you with new ideas, some of them good, some not so good, and some won't be new at all because you thought of them yourself earlier. Take notes of all the ideas, and try out the ones that are easy to try out.

This classic maze game was surprisingly easy to make. The original choice of using abstract characters really paid off in terms of speed of development. The technique of using placeholder graphics and sound to develop gameplay first is extremely useful. It's easy to replace graphics or sound after the gameplay is developed. Making your final art and sound first, and then trying to make a fun game out of it, is much riskier and potentially very expensive.

The project turned into an original maze game without even trying all that hard. There's very little code, just a maze, a few characters, and some simple sound effects. The game is fun just the same, just as many of the classic arcade games of the '70s and '80s.

You took some serious shortcuts in development, and it shows in a few spots. People expect to see a bunch of different mazes, not just a single maze. The abrupt warping of the player when he dies is jarring, and the game really could use more characters. For a prototype, experimental game, these shortcuts are acceptable. It's up to you to take the development to the next level. After working through all of the projects, you know enough to do just that.

EXERCISES

1. Use Blender to build a 30 x 30 maze. Use the same technique as your first maze, but experiment with different paths. Put in an open area, or a long spiral with a dead end. Then integrate the new maze into the game with the name Maze_2.

2. Use Blender to build a 20 x 20 maze and a 50 x 25 maze. Stretch the maze in Blender so that the width of the maze path matches the prototype maze. Integrate both mazes into the game. Do this by putting both mazes into the scene and moving the player from the first maze to the second when the player removes all the dots from the first scene.

3. Replace the main character graphics with a monkey head. Use Blender to make the monkey head. Optional: Rotate the monkey head to face the current direction of movement.

4. Put in a state machine for the game. When the player dies, have all enemies and the player go back to their starting positions, and put in a three second delay before gameplay starts again. Optional: During the delay, smoothly move the camera to the initial position.

5. Put in a new character, similar to a bonus fruit in Pac-Man. Use Blender to make graphics for it, have it appear at a fixed spot for a limited time, and make it worth 1000 points.

6. Create four different character shapes for your four characters. Do this by adjusting the x, y, and z scales of the renderers, or by replacing the shape with a capsule or a cylinder.

7. Modify nastyenemy.js to have the enemy aim at a 2D fixed offset from the player. Make the offset variables public vars and assign different offsets to the different enemies.

8. Record yourself saying "waka waka" and take the resulting audio file into Audacity. Modify the recording in Audacity using one or two effects. Then save the sound with the name waka.wav and put it into the game as a looping background track.

Epilogue

It's time to review your achievements. You took a closer look at some of the most influential games from the classic arcade era and used them as inspiration for your own creations. You built five classic games from scratch. You got a taste of what it's like to be a game developer. Last, and certainly not least, you got a step-by-step practical introduction to Unity, Blender, GIMP, and Audacity.

SO MANY GAMES, SO FEW PAGES

Tough choices had to be made when deciding which classic video games to feature in this book. What about *Asteroids*, *Missile Command*, *Defender*, *Q*bert*, and *Crystal Castles*? And then, of course, we shouldn't forget the racing games, video pinball, *Tempest*, and *Venture*.

Some major aspects of game design had to be mostly ignored due to time and space constraints. The worst of these omissions are multiplayer, theming, and story development. Entire books can be and have been written about these subjects. *Multiplayer* was typically ignored or handled poorly in the early years of video game development, with the exception of *Pong*. Oddly, the first and most famous arcade game from that time period was a two-player simultaneous game, only to have single-player games dominate the video game scene for dozens of years until the emergence of arcade fighting games. *Storytelling* was present in the classic era, but for the most part the hardcore players didn't really care about the stories. If there was a story at all, it was often tacked on by the marketing department and not really an integral part of the game. Good stories make it easier to sell games, but in games such as *Pac-Man* or *Space Invaders*, the game doesn't depend on the player knowing anything about the story. While there are plenty of story-driven games nowadays, back in the day, the stories tended to be ignored by the true gamers. The players cared mainly about how far into the game they could play and their high scores. Most games didn't have an ending, which makes for a poor story.

NOVELTY

Here's the last and possibly most important rule of all:

Classic Game Design Rule 8: Novelty Rule: Make it new!

In the '70s and '80s, novelty was king. It was taken to an extreme by the coin-op industry, especially Atari coin-op. Atari had an internal edict that forced all new coin-op products to be as different as possible from everything that came before. Sequels did happen, but because they usually performed below expectation, a prime example being *Asteroids Deluxe*, Atari management concluded that novelty was an essential ingredient when trying to develop a hit game.

Of course, there were a few really big exceptions, such as *Ms. Pac-Man* and *Stargate*, but in general, the public clamored for novelty, and the industry responded. Decades later, novelty is much more difficult to achieve, and sequels are often more successful than the originals. But let's not forget that novelty can really add to the fun, especially when you combine it with good design and high-quality engineering.

HOW MODERN GAMES ARE INFLUENCED BY THE CLASSICS

It may be amusing to look at these quaint old games, but do they still matter? Isn't it all just ancient history? Modern games may seem much more advanced, larger or even better (whatever that means) than the old classics, but if you take a closer look you'll see the influence of the classics in most every mainstream modern game. The single most successful game category during the past decade is without a doubt the "first person shooter" or FPS. When you play one or two of these games, you'll immediately see the connection with the classic 2D shooters. When you summarize it in one sentence, it's essentially the same game mechanic: Shoot them before they shoot you. Modern FPS games implement this with cutting-edge 3D and an epic and complex story thrown in to keep you entertained and motivated in the process. The basic lessons of classic game development still apply today and the foreseeable future: Fix your bugs early, make the game fun first before spending too much time polishing the art, and most importantly, test and play your game early and often.

The variety of the classic game spectrum is striking. The game designers from that era were continually innovating and weren't afraid to put crazy new features into their games. This happened, in part, because the designers worked in isolation on different continents and hidden away in secret labs without an Internet connection. Nowadays, huge economic pressures at major game studios make it more risky for them to do something radically different. Fortunately, there's a healthy community of independent game developers who aren't quite as afraid of change.

It's a useful exercise to try to design a game that has little or nothing in common with any classic video game. Consider the "null game." It's a game where every player ends up with a score of zero regardless of what happens during the gameplay. It's mostly a theoretical construct, kind of like the old joke game "52 pickup." Two similar games are the "you win" game and the "you lose" game. In these games, there's also no gameplay and the winner, i.e., the score, is predetermined. You're probably thinking that it's completely crazy to even talk about the "null game," or the "you win" game. But, if you think about it, when a casual player buys some AAA FPS console title because a friend told him it's great, plays it for a few hours and then gives up, isn't that a null game? Didn't that player just treat the game as an interactive experience rather than the game it was designed to be?

From a strictly monetary perspective, the single-player classic arcade games were "you lose" games in the sense that you always lost a quarter. But of course that's ignoring the fairly high importance placed on the numerical score by the classic designers. The classic designers suffered somewhat from the delusion that their players cared about the score. In reality, most players played for fun and didn't really care about the score. Eventually, many of the home console games caved and dropped numerical scoring. Then, to cater to the more fanatic players, they brought scoring back disguised as achievements.

Pretty soon another thirty years will fly by and game design will likely evolve in unpredictable directions. But, games are games. It's my humble opinion that the lessons learned in this book will continue to be useful to future generations of game designers.

Appendix I: Programming Using UnityScript

This appendix is a relatively short and quick introduction to programming to help prepare you for the programming parts of this book. It's especially useful if you're very new to it. Feel free to skip this appendix if you're an experienced programmer.

PROGRAMMING IS EASY

Programming is the way humans talk to computers and make them do what they want. Computers can seem to be very stupid, but they're fast, and they have a very good memory. Programming has evolved over the years from hitting toggle switches to creating punch cards to writing text files using a computer programming language.

Programming is easy because computers do exactly what we tell them to do, no more and no less. In that sense, programming is very much like playing the piano. It's easy to hit the keys on the piano and to make the individual notes sound good, but to string the notes together and play piano at a professional level takes years of practice and dedication.

To get started with programming, you need to first learn some of the basic vocabulary. Programming involves the writing of *code*. Code is just another word for the programs, which in turn are text written using the rules of a particular programming language.

Code is broken up into statements. Each statement tells the computer to do something or to set up something for use in other statements. Optionally, there can be comments that don't affect anything but are there to annotate and document. The program is the collection of all the statements, possibly spread out over several text files. Once you're done writing the program you can run it and, let's hope, the program does what was intended. Very large programming projects can have millions of lines of code written by hundreds of programmers. Fortunately, the classic game programming projects from this book are much smaller than that, encompassing at most a few hundred statements written by one or a few programmers.

UNITYSCRIPT AND JAVASCRIPT

UnityScript is the programming language used in this book. It is a dialect of the C programming language, so if you've seen some other dialects like Java or C#, you'll notice the similarities. UnityScript is a dialect of JavaScript that is similar to and often confused with JavaScript, although there are some differences.

The Unity environment refers to its UnityScript programs as JavaScript programs. From the viewpoint of Unity, there is no difference between the two. The word UnityScript has evolved to distinguish ordinary JavaScript from the form of JavaScript used inside of Unity. So, for example, when you create a new UnityScript file inside of Unity, you actually tell Unity to create a JavaScript file, with the .js extension. In the context of this book, the word UnityScript and JavaScript have the same meaning because both refer to UnityScript code used by Unity.

UnityScript, as the name implies, is a scripted language, as opposed to C, which is compiled. The difference between scripted and compiled is that a scripted program can be run immediately after a change is made to the program, whereas a compiled program needs the additional step of first feeding the program to the compiler before running it.

The main advantage of a scripted program is that you don't have to wait for a compilation step before running the program. Scripted programs allow for the possibility of changing the program "on the fly" i.e., right in the middle of program execution. Compiled programs tend to run faster, but in recent years this has become less of an issue due to vast improvements in processor speed and the fact that the processors tend to be so busy doing other things that the performance of the scripts is usually unimportant. This is one reason why the developers of Unity chose scripted languages rather than compiled languages.

After this general introduction, it's time to look at the basic elements of programming, starting with numbers and how they are represented in our programming environment.

PROGRAMMING NUMBERS: INTEGERS AND FLOATS

Numbers are the real foundation of programming games. That's because numbers are used to count things in your games, to measure the locations of objects, to describe the graphics, audio, and even the gameplay logic in your games. There usually are two types of numbers in games, integers and floating point numbers. Let's first look at integers.

Integers are whole numbers without fractions, for Example 3, 1892, or -17. Integers can be negative, positive, or zero. You can write +3 or just 3 to represent the positive integer three.

In programming, integers are used to count things. In game programming, integers typically keep track of the score in a game, or statistics such as lives or coins.

Next, there's floating point numbers, which is a fancy word for numbers with fractional parts, such as 3.452 or -12000000.1. Floating point numbers are used to represent the position, speed, or length of objects, for example. Floating point numbers can also be represented with an exponent using the letter 'e'. For example, we can write 1.425e20 which is an abbreviation of 1.425 times 10 to the 20th power.

Yes, there are limitations to both integers and floating point numbers because computers are finite machines. It would be inefficient to allow for really huge numbers because they are rarely used in practical applications. It is possible to go up to

64 bits worth of precision for integers and floating point numbers, though the default is 32 bits. In this book, you'll only use 32-bit numbers.

If your integers are going to be less than 12 digits long you're fine with 32 bits. For 32-bit floating point numbers, the limit is 10e38 with seven digits of precision.

It's important to realize that in code there is a difference between 3 and 3.0. The 3, by itself is the integer 3. 3.0 is a floating point number. In math and science, those two numbers are considered to be exactly the same, but not in computer code. The difference shows up when considering expressions such as 9/4. Because both 9 and 4 are integers, the result after the division is also an integer, rounded down to the closest integer which happens to be 2. However 9.0/4.0 results in the floating point number 2.25, just what you would expect.

VARIABLES AND VARIABLE NAMES

Numbers are stored in variables. Variables have names such as "Position" or "Color". Unlike mathematicians and scientists who tend to use single letters for variables, programmers often use longer variable names. This helps in remembering what all those variables are supposed to represent.

Variable names must start with a letter and typically the capitalization matters, i.e., "Length" and "length" aren't the same thing. Variable names may not contain spaces, so this is why you'll see variable names such as BallSpeed or MyLongVariableName. Other ways of writing variable names you might encounter are ball_speed or ballSpeed. It's important for you to develop a good eye for spelling and capitalization. Countless hours of programmer productivity are lost every day because of misspelled variable names.

In most programming languages, variables must be declared before they can be used. A variable declaration is a statement that tells the program some initial information about the variable. Think of variables as cardboard boxes with giant labels on them. The labels are the variable names, and the contents are the variable values. The declaration is a statement that puts the label onto the box. Here are some samples of variable declarations in UnityScript followed by some code that uses them:

```
var Score: int;
var Speed: float;
var PlayerName: String;
var isAlive: boolean;


Score = 0;
Score = Score + 100;
Speed = 54.9 ;
PlayerName = "Joe";
isAlive = true;
```

Strings are sequences of letters and are generally surrounded by double quotation marks. Boolean variables are used in programming logic and can take on two values: "true" and "false."

Sometimes it's convenient to initialize variables at the same time as declaring them. In UnityScript this is done, for example, as follows:

```
var Score: int = 100;
var Speed: float = 70.0;
var PlayerName: String = "Joe";
var isAlive: boolean = true;
```

WHITESPACE

Whitespace is a programmer's term for spaces, tabs, and linebreaks. In most, but not all programming languages, including UnityScript, all whitespace is equivalent. So, for example:

```
X = 2 + 2; Y=2+X;
```

and

```
X=2+2;
Y=2+X;
```

have exactly the same meaning. It takes a little practice to learn where it's OK to insert whitespace. For example, the following statements are NOT the same:

```
MyVariable = true;
My Variable = true;
```

This is because variable names are not allowed to contain whitespace. It is, however, OK to insert whitespace between parts of arithmetic expressions, for example: X + 2.

Whitespace is useful for making your code look nice. It's a good idea to avoid tabs because tab settings can change, thus making pretty code look ugly simply by changing the tab settings. It's best to avoid this problem by never using tabs in your code.

STATEMENTS AND SEMICOLONS

Statements are usually groups of expressions ending with a semicolon. For example,

```
X = 2;
```

is an example of a simple statement. Why do we have that semicolon at the end? Well, periods are used in numbers and complex variable expressions, so the next best thing is a semicolon. We need the semicolon to separate statements from one another. For example,

```
x = 2; y = 3; z = 4;
```

is a single line of code with three statements in it.

COMPUTATIONS

Computers are really just fancy programmable calculators. Let's learn how to add, subtract, multiply, and divide.

```
x = 2+3;
x = 12-3;
x = 2*12;
x = 7/2;
x = 7.0/2.0;
```

Those are the four common computations. The only strange one is multiplication, which is usually done with the star special character on your computer keyboard, or Shift-8. The results of the above computations are 5, 9, 24, 3, and 3.5. The 7 divided by 2 results in a 3 because the inputs are integers.

FUNCTIONS AND FUNCTION CALLS

Functions are a very powerful way to group computations together. Here is an example:

```
function DoubleAndIncrementScore()
{
    score = score * 2;
    score++;
}

score = 1;
DoubleAndIncrementScore();
DoubleAndIncrementScore();
DoubleAndIncrementScore();
```

This sequence of code doubles and increments the score three times. The function definition resides between two curly brackets, the three function calls can occur anywhere else in our code. The function calls change the score from an initial value of 1 to 3, then 7, and finally 15.

LOOPING

Loops are a great way to do repetitive task. Here is a quick example:

```
score = 1;
for (var i=0; i<4; i++)
{
    score = score * 2;
}
```

This sequence of code sets the score to 1, then doubles it four times. The final value of score is 16. The variable i is set to 0 at the beginning of the loop and is incremented as long as it stays less than 4. You can use the index variable in the loop, for example like this:

```
score = 1;
for (var i=0; i<4; i++)
{
    score = score + i;
}
```

The final result of this computation is 1+0+1+2+3 = 7.

LEARNING TO CODE

You're now almost ready to start coding. The only way to really learn how to code is to code. A great way for beginners to learn is to follow along with our step-by-step instructions throughout the book. Don't yield to the temptation of just cutting and pasting the code from someplace rather than typing it in. Only by typing each and every line yourself will you experience the joys, thrills, and spills of programming.

If you're a poor typist, stop reading right now and spend a few hours learning the basics on how to touch-type. If you're hunting and pecking with two fingers, you're needlessly handicapping yourself. Most good professional programmers can type at least 50 words per minute. Some are ridiculously fast and can type code faster than you can read it. A famous game developer with over 30 years of coding experience was asked recently which programming course he had found most useful. He immediately answered that it wasn't a programming course at all, but rather the typing course he took as a kid at a local vocational school. These days it's easy to find free typing tutorials and lessons online. Even if you're not aiming to become a professional programmer, touch-typing is a valuable skill if you plan on using a computer keyboard with any frequency.

You might consider yourself an accurate typist, but nobody's perfect. Typos are a fact of life for all programmers. Even if you're a top-notch typist, you're not going to be 100% perfect. All it takes is one single unlucky typo, and your amazing program turns into something completely broken. This isn't like writing an e-mail, where a typo here or there doesn't really matter. Fortunately most typos result in an error that is automatically detected by the programming environment. Sometimes though, a simple typo can result in a bug that can only be found and fixed via extensive testing.

THE CODE IN THIS BOOK

The code in this book is designed to be accessible to beginners. There are no advanced coding concepts here, just some assignment statements, loops, a little bit of easy math, and a few functions here and there. After reading this appendix, you are ready to follow along with the programming steps in this book. If you're new to it, it'll take some patience and perseverance, but there's no feeling quite like writing some code, fixing the bugs, and then having it do exactly what you want.

Appendix II: Eight Rules of Classic Game Design

Rule 1: Simple Rule: Keep it simple.

Rule 2: Immediate Gameplay Rule: Start gameplay immediately.

Rule 3: Difficulty Ramping Rule: Ramp difficulty from easy to hard.

Rule 4: Test Rule: Test the game to make sure it's fun.

Rule 5: Score Rule: Score equals skill.

Rule 6: Experts Rule: Keep experts interested.

Rule 7: Ending Rule: Make an ending.

Rule 8: Novelty Rule: Make it novel.

Appendix III: About the DVD

The DVD contains project files used for creating the games in this book. Please refer to the README file on the DVD for a detailed listing of the contents and further instructions on how to navigate the project files.

The DVD also contains image files that correspond to the figures in the book. These image files are provided as an additional resource to the reader.

The files on the DVD are compatible with most Windows PC and Mac computers.

INDEX

shots, 215–220
simple rule, 40
skybox, 200
sound effects, 161–165
Space Invaders®, 5, 106–109
spaceship, 114–125
spaceship control, 199–202
spaceship modeling, 188–193
spaceship texturing, 194–198
Spacewar!, 39
Sphere Collider, 36, 59, 254, 258, 266
sprites, 125–132
stamps, 114, 202
starfield, 111–114
StartingPlay, 147
statements, 279
Static Friction, 36, 60
Subdivision Surface Modifier, 28

T

tag, 137
Taito, 106–107
test rule, 74
texture, 120
title screen, 101–104
tuning, 265–267

U

Unity
    demo application, 31–37
    game development tool, 6–7
    installation, 9–10
    programming with JavaScript, 19–22
UnityScript, 275–276
UV Image editor, 121–122, 195–198
UV project, 196

V

variable names, 277–278
variables, 277–278
vertical shooter
    alien death sequence, 157–161
    aliens, 132–139
    alien shots, 139–144
    levels, 165–171
    lives, 144–157
    playfield, 110–114
    postmortem, 171–172
    scoring, 144–157
    sketching, 110
    sound effects, 161–165
    spaceship, 114–125
    sprites, 125–132
video games, 3
    arcade, 4
viewport shading, 122

W

Wahwah, 30, 162
white box testing, 142
whitespace, 278–279
Wozniak, Steve, 72